T0381454

365 DAYS OF WORD EMPOWERMENT

ALISON'S JOURNAL, A WALK WITH WORDS JOURNEY

ALISON BOUCHER

BALBOA.PRESS
A DIVISION OF HAY HOUSE

Balboa Press books may be ordered through booksellers or by contacting:

Balboa Press
A Division of Hay House
1663 Liberty Drive
Bloomington, IN 47403
www.balboapress.com
1 (877) 407-4847

Because of the dynamic nature of the Internet, any web addresses or links contained in this book may have changed since publication and may no longer be valid. The views expressed in this work are solely those of the author and do not necessarily reflect the views of the publisher, and the publisher hereby disclaims any responsibility for them.

The author of this book does not dispense medical advice or prescribe the use of any technique as a form of treatment for physical, emotional, or medical problems without the advice of a physician, either directly or indirectly. The intent of the author is only to offer information of a general nature to help you in your quest for emotional and spiritual well-being. In the event you use any of the information in this book for yourself, which is your constitutional right, the author and the publisher assume no responsibility for your actions.

Image Credit:
Jean Paul Comeau
Marlene Martin
Penny Paris

Print information available on the last page.

ISBN: 978-1-9822-3897-1 (sc)
ISBN: 978-1-9822-3898-8 (hc)
ISBN: 978-1-9822-3899-5 (e)

Balboa Press rev. date: 11/21/2019

ACKNOWLEDGEMENTS

Thanks to God for the divine inspiration guiding me in my writing.

Thanks to my family for coping with my adventurous spirit. Special thanks to my sister Elizabeth for teaching me patience and unconditional love.

Thanks to all the doctors, therapists, life skills programs, sweat lodges, 12-Step programs, and especially my students. Thank you to Paul Boucher, Madeline and Wayne Fougere, Audrey and Ken Fram, Sue and Sandy Sanford, Louis and Marie-Noelle Gaultier, Carrol Ann Smith, David and Stephanie MacNeil, and my Aunt Louise and Uncle Berkley for taking me into their homes during my journey. Thanks to all my friends, especially Luther Murphy for being a friend and mentor.

There are so many people to thank and it would be impossible to list you all; you know who you are, and I am truly grateful. I appreciate each and every one who practised patience to work with me over the years.

Special thanks to my friend and partner Jean Paul Comeau for continued support and encouragement and feeding me when I was deep into my "wording."

Thank to Julia and McRoy Gardner, Lenoir, NC who invited us into their log home, where I heard the calling to write. Thanks to Eleanor Quilty for suggesting I write one positive word a day, which motivated me to pick 365 words and write about one each day. Thanks to Bev Cheverie, Maisie Leader, Carmie Branco, Penny Paris, and all of you who suggested I publish my work. Thanks to Audra Raulyns for suggesting I publish with Hay House, from which I used Balboa. Thanks to Jean, Penny, and Audra for helping me name my book. Thank you, Balboa, for approving my content and publishing my journal. Special thanks to my publishing consultant Jean Daniel and Jim Manon for continued support, direction, and patience.

Thanks to Jean Paul Comeau, Marlene Martin, and Penny Paris for the photographs.

Special thanks to Lydia Elizabeth for editing my book and writing a preface.

PREFACE

In my AHA! moment, when I realized my life was not what I wanted it to be, I sought many ways to change negative habits and transform my suffering; I wanted each day to be one of joy and connection with others. I decided I wanted to live "on the beam," which is described more fully in my March 14th entry; basically, it means a course of direction that leads to positive living.

Of course, deciding to change and saying the words does not always lead to results without applied action. I had to apply many changes to my thinking, attitudes, and actions. One day at a time. Through meditation and prayer, I received many insights that helped with the process of change.

One insight came with respect to words. A friend suggested I write a positive word each day, and I decided to do a word for 365 days. I would take one year and each day study, contemplate, and record my thoughts about that word.

The following questions guided my daily task: What does a particular word mean? How do I apply that word through action? How has this word and what it means affected my journey of change? From these thoughts, the content for this book evolved.

My method was simple. I wrote a different word on 365 pieces of paper, put them in a basket, and each day I selected a paper slip. The word on that slip of paper became my daily focus each morning. I would study, contemplate, and then write about what that word meant to me and how it had affected my life and the transformation process. I consulted dictionary and thesaurus, read what was said about a word, then set all aside. I meditated and brainstormed about the word. Some definitions were recorded, and then I wrote from my own mind and heart about the word.

I found it therapeutic to focus on the positive meaning of words each day, drawing upon books I've read over the years that have helped in my transformation process.

Friends and other people found my word writings helpful and remarked that I should write a book so that others could benefit. Here you have it – the book from 365 days of conscious contemplation and writing, one day at a time, one word a day.

May this work of mine bring some benefit to you and may you partake of life blessings, as I have in my spiritual journey!

JANUARY 1
REJOICE

Let my spirit rejoice on this first day of a new year! Let this be the year of vitality, happiness, pleasure, joy, gladness, celebrations, and merrymaking.

It is a time of rejoicing with peace and love, singing, and playing music as we share our gifts, talents, and time together. The snow is falling, bringing in the New Year with softness and brightness; it is oh so lovely.

Rejoice! Feel the happiness; feel the joy; feel the freedom; feel elated. Be a merrymaker and respect family, friends, and all. Feel the feelings, awaken your spirit, and have a happy new year.

I rejoice in my blessings, in my celebration of life, and in worship of my higher power – God. I know I'm rejoicing because I have a good direction in my life today; I'm capable of experiencing great happiness and feeling pleasure. I'm content to be just me.

Have a day of rejoicing!

JANUARY 2
SERENITY

Serenity is the state of being serene, calm, respectable, and honored.

> *God, grant me the serenity*
> *to accept the things I cannot change,*
> *the courage to change the things I can,*
> *and the wisdom to know the difference. ...*
> (Reinhold Niebuhr, 1892–1971)

A journey of self-observation enlightens us to experience serenity as we learn the art of acceptance, the hope in courage, and the freedom in wisdom. Lifelong striving for progress each day is the key.

How do I live in serenity?

- daily meditation and prayer
- staying "awake"
- practicing mindfulness and consciousness

Peacefulness, calm, respectability, and serenity are results of conditioning the mind. The art of mindfulness brings about balance, purity, and *serenity*.

Have a day of serenity!

LOVE

Love is the gift of caring for a person, place, or thing while being patient, kind, compassionate, understanding, and helpful. These qualities are virtues of love.

Love is an expression of a positive sentiment when shared. It is a commitment to be honest and respectable, while bringing out the best in all our relations.

Love is pure.
Love is beautiful.
Love is patient.
Love is sharing.
Love is caring.

How do we know we are being loving beings?

We know when we reach beyond ourselves and find satisfaction in caring for others, perhaps helping them develop and feel safe. Love is giving our time, sharing our talents, and perhaps even our money, to help support another human being in his or her journey.

Love is an attitude of gratitude.

Have a loving day!

PEACE

Peace is a state of tranquility, security, self-acceptance, harmony, agreement, and calmness.

Shine your light of peace.

Let us have peace in our eyes.
Let us be calm in our movement.
Let us be hopeful.
Let us be confident.
Let us agree.

When we share our love with one another, we know peace!

My soul lives in peace; self-acceptance allows my spirit this gift. Being mindful allows my spirit to rise above chaos and/or turmoil. My spirit listens with empathy, and I reflect my inner peace. Being a mindful, peaceful person allows me to express my inner peace to all those in my presence.

I meditate for world peace.

Let there be peace. Let it begin with me and be shared with you.

Have a peaceful day!

ACCEPTANCE

Acceptance is the ability to feel adequate and of value.

My soul desires peace and joy. My ego creates anxiety and separation.

Acceptance of life one day at a time is my gift today. I accept all people, places, and things. I take control of my life by giving it to the universe, my higher power: God!

Acceptance of peace and joy allow me to be productive and grow as a healthy being. My mindfulness to live peacefully motivates me to be kind and compassionate. My spirit of joy opens me to share positive energy.

Suffering has been part of my journey. When I accept myself, I am able to see it as a step to my enlightenment. In accepting myself, I see how my experience can help others. My gift is to give back and show others their light and a positive way out of suffering.

Acceptance and understanding are my foundation for a loving life.

Have a day of acceptance!

COMPASSION

Compassion is love and understanding. To be compassionate, we share in another's emotion with understanding by being caring, sensitive, and kind-hearted. In being compassionate, we identify with others and are motivated to do something to help relieve their suffering.

Compassion opens my spirituality. We are all sacred beings and deserve respect. Mindfulness allows me to be positive and at peace with myself. In spiritual openness, I am blessed with understanding for others. I have learned that through serving others, as in volunteering, I find the ultimate happiness.

I have learned to be *wisely unselfish* rather than to be self-centered. As a result, I live happily! Be compassionate with yourself and others!

Have a day of compassion!

WILLINGNESS

Willingness means I am willing to live with positive virtues and principles of good character, such as the following:

- honesty
- hope
- faith
- courage
- integrity
- willingness
- humility
- sisterhood/brotherhood
- justice
- perseverance
- spirituality
- service

Developing these principles is a process that takes time; yet, by being mindful of our behaviors and actions each day with willingness, we find that willingness increases one day at a time.

Awareness is the key to change. The first step is to be willing to embrace spiritual growth. As I grow, I experience peace and a sense of freedom, living each day as a respectable citizen in society.

Questions for Thought

1. How am I trying to remove or control my undesirable character traits?
2. Am I asking my higher power, my God, to remove my negative character traits and open me to accept the blessings of positive virtues and principles?
3. Am I willing to act differently, to accept life on life's terms and be kind in my actions, opinions, and behaviors in all my daily living?

Have a day of willingness!

FORGIVENESS

Forgiveness is a process of learning to let go, understanding, and tolerance.

Just how do we forgive and let go?

We reflect on the issue, learn from it, deal with it, and then let it go. Holding grudges results in spiritual malady and blocks us from being free souls.

Forgiveness is a healing tool that opens us to wonderful sources of love, peace, and serenity. Holding on to past hurts keeps me a prisoner in my mind. I forgive others so that I can move forward. Being willing to forgive and taking action to forgive shows growth and true character. It frees me to live in peace rather than in anger.

I forgive myself for anything wrong I have done to any person, place, or thing, and I open myself up to spiritual freedom.

Peace to all.

Have a forgiving day and live well in love and peace!

SPIRITUAL ABUNDANCE

Spiritual abundance contains deep, unconditional love, calm, security, faith, wisdom, patience, connectedness, balance, peace, wholeness, complete generosity, tolerance, acceptance, enlightenment, endurance, and integrity.

How does your spirit express this abundance?

1. Your spirit might be absorbed in happiness and joy.
2. Your spirit might know peace.
3. Your spirit might love freely.
4. Your spirit might enjoy the gifts of living.

How do we work toward achieving spiritual abundance?

I practice meditation to quiet my brain. Meditation shifts my ego from being disturbed and confused with feelings such as: insecurity, pride, selfishness, lack, fear, numbness, loneliness, impatience, greed, judgment, conditionality, skepticism, and internal conflicts.

What are the benefits of spiritual abundance?

1. The spirit is released from sadness to being joyful.
2. The spirit is released from anxiety to having faith.
3. The spirit is released from lacking to being nourished.
4. The spirit is alleviated from suffering to having serenity.

Spiritual abundance to all!

Have a peaceful, happy day of spiritual abundance!

JANUARY 10
JOY

Joy is happiness, gladness, bliss, ecstasy, faith, gratitude, grace, and love. Joy is present when I help others, share my talents and gifts of peace, and have patience and awareness; this is great spiritual abundance.

When we share the experience of sorrow, sadness, and tears, we feel less alone. We experience a new level of spiritual growth and feel connection with others. As a result, we then feel a deeper level of joy and happiness. We smile, knowing we are compassionately spreading joy to others during this spiritual journey.

I feel joy knowing I'm appreciated.
I feel joy seeing my friends and family smile.
I feel joy sewing for friends and family.
I feel joy spending time with my friends and family.
I feel joy being there for the sick and dying.

I feel joy for my healthy compassion for myself and compassion for others.

Have a joyful day!

CARING

Caring is to show interest in someone, something, or some place. It is to be interested in another's well-being, to show compassion in helping them to achieve their goals and to make their dreams come true.

To care is to be present with calm, kindness, understanding, empathy, and acceptance.

When family and friends are in their final life journey phase of dying, I show caring by respecting their interests, praying, or playing music and games, for example.

It is a great gift to help people through this final stage of living. It is a spiritual experience to see them free from their suffering and, just for the moment, living right in that very moment! Caring is being present in the moment sharing the feeling of joy and life's positive moments.

Have a caring day!

GRIEVING

Grieving is a process of dealing with a stressful loss, which takes time to heal and cope. All grieving is a personal experience, and we all grieve differently.

Today is a day to reflect on my journey, which includes feeling sadness and loss of my friend. Dealing with the pain and sadness is a challenge to renew my own life and what I am all about on this journey. Grieving allows me to feel the sadness, but also happiness because we shared love and appreciation for each other and valued each other. We shared losses together, but we rejoiced each time we met.

Today, I rejoice knowing my friend has "flown away" to be with all the angels. She is a free soul journeying in a better place with her God.

I was singing "I'll fly away" as my dear friend passed, and I knew that she was journeying into the glory land.

R.I.P. my friend: Minnie Mary Boudreau (nee Brittain)
Died: January 11, 2015

Peace to all!

It's a grieving day, but also a celebration of a courageous, keen, funny, smart, and all-loving woman!

JANUARY 13
GIVING

Giving is offering, donating, supplying, contributing, and conveying love and support. Giving as generosity is the state of giving and expecting nothing in return. To learn the gift of giving is to know peace in your heart.

There are many expressions such as "the more you give, the more you receive." I find this statement to be true. I give my time, talents, and knowledge to help those in need, and I receive blessings of a quiet mind, a deep spiritual awareness, and gratitude.

You see I was not always in a state of giving. I used to live in a dysfunctional state, sick and sad. Then one day I started to change from being "lost," and people were honest with me; they were there for me and treated me with generosity, courage, faith, hope, acceptance, strength, and gentleness. As a result, I am "found," awake, fully conscious of my daily living, giving freely to those who travel into my journey's path.

Today I was blessed with the opportunity to give, and I knew and experienced an overwhelming feeling of peace and bliss as I looked into my friend's eyes!

Today was a giving day!

GRATITUDE

Gratitude is a state of feeling thankful and appreciating, respecting, and acknowledging what we have.

I have gratitude for the life I live today. I am grateful for the good mental health support team, programs, family, and friends that helped me become the person I am today. I appreciate their understanding my personality.

An attitude of gratitude contributes to contentment, stability, blessings, and spirituality.

Let gratitude bring grace to my thoughts, motivation to my actions, and affection in my being.

> I am grateful for life.
> I am grateful for serenity.
> I am grateful for ambition.
> I am grateful for meditation.
> I am grateful for family and friends.
> I am grateful for this moment.
> I am grateful for 12-step programs.
> I am grateful for spirituality.

I have gratitude and am grateful for my experiences in acceptance, courage, and wisdom to become the best I can be, just for today. I am grateful for pool therapy and for all my swimming buddies!

Have a day of gratitude!

JANUARY 15
FREEDOM

Freedom is the state of being free: free from physical confinement, free from emotional pain and suffering, free from self, personal liberty, and, finally, free from an earthly body.

If you are free from self-centeredness by living and dying God-centered, "Bingo," you're a winner!

Mental illness took my freedom, the ability to live on my own, and confined me to care from others. Physical illness took my health, such as in a severe case of liver alcohol poisoning. It took time to heal, but I was blessed with healing. I received a second chance at life, to spend special times with family and friends. Spiritual wellness allowed me to accept my predicament and let go. I am now free to be a healthy human being.

I am grateful for my freedom, to live the best I can each day, proud to serve others and our country so that we all live in freedom. Today I feel the freedom.

Have a day of freedom!

MINDFULNESS

Mindfulness is a state of awareness, focused on the present moment. When you open your mind to be positive and live in reality, accepting both the good and bad.

The key is acceptance and being centered so that you can be mindful, pleasant, and helpful rather than negative and judgmental. When we take personal inventory and self-monitor our behavior with mindfulness, we free ourselves from blaming and judging. We grow to be free from negativity and shine to live a mindful and healthy life.

How do we know we are experiencing mindfulness?

We know peace.
We know happiness.
We know freedom.
We know intense alertness and awareness.
We are aware of stress and walk away.
We are calm rather than anxious.
Our choices feel right and just.
Life is good and enjoyable.
We are mentally fit, grounded.

Mindfulness is bonding in every stitch as we weave our life into what we create each day. Be still: practice mindfulness and know peace.

Have a day of mindfulness!

GENEROSITY

Generosity is a good quality, such as being kind, unselfish, and freely giving. Generosity is the understanding of the value and need for compassion. Generosity is being openhearted enough to share your time, talent, and financial support.

I learned about generosity from my experience when I was down and out. People reached out and showed me that, in their giving, they were happier people. Both rich and poor folks were willing to help out; their generosity is never forgotten. I can't pay back all the folks who were there for me in times of desperation, but I can pay it forward to help others.

Sometimes people practised generosity by spending time with me, while others shared their talents, and some even shared financially. As a result, I have abundant gratitude. I practise their generosity freely given me through volunteerism. Through this process, depression is lost, happiness found, and I grow stronger in my spiritual being.

Have a generous day, give freely!

JANUARY 18
PRAYER

Prayer is the act of spiritual communication requesting guidance for one's thoughts and emotions. Prayer is a time to be generous in positive thoughts for our loved ones, both the living and the dead.

Prayer is an act that seeks God and blessings in worship. A universal prayer is the "Serenity Prayer." It becomes an aid in positive daily living. It suggests acceptance, courage, and wisdom, all of which encourage a better way of living.

Prayer is an act of surrender; we understand we are not alone and accept a concept of God. It is a personal relationship, an individual belief, and a universal gift.

Prayer is a soothing exercise to decrease depression and opens one's heart to all-powerful love.

Prayer improves self-esteem, reduces anxiety, relieves pain, and improves spiritual being. One form of prayer is to know God and to live in "Good Orderly Direction"; we know we are not alone, staying awake and conscious as we grow each day and experience the love of God who lives within each of us.

Have a prayerful day!

JANUARY 19
RELEASE

Release is the act of letting go, setting oneself and others free from all negativity. Release is healing to a better way of life; we grow through mercy, grace, and pardon.

Release from trauma includes dealing with emotions that are buried from consciousness in our bodies and minds. In meditation, we recognize these experiences as fear, anxiety, depression, illnesses, and negativity. We pray for healthy actions such as mindfulness, forgiveness, awareness of positive behaviors, and thoughtful actions. As a result, we experience healing that stimulates positive brain action and recovery from negative habits.

Releasing myself from being a victim delivers me from living in negativity. Rejoicing as a survivor feeds my spirit to grow positively, and I enjoy thriving in my new way of life.

Resentments are the number-one killer of a happy, joyous, and free spirit. Therefore, release is the answer to all my problems. I release my troubles over to my God and am blessed with love and peace of mind in my heart and soul. As a result, I feel a healthy intense emotional state of being.

Have day of release!

ENRICHMENT

Enrichment improves the quality of one's life, enabling us to become more useful, to make things better, to enhance, improve, amend, help, and refine our light and life.

Once upon a time, I found myself totally bankrupt – mentally, emotionally and spiritually. I made a choice to change my thinking habits and negative ways of living. My quest for enrichment brought me back to school, French immersion studies, an education, and teaching career. I was blessed with success and put my all into my work.

Then, in a blink of an eye, one slushy, snowy morning in April 2001, all came to a halt with a car crash, which left me physically challenged, mentally and emotionally disturbed, but not spiritually broken. So I did the best I could to seek enrichment and heal. It took a long time to find my serenity; it was possible through acceptance and the need to reclaim my joy and sense of purpose.

Having recovered to be the best I can be in my new state, I now find myself blessed with compassion to help others and share my time, energy, and creativity. I came up with a few projects and have been blessed in my life with enrichment. Thank you to all who helped me become whole and useful; I now have an attitude of gratitude for my life on this earth, because your encouragement gave me strength to seek enrichment.

Have a day of enrichment!

CONTENTMENT

Contentment is a state of peaceful happiness: being grateful, glad, satisfied, cheerful, unworried, serene, and tranquil.

Contentment is when you find yourself thriving as a healthy human being, feeling serenity and peace of mind. Contentment is being satisfied with one's life. Living well is being able and willing to accept life in the moment and being awake in an emotionally satisfied mind.

Contentment comes when we release our negative thoughts, behaviors, and actions and replace our unhealthy behaviors with intentions to achieve harmony through positive thoughts and actions.

Self-improvement, self-actualization, self-fulfillment are works in progress that evolve through living in the moment. In finding my inner core being in consciousness and psychological well-being, I am content.

To be content is an attitude of gratitude! Prayer and meditation are healthy ways to achieve peace of mind. Today I accept my life, and everything is good. Life is good, and I am content!

Have a content day!

ADDICTION

Addiction is a serious malady, a spiritual illness, a physical disease, a habit, and a compulsive need for stimulation.

Addiction has no boundaries: it will take your spirit on a negative journey of despair and sorrow. It is a problem when you are chasing the stimuli, because, when you cross that line, it takes over your good spirit, mind, body, and soul.

The good news is that there is a solution. Yes, and it really works! The secret is to not use or indulge in your substance of choice for one day at a time. Start a journey of living in the light. It is hard work but very rewarding as you grow a little each day and let go of negative behaviors. Yes – change the resentments, anger, sadness, isolation, lies, and all the negative thinking.

Start today with a meditation on a positive word. Pray about this word, and then journal how you can make one little change each day. Learn to love life and have fun and laughter doing it.

Life is good with an honest, open-minded, heart-felt willingness to grow each day. By sharing our hope, life experiences, and love, we grow stronger each day like a watered flower in our garden. Rising up each day to be more positive and happier results in living with a healed heart.

Unite, rejoice, and celebrate a happy, joyful lifestyle, free from misery and miserable company. Surround yourself with people living in recovery and live free from your addiction.

Have an addiction-free day!

DETERMINATION

Determination is the act of coming to a decision to fix or settle something, which includes being firm on resolutions and intentions and expressing our character strengths.

Determination is having a "stick-to-it" mindset to achieve a new way of living and to be confident in your being. When one becomes determined to change and follows through with positive actions, things start to manifest for the better.

When I decided that I definitely needed to make some changes in my life and followed through with determination, I found my solutions. My life was a mess, but I changed. Now my life is one of a messenger. I share my experiences and where I find my strength; in doing so, I have hope for a better way of living. I am determined to live a little better each day in a positive direction of spiritual growth and, for that, I am grateful.

My determination is to write a book one day; this journal is my practice to develop my skills in writing.

Let determination direct your day!

PATIENCE

Patience is a state of being calm, meek, tranquil, humble, stable, courageous, faithful, tolerant, and even-tempered while sharing love with detachment. Patience helps us to persevere calmly and endure difficult times.

At one point in my life, I realized I had no patience with myself. I was restless and discontent with my life. I was irritated about everything and everybody. I came to a point where I could not trust and experienced the dark painful state of loneliness and isolation that was tearing my heart and soul apart. I felt fragmented, lost, and numbed out.

My friend Lou said, "Feel the fear and grow in your journey; be gentle with yourself and trust the process." Unsolved issues took residence in my heart; I was paralyzed in an unhealthy state of existence.

Patience was the virtue that led me to acceptance and detachment. Serenity followed. As I shared my experiences with others, together we gained hope, strengthened our courage, and learned to enjoy each moment with centered minds. These were times of challenges with uncertainty, but we kept our faith and rejoiced in our patience. Patience is an act of letting go, surrendering, and praying for guidance.

Patience allows us to live in kindness, peacefulness, understanding, and a caring environment. Patience enables you to endure waiting through delays and/or provocations. Patience allows us to move forward each day with respect for ourselves and others. Patience allows us to be courteous and compassionate.

Enjoy a day of patience!

PERSISTENCE

Persistence is the action of purposefully moving on, no matter the difficulty or opposition, and continuing one day at a time; sometimes just one moment at a time. Persistence is continuing to have faith in your friends and family; it is not giving up, but rather holding on regardless of rejection. It involves being patient, persevering and tenacious, being insistent, unrelenting, in for the long haul, continual, constant, tireless, and determined.

I am persistent in learning about a healthy lifestyle and in forgiving myself and others. My sanity and peace of mind are contingent on my willingness to grow and self-acceptance. Being able to be persistent is a work in progress because I am only human; I am not perfect.

All life experiences shape me in who I become or fail to become. Water runs deep; there came to a point in my life where I could either sink further into negative, unconscious living or I could swim towards the Light. People persisted in sending me life rafts, and one day I grabbed on and came to shore. They showed me some tools for growing and guided me to the better path, which I choose to travel.

My progress in learning to be persistent has nourished my growth. My friends' persistence in walking the walk has nourished my confidence. I am forever grateful!

Have a persistent day!

FOCUS

Focus is the ability to concentrate, zoom in, engage, adjust, fixate, sharpen, sponsor, manage, counsel, control, organize, adapt, and see clearly.

Focus on perceptions: zoom in and open up to the positive energy, sharpen perceptions about what is going "Right" in life, fixate your energy on transforming your emotional state.

Focus on acceptance, become spontaneously flexible in an awakened state, connected to all feelings and memories. Yes, accept the feelings and grow; you may like the positive growth from experiencing a focused state of mind. Focus on positive thoughts of gratitude.

Focus on what is "right" and make a complete list of all the good that is in your life, just for the moment. Feel the joy of knowing you have the ability to focus on the good stuff that brings you to spiritual wellness.

When I am focused on my blessings, I am focused on what is going right in my life. Life improves with meditation, prayer, and gratitude. Gratitude changes perspective and evokes positive feelings about people, places, and things. It is a pleasure to be focused on giving thanks. Life is manageable, acceptable, and peaceful.

Focusing on being the best version I can be allows me to be connected in society and live the joy of living one day at a time.

Have a focused day!

JANUARY 27
IMPROVEMENT

Improvement is the act of becoming better. This can be a work in progress: advancing, enhancing, and refining our emotional well-being.

When one stands at a turning point and decides to change for the better, change for the moment, or change for the long haul, it takes courage, strength, and hope; yet, with time, improvement is experienced. Gradually, we see improvement from being lost, unhappy, and isolated. We note improvement when we tend to the process, when we change and develop our inner strength rather than stay in negative behaviors. Each day is a little better, thus improvement.

Improvement in my social skills came as a result of enhancing my beliefs and refining my ways. This was, and is, a timely process. Indeed, one day at a time, I experienced improvement in my thinking, acting, and behaving; as a result, I'm feeling peace.

Time, effort, and attitude are crucial to personal improvement. In letting go of fears, anxiety, and negative thinking, I have enjoyed the opportunity for spiritual growth, improvement in my awakening to live a better, harmonious, and spiritual life.

Have a day of improvement!

JANUARY 28
EFFICIENCY

Efficiency is learning to do things right, without wasting time and effort.

When I choose neither to live in the past nor the future, I am left to live in the present; in doing so, I find that it is possible to experience efficiency in my daily life. Being spiritually fit allows efficient organization and fulfilling days. My life is manageable.

Efficiency is the success of being organized, awake, spiritually fit. My focus is learning to accept life as it comes, doing the best I can each day and sharing my skills through positive communication. Living on the beam helps me to do things right and hone my skills of efficiency.

I used to waste a lot of time and energy because I was not living on the beam. A changed outlook on life, a new attitude, acceptance, and a changed lifestyle enables me to be efficient. My beliefs are my guidance in living a spiritual lifestyle. Without divine intervention I was inefficient, but with God's Grace I am now living a life of efficiency.

Have a day of efficiency!

COOPERATION

Cooperation is the ability to work with others; in service, unity, helping, assisting, teamwork, combined effort, responsiveness, and concurrence, we can find solutions together. Life is a journey, and cooperation with our fellow human beings makes life more comfortable and endurable. Together, we can focus on an issue, share our experiences, and support each other in cooperation to change, one day at a time.

Service is a gift when I share what I have learned with all. When I stick together with all folks, I share in unity; I help others, and they help me, so that we all grow spiritually. We assist each other by taking part in the process, and we find encouragement through teamwork. We are not alone on this journey because we are combining our efforts to find peace and serenity.

We rejoice, and we experience life being a little bit more comfortable each day by living in the solution and cooperating! Living in the moment, our personalities grow spiritually fit. We experience a psychic change and continue a life of cooperation.

The key is a positive attitude of gratitude.

Have a great day living in cooperation!

BALANCE

Balance is a way of emotionally allowing myself to experience life by feeling my feelings and consciously dealing with their expressions.

Learning to recognize feelings, consciously understanding what is happening in body responses, and dealing with them by responding rather than reacting keeps me in a state of balance. The key is in understanding that feelings do not last; I must stay awake and aware to release them to maintain good balance.

Prayer and meditation are exercises to have a tranquil mind, which allows me to keep emotionally balanced. I adventure into self-examination and learn to deal with life on life's terms. I cooperate, focus, and improve my conditioning to be strong, courageous, faithful, and surrender to my higher power and the universal energy. I am now open to live in unity with my community and the world. Having had an experience of spiritual awakening and freed myself, I am emotionally balanced and feel strong, unselfish, tolerant, and forgiving. I love life.

Have a day of balance!

ABUNDANCE

Abundance of good healthy thinking is my wealth. Abundance of enjoying life as it is right now in this moment is a result of listening to my inner voices, accepting my struggles, and learning to cope.

When I find myself spiritually bankrupt and in ill health or overtaken by fear, anger, worry, self-pity and resentments, I must become willing to risk opening up, listening to my inner voice, and acknowledging, accepting and forgiving myself. I then become open to an abundance of blessings: gratitude, joy, peace, patience, passion, purpose, creativity, and balance. Each day I experience true freedom: freedom from depression, despair and doubt. Abundance of faith tames my mind and nourishes my soul, and courage allows me to cope with life one day at a time.

My inner voice persisted in being heard. Once I took the time, patience, and willingness to listen, acknowledge, and accept things as they were, my life changed. It has been a long journey, but I am grateful and give thanks for all, both the good as well as the bad. I have learned from experience that abundance in faith allows me to excel in positive living. Abundance of living in solutions, being optimistic and forgiving, is a peaceful way of living; I must practise sharing and caring.

Have a day of abundance!

HEALING

Healing is the process to cure, mend, and grow to a state of sanity: getting well and freeing oneself from bondage of self and becoming healthy.

Healing my mind is first because my problems are all centered in my mind. Some people say, "mind over matter," and other people say, "it don't matter if you don't mind"; I say, "it matters, so I mind." I am now mindfully looking at my life, aware and open to changing.

Healing my body involves focusing on the cause of my discomfort; I then become aware of my body by listening to what it is trying to tell me. I believe in myself, because I am my own advocate and open to heal my blockages. I verify my awareness with my support team and welcome healing.

Healing my soul started with surrendering my life to God; oh God, thank you for this day; may I be of service to you by taking care of myself by praying and meditating and soothing my soul through your guidance. I have come to learn that there is nothing that together we can't handle and heal. I trust in You. Thank You. With this practice, my soul is at peace.

Have a healing day!

HOPE

Hope is belief: a mindset of faith, trust, optimism, confidence, desire; a positive attitude, understanding, and an opening of the mind to see the bright side of life and the light at the end of the tunnel.

Hope for inner peace was distant when I was engaged in attacking and defending, whether it was stemming from fear or guilt. With a change in my perceptions, I experienced a new peace and freedom. I accept myself and all exactly as we are in this moment, and I know love as a result of my change in belief.

My hope began when I chose to change my life. When I came to an understanding that my life was a mess, I found hope in reconnecting with a positive, loving God. Then I humbly began reconstructing my life, starting on a major journey to a better way of living. My confidence came from mental health counselors, support groups, friends, and a great overall health team. As a result, I was blessed with positive self-esteem as my hope grew through persistence, tenacity, patience, and determination. Life changed for the better.

Difficulties are part of life; how we cope and deal with them is contingent on our hope. It is in accepting hope, faith, and love that I heal and feel hopeful, optimistic, and energized to share my hope and honesty with others.

Have a day of hope!

SISTERHOOD/BROTHERHOOOD

Sisterhood and brotherhood integrate affinity, affiliation, camaraderie, togetherness, fellowship, society, kin, family, community cooperation, sorority, fraternity, and unity, built out of respect and love. We share honesty and trust, support each other, encourage each other to grow, and are accountable with common goals. We are equals.

A person who thrives in sisterhood/brotherhood has a kind character and listens free of judgment and conditional love. He or she has the spirit of giving without expecting any returns. In sisterhood/brotherhood, bonds exist with other human beings.

Before I took the spiritual path in my life, I experienced disconnection, fragmentation, aloneness, friendlessness, isolation, solitude, lonesomeness, and withdrawal. I was a lost soul out there in the universe, roaming from pillar to post.

One day I started walking to a different drum: I connected and, little by little, things changed for the better. With friends we shared our experiences; we identified our habits and patterns, and encouraged each other to become empowered, enlightened, and to continually grow. We found sisterhood and brotherhood works best as a trio; me, you, and God living a peaceful life.

Have a sisterhood/brotherhood day!

FEBRUARY 4
SHAPING

Shaping is an act of conditioning, molding, sculpting, bringing together, building one's behavior, building one's mind, and applying mindfulness. We shape our emotional well-being through positive transformations; we change from old negative thoughts to positive thoughts and from negative beliefs to positive beliefs. We rebuild by letting go of victimization and shifting from negative attitudes to positive attitudes. We are shaping ourselves to achieve peace of mind.

Shaping involves accepting oneself and others. Shaping my own reality by being awake, conscious, and focused on meditation, prayer, and contemplation have great effects on my health. Shaping removes emotional pain and makes life easier. Shaping nourishes my soul and revives my energy. Spiritual shaping is the choice of action and beliefs of hope, faith, and courage. Shaping opens us to live a better life and frees us from negativity and "dis-ease!"

When I began shaping my mind, becoming spiritually fit, I realized that I had played a part in my being who and what I was, and I had a choice in changing my beliefs. I began to focus on deciding to change; as I followed through, I began changing a little each day. This shaping is a work in progress.

Letting go and forgiving are my greatest assets in continuing my journey of shaping. My willingness to change allows me to experience a new freedom, relief, happiness, joy, peace of mind, and serenity.

Today, I tend to my thoughts; my beliefs are positive, and my attitude is gratitude.

Have a shaping day!

REBUILDING

Rebuilding is to rehabilitate, restore, conciliate, overhaul, revise, rejuvenate, tune up, reconstruct, renew, repair, amend, correct, remedy, reconcile, make well, make healthy, free, recover, harmonize, bring around, revive, mend, and ameliorate. Rebuilding involves examining consciousness and making improvements in one's life, changing one's ways of thinking, restoring the child within, revising what we eat, tuning up with exercise, reconciling with one's faith, trusting, and forgiving.

Rebuilding involves actions to restore your mind, body, and soul. Action is working to reconstruct thinking with others: friends, psychologists, psychiatrists, life coaches, and family. Action is working with pool therapy, yoga, stretching, biking, and walking to tune-up the body. Action of prayer and meditation harmonizes the soul.

What drives one to rebuild spiritually are the feelings of loneliness, arrogance, a feeling of entitlement, and poor self-esteem, which are debilitating and lead to brokenness and suffering. Rebuilding came through divine intervention after many conversations with the big white throne: "God help me!"

The process began with a desire, then came the willingness, patience, courage, truthfulness, acceptance, actions, affections, persistence, and respect. The first key was to trust myself and take a personal inventory of where I was in my life; the second was to forgive myself and others. Understanding that no one is perfect and accepting my imperfections helped me on my journey. Time and effort are the essence. Plan your goals but not the outcomes. Rebuild your life with respect, security, love, safety, and new friendships. Rebuilding is life-changing; grasp the knowledge and accept that you are valued very much and enjoy all the good changes.

Have a rebuilding day!

MELLIFLUOUS

Mellifluous means pleasant to hear, mellow sounding, smooth, rich, harmonious, tuneful, and musical. Mellifluous comes from the word mellow. A mellifluous mind is free from racket, inner voices of negativity, off-key thinking, being out of tune, and dreary perspectives.

When I became aware of how loud, rambunctious, and crazy I was acting, I realized I was not mellifluous. I was suffering from a spiritual malady of my mind, and I was preventing myself from mellow living. There was no peace for me and those around me. I was rough, tough, and lacked the ability to be mellifluous.

I began to grow, and I gave up fighting myself and those around me. I acknowledged the voices and surrendered to God, whom I understand to be "Good Orderly Direction" that guides me. I gave my mind a complete overhaul and experienced a psychic change in my thinking. The voices have all integrated and are at peace, living with new attitudes and perceptions. Integrity brought me to a state where I could be totally honest with myself and others. My problems are solved with my new-found thinking skills, and I am functional; I walk the walk one day at a time, mellifluously. As a result, I have an improved nature with focus, attention, better concentration, and enhanced learning. Prayer and meditation are the key to having a mellifluous mind, to being at peace when you think, feel, and speak.

I hope when people hear me sing that it is mellifluous! Lol!

Have a mellifluous day!

TRUST

Trust is to have hope, to have confidence in a person, to believe they will hold confidence, and to be able to rely on someone.

My trust was corrupted in silence, betrayal, and lies. My perceptions were confused, my memories were debilitating, and my sanity was off the beam. I was filled with resentment, self-condemnation, self-justification, anger, pride, fear, hatred, intolerance, and suspicions. My belief in God was shattered; I trusted no one, which was a very dark place to be in my mind. My friend Roy told me, "Allie, when you find yourself alone and lonely, you are in bad company!"

My trust was regained when I took stock and realized that I was betrayed. I came to recognize that I was living "off the beam" and felt totally frustrated and broken; then I became willing to change. My journey out of disillusionment, disappointment, and betrayal compelled me to seriously overhaul my thinking habits!

I cleaned out my thinking closet, learned to trust God, and now I make a life of trying to help others along the path. As long as I am praying and meditating, I have good thoughts and experience a better way of living. The key is keeping "awake and conscious" of my being. First, I took my body to get help; then my mind followed along, and one day my soul felt like it came home. I now trust myself and others. As a result of dragging the body and nourishing the mind, I experience a happy soul.

Have a trusting day!

HILARIOUS

Hilarious is to be funny, rollicking, farcical, merry, cheerful, happy, joyous, folly, gay, comical, entertaining, and humorous.

Once upon a time, I went to St Andrew's Junior High School in Antigonish. It was decided that it would be best to send me out of my regular English class because I had a hard time learning words and reading. Sister Sarah sent me to the resource room, which was very humiliating; yet, I went.

I was not happy, but I would go upstairs to the resource room. Once there, I would get settled into my cubicle where I was asked to look into this little box, and then read the words as they slowly passed on a screen. These words would start slowly but then the teacher would speed them up. So, being a creative student, and having a hard time with the story, I figured I had to come up with a solution for this process. There had to be a method to have greater success so that I could stay in my regular classroom.

One day I was reading, trying to keep up with the words but when I lost track, I just kept talking, making up my own story with my own words. When that poor teacher, who was a nun, realized I was making up my own story (I might add it was a pretty funny one), well, she just whacked me on the head. This makes me laugh today!

This was a hilarious day, one of my best days of schooling. I have been making up songs ever since; the only problem is I can't remember the words once they roll off my brain. All is good, because I have learned to love words and, today, sharing them with you.

Have a hilarious day!

SELF-POSSESSION

Self-possession is the gift of controlling one's emotions, reactions, calmness, serenity, tranquility, and peace of mind.

Self-possession is a behavior of maturity in a healthy self-assured being who maintains composure in one's feelings and behaviors. Confidence in one's identity and calmness in stressful situations are good characteristics to maintain control of your emotions at all times; they are virtues that need to be acknowledged in daily living to enhance spiritual growth. Self-possession is gained through self-knowledge, so seek to learn and learn to love!

Self-possession helps us grow towards being a better version of ourselves. We learn to speak our mind in our own individual spirit. We seek self-knowledge and, as a result, learn a little more each day how to live more effectively in self-possession, which is a spiritual act.

Self-possession is a result of walking the walk, living a simple life, and learning to live in peace with myself and others. Living in a restored personality is a state of grace, truth, and light!

Have a self-possessed day!

RUMINANT

Ruminant is a neat word because it has two meanings: one is that of being a hoofed mammal, and the other one is about being contemplative, reflective, and in a meditative state. Ruminant is when you are in a state of sober thoughtfulness.

My mind used to wonder about what my life would be like when I got to this age. However, the universe had a change of direction; what I believed my life would be like has turned out to be very different from what I had foreseen. I experienced a serious car accident in 2001; major changes and a new life path occurred. I found myself in a ruminant state of musing over what life would be like for me with this new state of existence. Then the light came on one day and the voice said, "Turn it over to God!"

I heard a voice say, "Just do good and be the best you can be." So, each morning I sit in my rocking chair by my window, I pick a word from my basket and enjoy time being ruminant. In my sober thoughtfulness, I write my reflection on my word.

Have a ruminant day!

AWESOME

Awesome is when you are in awe and admire someone, something, or some place. Awesome is when you find one of these to be wonderful, cool, neat, outstanding, astonishing, magnificent or beautiful.

This has been an awesome week visiting with family and friends, especially with my sister Elizabeth. Elizabeth lives at the L'Arche Covenant House in Antigonish, which is a home for the mentally challenged. She was so excited to see my videos and pictures. She sang along with the music and knew the words. I was surprised and asked her how she had learned these songs and she said, "From your CD." It was awesome to visit her and to see her excitement, appreciation, and enthusiasm. Her love is awesome; it is pure unconditional love.

Today is an awesome sunny day, great for a drive while listening to some great tunes. Bluegrass is an awesome genre of music. High rhythm keeps me revved up.

Tonight will be an awesome reunion with a few friends, and one will cook us an awesome supper. Life is good!

Have an awesome day!

STRENGTH

Strength is having the quality of being strong, of being able to deal with life on life's terms. Strength is having honesty to train your brain to be mentally and spiritually strong. Strength is also a physical quality; for example, you need physical strength to hold your head on your shoulders, and you need mental strength to keep in a healthy spiritual condition.

I keep my strength by having a daily conscious contact with the God of my understanding. I find and continue to find my strength in caring and sharing with others my experiences and dreams. In sharing, we help each other see different perspectives and help each other make our dreams come true. Together we are strong in numbers: you, me, and the universe; all our life's a circle! We must take action to enjoy the journey.

I used to act like nothing bothered me, and I went about life as a lost soul, hurting and feeling hurtful. The miracle happened with divine intervention and the Grace of God, so that I now walk in peace and calm. I am what I am; I am open and honest as best I can be, and my strength grows like a well-nourished plant.

My strength is in trusting God, the creator, the universe, and energy. Life is a "we" experience; we are all connected!

Have a day of strength!

MAGNANIMITY

Magnanimity is a virtue of having the willingness to face a crisis or danger with a peaceful, good heart and sound mind. Magnanimity is having the quality of being insightful, generous in your forgiving – big, liberal, and noble.

Living in a state of being magnanimous includes being high-minded, great-hearted, ungrudging, kind, forgiving, unselfish, bountiful, and charitable. It takes magnanimity to counter troubled times. Life can be a challenge. I have learned that being magnanimous is more soothing to my personal being. I can't afford the mental instability of being anything but magnanimous in my daily living. I like to keep all my energy for a peaceful life and mind.

I used to be a "self-will run riot," unsettled in my mind, but today I use my energy to practice a centered mind, being still and knowing peace. Now I usually have the ability to step back in a crisis; I avoid being tactless, mean, and flaring up with damaging reactions. Today, I believe I live in soundness of mind. Practising magnanimity keeps me sane, and, as a result, I experience the gift of dignity. My mind, body, and soul are nourished when I meditate and pray. Healing from my unattractive and unacceptable character aspects has opened my heart to living compassionately. My actions come from being right-minded and living positively with a humble character.

Magnanimity is an attitude of gratitude and generosity!

Have a day of magnanimity!

TRANSFORMATION

Transformation is the act or process of changing, a psychic changeover, changing from negative to positive thinking habits, the experience of transforming.

Transformation of the mind involves honesty, open-mindedness, and willingness to alter your debilitating beliefs from self, ego, and spiritual malady. Transforming occurs when we make a radical change from our character flaws and stop fighting our past. Once we surrender our will to God's, we are free to rebuild ourselves. We live in the moment with a desire to continue to change, and with determination to have courage and dedication to share our new life.

I used to live in a cocoon – in a state of being sick, sad and sorry, but I transformed. Now I live free and fly like a butterfly. Slow is fast – transformation is a process; we strive for progress not perfection. One positive word a day, and taking time to write a reflection, helps me to transform daily for the better.

Self-transformation is a life journey, a healing process, nourished with patience, kindness, strength, hope, belief, and best of all LOVE!

It's an inside job: learn to love, love from the heart, and, as a result, enjoy better health. Forgiveness is the path to transform from judging and holding onto the past; learn from the experiences and move on. Love your mind; it has no limits, and, with spiritual growth, it continuously transforms for the better. Love to give; the more you give, the more you are blessed, because it keeps you connected with others. With your transformation, go forward, and, in your sharing, carry your message of Love, your transformed spirit!

Have a day of transformation!

SAGACIOUS

Sagacious comes from the word sage. Sagacious is to be wise, clever, clear-minded, keen, intelligent, shrewd, on the ball, sharp as a tack, perspicacious and to have sound judgment.

When we are faced with a situation, do we practice sagacious thinking? I have learned that, although it appears that I am being passive in an uncomfortable situation, it is better to practice sagaciously in neutrality. My sagacious ability helps me to understand and observe situations and see through obvious dysfunctional behaviors and lies.

Another situation in which to be sagacious is before a storm; checking the fridge and stocking up, making sure the candles and lanterns are all ready, and buckets of water in case the power goes off! Sagacious means to have far-sightedness. Today, we are grateful to have the ability to be sagacious.

Today, my mind is quite sagacious as a result of spiritual conditioning, a work in progress to look at my faults and to correct them each day to the best of my ability. My resourcefulness to use both my mind and physical abilities has led me to this ultimate brain challenge to write my reflection each day. This exercise strengthens my knowledge of words and exercises my fingers to type my reflection.

Have a day full of sagacious living!

Universe means all that exists and has existed: the cosmos, the world, nature and our reality. Yes, the universe is everything: all matter, molecules, atoms, particles, energy, human beings, and every living thing.

The universe is energy, so we are all connected. We see and feel this especially when we are around music. The universe, similar to our life, is like a guitar. I have learned to always tune and then play, just as I have learned to pray and live. When we tune our instrument and our thinking skills, our sounds are pleasant.

The universe is one big messenger, teaching us lessons throughout our journey. We all receive messages, but are we "awake" to recognize them, and do we enrich our lives to be the best we can be? It is a wonderful enlightenment to be aligned with the universe and living one day at a time, just going with the flow. Being centered in my core being opens my mind to continue with new experiences because I am a free spirit. I keep myself open to receiving abundance, grace, and love without limitations. I am keeping my dreams alive, living as best I can because of the grace of the universe, God, the creator.

The universe will throw us curve balls, but we are wise to stay rooted in our own being and listen for the lesson. It is in identifying that we grow and in comparing that we die. We are unique and individual, so we each will develop our own reality; it is best if we learn to walk the walk.

My spiritual guidance in my universe includes trust, wisdom, peace, faith, and patience. My life is manageable and confident, and I am secure and at peace as long as I stay spiritually fit. Let yourself be wrapped in the love and peace the universe has for you. Enjoy life daily with compassion and enjoyment of our universe.

Have a universal day!

INSPIRATION

Inspiration is stimulus, incitement, being inspired by something or some person, as well as being the act of influencing, and the action of moving your intellect and emotions.

When you feed your ego with gratitude, love, peace, excitement and adventure, you stimulate your mind, which results in feelings of inspiration. Along our journey, we learn to improve our direction; we are inspired by divine intervention, and we are inspired to strive for progress. When I united with others and we shared our experiences, we were inspired to climb over our obstacles with love and determination.

Our goal is progress; we nourish our progress by experiencing our gratitude and living on the beam – being honest, open-minded, willing to grow spiritually, and sharing our living in the Light.

The gift of inspiration came as a result of doing what was necessary: trusting the universe, filtering out any negativity, and realizing that I'm okay and can help others. My inspiration has grown from the influence of a group, friends, family, a medical team, reading, and, most of all, from my learning to embrace my belief in a divine influence. I am inspired to live happily, joyously, and free spirited; as a result, I experience great contentment, which is my wealth! It feels good to feel good; being spiritually fit is my wealth.

I share my message of hope as my inspiration to help myself and others. Life is good!

Have a day of inspiration!

WIDE AWAKE

Wide awake is to be conscious of every moment: our mind is quiet and open to our intuitions, our inner wisdom, and our truth. We are aware of our surroundings, and we are aligned with the universe, our higher power, and our higher purpose in life. We strive to be wide awake, to be present to the voice of truth, and we open our hearts and experience the peace, joy, and clarity of our reality.

We learn the tools to shape our journey. We learn to stay grounded in our new self-knowledge. We practice prayer and meditation and focus on positive thought. We are tuned into our inner voice for guidance and answers.

When a problem arises, we are secure in our wide-awake state, and we know we can deal with the difficult times, and we take action to transform the problem with a solution. It may feel insecure and confusing at first, but then our wide-awake brain kicks in; we turn it over to our faith and trust the process. Following divine guidance, we resolve issues and continue to grow spiritually each day.

Have a wide-awake day!

TENDERNESS

Tenderness is a state of warm-heartedness, lovingness, compassion, and affection. Tenderness is a virtue of kindness, passion, and sensibility. Tenderness is possible when we are aligned with love and integrity.

When we are honest with self, we can speak our own truth with confidence and humility. We tend to our emotional health; we feel more connectedness; we release ourselves from being enslaved in our disconnection, from being a walking dead spirit, and from being a lost soul. We tend to our soul health and heal from a state of weakness, from a hardened personality, low self-esteem, splitting, paralyzed in doubt, and living in an emotional prison. We become awake to a state of tenderness to break through our own trapped sense of self and no longer feel alone, lonely, and isolated, but rather free to care, be caring, and being part of a community. Such a wonderful journey into spiritual living; we forgive and no longer fear life but rather embrace life. We feel safe, knowing our reality has no limitations as we become open to endless possibilities.

My journey guided me to grow in self-confidence and humility. I learned to love myself through self-acceptance, and now I am capable of tenderness. The walls are down, and I am confident. I do not need to speak first because I have learned compassion to listen and have empathy. My practice today comes from being at peace with myself and through prayer and meditation. My hope is to speak cheerfully, to shine my light of hope, to keep my heart open, and to carry the message of love and tenderness. It is good to feel tenderly connected in my mind, body, soul, heart, and spirit!

Thank you to all who have tenderly helped, encouraged, and challenged me on my spiritual journey. I am forever grateful and go forth to share my tenderness.

Have a day of tenderness!

SELF-SUFFICIENT

Self-sufficient is the state of having confidence, being independent, self-supporting, self-reliant, and self-sustaining while being able to provide for oneself without the help of others.

Self-sufficient is a benefit from learning how to live on life's terms as we discover the joy of living and a gift from living with faith in our higher power. In unity, we feel connected as we grow, by working with family, friends and our support teams, and encouraging each other to share our visions. Life is not without negativity but, with our self-improvement, we learn to deal with it and move on, continuously growing with the flow of life.

Being aligned with a healthy support team nourished me to grow through my darkest fears. With their guidance, I was able to overcome difficult obstacles that kept me from being self-sufficient. Once I faced the fear and trusted the universe, I became more sensitive, experienced a new awareness and let go of self-centeredness, personal gratifications, and the spiritual malady of my ego state. Letting go of self-judgment, selfishness, social judgment, and material pride opens us to move to a state of self-sufficiency in unconditional love, great inner peace, and a fulfilling and meaningful life.

Acceptance was the answer to all; first I accepted a higher power and then I accepted myself, which opened me to experience the love of others. The process taught me the understanding that, in unity, we are able to experience self-sufficiency living in the Light. This is the real wealth of happiness, which is the result of letting go of anger, resentments, numbness, unfeeling; we awaken and consciously grow in love to a balanced life and a feeling of being self-sufficient.

So, let's get out our hoes and tend to our garden, weed out worries, trim off the stress, and water to relieve anxieties. Yes, it takes work to grow into a carefree, generous, and bountiful spirit; we must be awake and participate in the process.

Have a self-sufficient day!

INSIGHT

Insight is understanding, intuition, perception, apprehension, and having the ability to clearly see a person or thing's true nature. Insight is the ability to notice something or someone for exactly who they are and understand the reasons for their behaviors.

With insight, you can see the problem in a bigger context. Once you get out of the box and recognize the source of your emotional pain and difficulties, you are free to open yourself to new insights. With your new insight focused on positive outcomes, you follow through by changing and living in your new solutions.

When we see that we are stuck by our defeated ability to enjoy life, we are responsible to grow into a new way of living. We take time to learn about ourselves, and we seek support with others. In our effort to grow along spiritual lines, we gain insight into our own motives and behaviors. With this rigorous honesty, we take action to resolve uncomfortable living conditions.

We learn to have insight and we learn to mirror back love, patience, tenderness, kindness, tolerance; we are merciful. We are humble and yet strong, living in solutions. We have the insight and ability to be sensitive, considerate, sympathetic, compassionate, and empathetic but we are not door mats. We have the insight to express ourselves assertively with dignity, and we know peace.

Build yourself a strong character in faith and go forth with empowering spiritual insight. Keep your insight of your past, present, and future in perspective: enjoy living in the moment, one day at a time.

Have a day of insight!

RELAXED

Relaxed is to be in a state free from anxiety and tension while being calm, cool, composed, connected, tranquil, patient, and unhurried. When we are relaxed, we do not stress over how things are, but rather we are grateful. For example, we do not get overwhelmed about how the egg is cooked, just as long as the egg is cooked. When my plate is in front of me, it is best when I am mindful and relaxed, and savor each bite of these eggs.

One of my favorite ways to get relaxed is to hang out in nature: the woods, the hiking trails, the cross-country trails, the snowshoe trails, and the beach. Being in nature allows my mind, body and spirit to be in tune with my inner core self. I feel relaxed and at peace where I feel the energy of the universe, and my God the creator, soothing my soul. A wonderful feeling of being relaxed settles in my bones, and I rejoice, enjoying the experience of being connected and alive.

As I stop to enjoy the stillness, I close my eyes and appreciate the smells, and I know peace. I am totally relaxed in the moment and am mindful of the breath of air. Every cell, every molecule, every speck of me, is totally relaxed.

Life is a process of learning through trial and error, but there comes a time when you come to surrender. You learn to sit back in prayer and meditation because you are relaxed and feel peace. How wonderful is this state of peace? Peace sure beats being in a distracted state of mind that prevents us from being relaxed. With a mind quieted from the past and the future, we open ourselves to being relaxed and more productive, as a result of living in the present moment. Being relaxed allows me to feel so much gratitude.

Have a relaxed day!

POISE

Poise is a state of being stable and balanced, dignified and self-confident, while being in a state of self-assurance, serenity, elegance, tranquility, presence of mind, body and soul, tact, equilibrium, and *savoir faire*.

Poise is a wonderful gift to experience, attainable through the power of having conscious contact with a Higher Power. Taking time to review our life through meditation, we can gain spiritual poise with courage, new strength, and hope. We are empowered and motivated to study and devote time to better conduct our lives with gracefulness. In our fact-finding quest, we learn to identify our wrongs and accept our part in life, in our humanness. As we look at our behaviors and actions, we grow confident and learn to change and grow; in maturity, we find a new elegance in our tranquility. We trust God, become centered, awake, and poised in our spiritual life. Our confidence excels to a healthy state where we are gracious, certain, and positive, knowing we can handle life on life's terms. Together, you, me, and God can handle life and live in calmness and peace, poised.

So hold your head up high with poise, strength, and awareness. Enjoy the softness of living, serenity in peacefulness, and be confident that you are not alone. Just breathe in and smile in a state of poise, gracefulness, elegance, balance, and control. Be still and trust the journey!

Have a day of poise!

RENEWED

Renewed is to begin again, to restore, regenerate, replenish, renovate, refresh, and rejuvenate, and also to recover from insanity and dysfunctional, unfulfilling ways of living. Renewed living is a better way.

I believe I was born a free spirit and lived with happy, joyous, and free energy until I got derailed along the lifeline. When I met up with some soul-searching friends, I began to renew my spirit. With lots of study, devotion, and faith I renewed my energy and began to walk the walk a little bit each day. When I opened my heart, acknowledged there was a God and I wasn't it, I was humbled to live more peacefully.

I have learned that you can go through life lost and searching, or you can "grow" through life renewed. If you leave your garden unattended, it grows hard and not much comes from I; but if you keep the soil worked and loosened, your garden flourishes in its softness and is plentiful. Results in life are the same; take small steps, live healthy principles, and reap the benefits of being renewed physically, mentally, emotionally, and spiritually.

Mourn your past and move on. Change in our life is optional. I choose to be grateful for each day, empowered as a spiritual being steeped in prayer and meditation. I write a reflection on a word each day, and I give thanks for this ability; I am so grateful to be renewed in my mind's spirit. I was not one to conform, but I was willing to transform, renewed!

Have a renewed day!

FEBRUARY 25
ELATED

Elated is to be in high spirits, very happy, overjoyed, ecstatic, delightful, gleeful, joyous, euphoric, proud, and on cloud nine.

How do we get to this point in our lives?

For me, it was recognizing that my self-will was killing me. I was running around life on fast-forward, trying to be perfect and people-pleasing, a self-will run riot. This activity was overwhelming, exhausting, onerous, demanding, and bothersome.

It delights me to share that my will power has been recovered by my Higher Power in "Thy will." I am elated with the comfort I live in today with an open heart, compassionate and high spirited. Elated living is the gold standard, the measure and the touchstone for carrying the message of hope in spiritual living. Change is optional, but sometimes in life we must choose to change; trust God, clean house, and help others, which nourishes and feeds the soul to be elated. Sharing your experience in a joyous and gleeful state with gratitude is emotionally fulfilling. Also, living in an elated state with a compassionate heart opens doors for many happy adventures.

Embrace simplicity, rejoice and be calm, gentle, unhurried, and patient. Life is good. Live in acceptance, strength, courage, and wisdom with the God of your understanding and know peace. Enjoy the ride on cloud nine!

Have an elated day!

CALMNESS

Calmness is a wonderful mental state of serenity, peace of mind, tranquility, untroubled, quietness, placidness, and a state free from turmoil, disturbance, agitation, irritability, restlessness, and disconnectedness.

Calmness is a gift that results from surrendering to a Higher Power. Letting go of all our troubles and worries and allowing our egos to be nourished through our spiritual connection transforms us to a state of peace and calmness. Learning the difference between reacting and responding is very important. Reacting does not allow peace but responding maturely is a peaceful and positive way to deal with life. Another great teacher is time, because it allows things to heal and mellows out our understanding, acceptance, and ability to move on. Our peace comes from within; feed the positive energy and nurture your calmness.

Let's heal, wheel, and deal! Heal our spirits from chaos to calmness. Wheel in our brains, drive our own buses, tend to our thoughts, and cultivate positive thoughts through meditation. Finally, let's deal ourselves peace and don't beat ourselves up, because we all make mistakes. Learn from them and move on. Deal good deeds to others. Rejoice and let's share our God-centered calmness.

Have a day of calmness!

Bouncy is the state of being cheerful, jolly, upbeat, good natured, good humored, hopeful, chipper, zingy, lively, exuberant, frolicsome, enthusiastic, optimistic, and sanguine.

Being well grounded, self-confident, and successful in my teaching career, I experienced emotional strength and endurance to deal with most experiences in a bouncy attitude of gratitude. I was attached to who I had become, and my students were my joy. Coaching enriched my experiences and presented me opportunities to really shine in my ability to be bouncy.

Many years ago, I experienced a car accident, which became a detour in my spiritual journey; I became frustrated and angry and could not function well. My reality changed my mindset. I was attached to my career and my fun-loving, jolly, and happy teaching identity, I couldn't let go and let God. However, with much effort, a psychic change, and lots of therapy, I was able to let go of my pain and sorrow and grieved the loss of that old identity. I had to mourn lost skills that I could no longer do and accept and embrace what I could do. With great tenacity, I was able to give up the mentality of being stuck; I moved on to open new doors and start new chapters in my life.

I had an opportunity to study myself in great detail, and I have come to a new understanding and a deeper sense of life by accepting my Higher Power. With my surrender, I am gifted with a grateful heart and clarity. Living with anger does not allow the flow of healthy well-being; however, living in acceptance is all powerful and feeds positive energy and a vivacious, light-hearted, happy, joyous, and free spirit. Gratitude is the attitude for my life that I celebrate each day; with this, I am bouncy and as good-humored as I can be, just for today.

Have a bouncy day!

EDUCATION

Education is illumination, nurturing, inspiring, enriching, uplifting, improving, elevating, transforming, renewing, and is personal development for the mind. Education happens in families, churches, schools, retreats, groups, your community, and the world.

Education is the act of teaching and receiving subjects, ideas, and experiences. It is acquiring knowledge, learning, and training to analyze and make informed decisions. When you are connected, you learn better.

Spiritual education is an adventure into understanding how God is working for you in your life. When we renew our faith and trust our God, we educate ourselves and open our connections to the universe. Education involves looking at our beliefs, ideas, and behaviors so that we can study where we are in our trust. Spiritual education opens doors to learn how we think, feel, and act. When we are honest in our fact finding, we are ready to grow to new levels of happiness, peace, and freedom. A daily reading of healthy spiritual books, sharing with others, participating in discussions, and being connected, are good ways to educate ourselves. Education is a form of teaching, training, guiding, priming, and enlightenment. Education is an ongoing process, where we strive for progress rather than perfection. Seek in your heart, acknowledge in your mind, and live in your spirit!

Have a day of education!

ADVENTUROUS

Adventurous is being willing, daring, confident, bold, and fearless to take risks.

An adventurous person journeys to conquer new perspectives. Boredom and fear can open the path to be adventurous; becoming conscious is empowering and becoming mindful brings peace. It is an adventure to look at our life, because life is a teacher. The lessons keep coming back until we become adventurous enough to engage in self-care and are willing to change to learn the lessons. We are empowered by understanding that we all make mistakes because we are human and that changing is part of life. The key is to rise above our mistakes and move forward; we become adventurous to learn about feelings and emotions while coping with the lessons. Travelling is a great teacher; taking risks to adventure across our province, country, and overseas softens and humbles us with gratitude for what we have.

Learning about me has been an endless adventurous journey to seek wellness. I believe I was born with an enormous adventurous spirit. I am happiest when adventuring and trailblazing. Throughout my journey, I've embraced both the dark and light. Becoming self-aware of my habits and grounding to be centered has freed me to live balanced in the light. I have learned to acknowledge the past, deal with it, and adventure forward into wellness. Learning to be brave to do things I wouldn't normally do allowed me to live on the wild side, adventuring into activities such as white-water rafting, helicopter riding, and moving to a country where I couldn't speak the language. It was an adventure to live, grow, and learn in a new culture. Being adventurous is humbling because it develops appreciation, strength, and confidence.

Have an adventurous day!

GOOD-NATURED

Good-natured is to have, and to show, a kind spirit and to be pleasant, acquiescent, amiable, friendly, gracious, obliging, helpful, agreeable, and tolerant.

Living with the love of my higher power and knowing God as being all loving, cheerful, hopeful, lively and forgiving, and being God-like allows me to be good-natured. Developing my spiritual wellness enables me to live with a harmonious state of emotional stability. Being communicative to share my experiences, strength, and hope in open discussions shows my good-natured consciousness.

I am now mature to enjoy being pleasant, patient, and kind with all folks. Sharing my talents and gifts and being reliable, I am willing to help others with gratitude and expect nothing in return. I am not as suspicious of people, but rather look at them with optimism. I look for the good in people and have learned from my family and friends to be at peace with myself and enjoy the wonderful feeling of being good-natured. Being good-natured is natural, whole, and confident.

So now I strive for progress at being good-natured, to stop disliking people, and connect with better behavior. I love Mother Theresa; she was all-loving and good-natured, patient, kind, and always giving her time to others, a pretty good role model to follow.

Have a good-natured day!

THRILLED

Thrilled is when you have a sudden feeling of inspiration, delight, excitement, pleasure, and exhilaration.

Challenges in my life are now manageable, whether I am presented with lightness or darkness. I am thrilled to be spiritually fit and responsible to deal with my thoughts and emotions. Keeping an open heart allows my mind to follow with positive resolutions; we all come out shining, radiant, and full of life. Being spiritually thrilled and cheering people on in positive directions to experience a happy and prosperous life with abundance of love and peace is very thrilling, satisfying, and exhilarating.

Finding a balance in life allows me to feel thrilled, full of energy, serene, and to be composed. Learning to manage my journey with acceptance, trust, and faith in my higher power thrills me to move forward in positive, active living. I am deeply grateful; gratitude is my attitude for this true freedom; I am thrilled!

So, my friends, be polite and generous; walk the walk of love and be kind. I am thrilled to share my joy with you all.

Have a day being thrilled!

CONSISTENT

Consistent is to behave continuously in the same way: harmoniously, with compatibility and stability, constantly and steadily. Consistent living in stability is desirable and possible.

Living in the fourth dimension of life is being spiritually fit, which I achieve by communicating the truth. I acknowledge my anger, fear, guilt, and shame. I make efforts to change by showing up for life. I learn to say what I mean, and I learn to trust myself. I learn to accept life on life's terms, understanding myself with an open heart and humility. I am dedicated to nourishing my mind with God because I understand love. I practice living in unity with God, myself, and others, consistently sharing my truth, trust, love, and peace.

I have freed myself from judging and engage in positive meditation. I pray for guidance from God's will and to know a new freedom. I am free from the past, free from self-limitations, and free to live in the moment. I have moved forward on my journey and walk the walk with the creator.

Being consistent in staying connected with others gives me a sense of belonging and, together, we grow through sharing our experiences. I am bonded on my journey with others, grateful for a new beginning, and am comforted knowing I don't have to journey alone. I show my gratitude by being of continual service. I am consistent in sharing my strength and hope on how God is working in my life, and I am accountable for my thoughts and actions from this day on!

Let's share our truth, release all negativity that we are holding within, and be consistent in our integrity, insight, forgiveness, love, awareness, and liberation.

Have a consistent day!

International means the involvement of many countries. International means everywhere on earth, all our universe: all cultures, beliefs, values, and practices.

Internationally, our world lives in changing times. Cultures are mixing, becoming multicultural; with multiculturalism comes ethical principles. Acceptance and integration of faith through prayer and meditation is the key to international world peace. The universe is one and, with positive spiritual transformations, we can grow together as one.

Let's embrace a world of peace. It starts with each one of us; together we grow by sharing our love and peace. Let's keep our hearts open and live spiritually fit, respecting all international spiritual journeys and practices.

International knowledge is fundamental to learn respect for all, as we grow in modern times and with new trends. We can live in the kingdom of our creator with peace among all brotherhoods and sisterhoods with acceptance, respect, and tolerance.

The Golden Rule is to respect all: Baha'i Faith, Hinduism, Buddhism, Confucianism, Taoism, Sikhism, Christianity, Unitarianism, Zoroastrianism, Native Spirituality, Jainism, Judaism, and Islam. Peace to all, as we rejoice for all the universe's creations, colors, and cultures, amen!

Have a day being part of an international community!

Therapeutic relates to healing from disease. Therapeutic is when something aids our healing and is natural, curative, medicinal, and restorative. Therapeutic also relates to spiritual healing from dis-ease!

Coping skills can be improved with communication in therapy, meditation, and prayer, as we study and practise our beliefs and values. Once you tap into your core belief system, you can see how it has been serving you, and you can open your heart to connect your mind, body, and soul. It is therapeutic to do this with trusted family, friends, and therapists.

Spiritual therapy is a progress in action through daily meditation and prayer. I find it therapeutic to focus on the positive meaning of words each day and to read good books to help sharpen my abilities to cope with life. Therapeutic benefits come from working with counsellors to clarify my spiritual self. Attending groups and sharing my spiritually fit lifestyle with others, which offers me spiritual healing, insight, and a social support system, is also therapeutic.

Once I learned the nature of my thinking, I was able to apply my consciousness to my perceptions and create healthier realities dedicated to being the best I can be, one day at a time.

Have a therapeutic day!

PLACID

Placid means to be tranquil, level-headed, even-tempered, self-possessed, not to get easily upset, and to be unexcitable, calm, steady, self-composed, untroubled, unworried, and peaceful. Placid is to be centered, grounded and living serenely, free from disturbance or interruption. To be placid is to be emotionally stable.

I was derailed in my silence and carried anger and resentment. I behaved loudly, aggressively, and experienced bitterness. I could not succeed in my studies and dreams. I was blind and could not see. When I realized I was off the beam, I traveled with "the Footprints in the Sand," and then, one day, I saw the Light!

Through the help of family, friends, 12-step programs, and therapeutic guidance, my voice became empowered, and I experienced release from my anger and resentments. Through healing, I became quiet and assertive, as well as humble. I grew, and continue to grow, to succeed and live my dreams.

Today I go placidly, walking the walk, and knowing peace in silence. The "Desiderata" has become my way of living, which I read and work on manifesting in my life. Placidity came sometimes quickly, sometimes slowly, but, like a turtle, I was carrying a hard shell; I won the race! Ha-ha!

Have a placid day!

MARCH 7
CAREFREE

Carefree is to be spiritually fit and to have no worries or troubles. Carefree is to be free from care, lighthearted, unconcerned, happy-go-lucky, insouciant, and blissfully happy.

Carefree is a wonderful state to be in life. It is with clarity and understanding that I find myself creating the reality of enjoying my journey and experiencing positive, peaceful, and powerful energy. I feel genuine gratitude to share peace and love in my own special way.

Carefree comes from happiness. My happiness is based on my journey one day at a time. I understand my happiness is not my destination, but it is my experience and my journey. So, I praise my higher power, tap into my peacefulness, and develop my calmness with my conscious contact through prayer and meditation. I am grateful to rejoice and be carefree in my well-being.

Going to retreats at the Bethany [property of the Sisters of Saint Martha, a Marian Community near Antigonish] has provided me with a carefree environment in a beautiful center. It was a peaceful place to walk the labyrinth for reflection, contemplation, and prayer. I am grateful to be carefree just for today feeling the peace and serenity.

Have a carefree day!

MARCH 8
INTEGRITY

Integrity is the state of being honest, honoring, living virtues, sincerity, truthfulness, ethical, morality, decency, and fairness. Integrity is living in the state of unity, togetherness, solidarity, and coherence. Integrity becomes a choice with maturity and willingness to live consistently striving for progress in one's actions, beliefs, behaviors, gestures, and practices.

When I stopped and took account of my life and took a good honest look at my truths, I then became ready to peel back the layers of disillusion. Dignity came as a result of having the integrity to share my faults, put them to rest, and set myself free to be the beautiful, humble, intelligent human being that I was born to be.

My spiritual integrity grows with practising conscious contact with, and doing the will of, my higher power. Living in a state of integrity becomes a way of life; knowing the truth and acting on the truth empowers me to live an honest authentic life. I am a ray of light from God, beaming with an illuminated spirit deep within my heart, at peace, and embraced in my connection.

I want to share and enjoy the gifts of spiritual integrity. I thrive in my human wholeness, totally energized and inspired with clarity in my heart and having the willingness to continue to grow one day at a time with compassion and forgiveness. I practise being mature and accept blessings with peace and freedom to look the world in the eye and be proud to be humble no matter where I am in life.

Integrity is an attitude of gratitude to continually take my own inventory and stay true to my authentic self, to be accountable for my daily living, and to share and care for my fellow human beings. Learning to live with integrity in the moment, day to day, every day, harmonizes my experiences and hopes to live a good moral life. This practice is my insurance to stay attuned to my integrity.

Have a day of integrity!

PIONEERING

Pioneering is to be a leading force, a forerunner, pathfinder, and trailblazer. Pioneering is the act of being the first, or among the first, to inquire and progress.

When you are willing to go to any length to find solutions, endure the journey to learn to walk the walk, you have a pioneering spirit. The pioneering spirit is active when you push forward in your struggles from the darkness to the light. Along the journey, we peel back the layers and explore new ideas, beliefs, and values. We try differently rather than harder, and we identify rather than compare.

Part of my journey involved hiking, camping, and skiing outback. Biking and camping in the wilderness strengthened my pioneer spirit. Along the river, in a lean-to with a little fire of twigs and branches crackling, I fed my pioneering spirit. I believe I have an old soul with a true pioneering spirit, always loving an adventure. I love to travel and camp out. Making a bonfire and sitting under the stars is such a peaceful experience, and the simplicity feeds my serenity.

I believe a spiritual pioneer is one who lives with serenity, honesty, courage, wisdom, and loyalty.

So let's all enjoy a pioneering spirit to become whole and grounded; let's be the best spiritual pioneers we can be, just for today, one day at a time, until we meet again. All my relations!

Have a pioneering day!

MARCH 10
TREASURED

Treasured is to be valuable and precious with appreciation, adoration, esteem, conserved, preserved, and loving a person or place.

To examine my life, thoughts, feelings, behaviors, influences, and discipline to discover what is treasured in my own life has helped develop and maintain a healthy mind-set. A treasured mind-set is feeling satisfaction in my life, thriving in my truth, seeing my potential, and keeping my dreams alive. I am open to all the possibilities life has to offer me.

Being emotionally, mentally, physically and spiritually fit is to be treasured. Living out my dreams, using my potential to live on the beam, one day at a time, keeps me in a state of appreciation and adoration. I still have hopes to recover my physical fitness; this too shall come! Ha!

I adore my higher power, and I value my treasured time every morning with humble gratitude. I pray and meditate for continued divine interventions that I might have healthy perceptions, positive attitudes, and maintain patience in a state of psychological well-being. Being interconnected, integrated, and restored to living a balanced positive lifestyle enables me to share a positive perspective on living and life.

I treasure my family and friends. I treasure my peace and stability to enjoy life on life's terms. I treasure this beautiful sunny day. I treasure all that life has to offer me today. Most of all I treasure my higher power's blessings and love.

Have a treasured day!

SPECIAL

Special is to be exceptional, unusual, notable, remarkable, unique, individual, and particular, to have a particular function and purpose, a unique character and personality.

Life can be seen as a train: each stage, chapter, and experience representing a boxcar. It is beautiful, colorful, cheerful, challenging, and reasonably comfortable as long as I stay on the track, connected and integrated. However, sometimes I am faced with people, places, and things that shake up my boxcars, and sometimes I get derailed, lost, and disconnected. A conscious awakening to see my own makings, the environment I live in, and sharing my journey is my engine to pull me forward.

It is exceptional and remarkable to have an experience and an awakening to get back on the tracks. I learn to trust faith and to let go of some boxcars, the old inventory; I gain new perceptions and realities, and the new boxcars are welcome. It is particularly special that I keep moving forward in a state of progress. Trains, like life, move forward; sometimes quickly, sometimes slowly, so I must stay awake to enjoy the journey!

It is special to develop with a focus on improved healthy perceptions and to learn to adapt and transform with an attitude of gratitude. This grateful state opens my heart with love and a compassionate, caring, and sharing lifestyle. Today, this special state encourages me to write my unique reflection on a word once a day, so that I enjoy life on the slow, steady, and stable track of serenity.

Have a special day!

STILLNESS

Stillness is to be free from disturbances, rackets, commotions, agitation and motion. Stillness is having calm, quietness, placidity, placidness, peacefulness, being untroubled and having tranquility and serenity.

Stillness is a state of being awake and conscious of where I see my truth revealed. As I sit quietly focused on my breath, I feel my heart beating in the stillness. I welcome the abundance of peace and love as it aligns my well-being. In this moment of devotion to my well-being, I seek guidance and accept that all will be well; I release my thoughts.

Having the courage to practice stillness opens me to guidance, wisdom, and enlightenment to be strong, faithful, and free. It is vital to nourish my mind, body, soul, heart, and spirit. My mind is nourished by prayer and meditation; my body relaxes; my soul feels respected; my heart opens; and my spirit is illuminated, sparkling in a happy, joyous and free state. Life in stillness nourishes my clarity for healthier perceptions, and I worship my peace within.

When I was alone, wounded, and fragmented, I knew misery and pain; with stillness, I grew with God and others to live in unity, healed and unified. I am recovered in my mind, body, soul, heart, and spirit. My greatest wealth is to take time to simply be, to sit in stillness, then to go about my day in mindfulness, centered to share my peace. I trust God and energy to liberate me from worldly disturbances, rackets, and negative voices. Blessed with gratitude, I now live in a state of a cheerful mind, living well with my lights on. I am home, living as God's agent of Love.

Have a day of stillness!

TRAVELED

Traveled is to have moved or gone from one place or point to another, to have proceeded or advanced in any way, to have transformed, moved forward, journeyed, wandered, or adventured.

In my spiritual sojourns, I have traveled on some colorful journeys to learn my truths, my dreams, and my motivations. My insight and awareness have consistently improved, and I have grown in my state of awakening and clearness to love.

During my journey, I have traveled from great levels of darkness, despair, and depression into the light of hopefulness and happiness. Awakening slowly opened my heart and soul to change on a daily basis. My new awakening gives me a strong sense of self-esteem. I have traveled and now understand that my experiences have brought me out of my extreme disconnectedness of self. I have traveled to new experiences of encouragement, serenity, and spiritual growth. My healed state of consciousness is focused on being divinely guided, directed, and protected. I travel with an open heart and an illuminated soul, full of joy, happiness, and a contented spirit, but most of all with the Grace of God.

Have a day of travel!

ON THE BEAM

"On the beam" is to be on the positive side, the preferred course and direction, proceeding well, positively, correctly, radiantly, and happily living in the Light. On the beam means having qualities of living in honesty, faith, courage, consideration, humility, giving, grateful, modesty, self-forgiving, moderation, action, trust, and love.

Living off the beam is living with character defects such as dishonesty, fear, inconsideration, having false pride, envy, self-pity, self-justification, self-importance, self-condemnation, gluttony, sloth, and being greedy, angry, impatient, resentful, hateful, and suspicious.

These are two choices we have: living on the beam or off the beam. Today, I choose and am inspired to live on the beam to the best of my ability, which came with rebuilding my trust in humanity and developing confident self-esteem. I am learning to be still, in the moment, in meditation and prayer, asking for forgiveness, taming the constant racket and ranting dialogue in my brain cells, and to move forward. It is with sincere gratitude that I live with respect for myself, God—my energy source –and others. These gifts bring me the wonderful outcome of a quiet, placid, stable, and peaceful mind. Living on the beam awards me to constructively review my day, to live with a clear conscience, and a proper attitude of gratitude.

So jump on the beam and let your light shine, sparkle, and illuminate your well-being!

Have a day on the beam!

WONDERFUL

Wonderful is to be good, marvelous, fantastic, fabulous, miraculous, aces, amazing, astonishing, and awesome.

Gratitude is the attitude for a wonderful life. Being honest and respectful of all beings creates a wonderful environment. Most beings are basically good, but some are disconnected through the stress of human conditions that drive them to pain, deprivation, and destruction.

My hope is that each day, more and more, we can all try to travel the journey with our fellow beings in honesty, respectfulness, and encouraging each other to be the best we can be. Healthier self-esteem and self-confidence are wonderful assets.

We are wonderful when we have, and improve our, high self-esteem. We project optimism, control, responsibility, enthusiasm, happiness, and sometimes a wonderful sense of humor. We are wonderful when we are spiritually fit and well enough to offer praise to each other. We are wonderful when we are grounded in accepting our source of energy and understand that grace guides, directs, and protects us.

When I don't feel wonderful, I take an inventory of my circumstances and issues and change accordingly to live a happier and healthier life. I build my confidence from my energy source and am blessed with self-confidence knowing I am not alone. I have a wonderful life, staying humble and grateful, walking the walk each day!

Have a wonderful day!

Equanimity is a state of psychological stability and composure; having the quality of being patient, calm, cool, assuring, confident, peaceful, tranquil, and serene. Equanimity is having an unshakable balance of mind that is based in insight.

A mind of equanimity is one of abundance, good-will, a strong sense of well-being, inner peace, calm, and a stable detachment of the egotistical self. Such a mind is humble and lacks conceit. With equanimity, we feel adequate, successful, and competent in decision-making.

Equanimity comes from the discipline to live with integrity and faith, developing on-the-beam positive attributes, and continuously journey toward a well-developed mind with a positive sense of well-being. Building an attitude of gratitude and loving acceptance and having a deep psychological/spiritual experience helped me to awaken and brings inner strength each day so that equanimity follows.

The key is mindfulness, which opens the freedom path, and to keep learning and developing my inner strength to keep a balanced mind; such is the ongoing process to a mind of equanimity.

Have a day of equanimity!

RESTFUL

Restful is the state of being at rest; quiet, placid, calm, still, peaceful, and tranquil. It is restful when you experience a good rest.

Being spiritually fit is to be at rest. I am rested after a peaceful sleep. When I wake up, I take time for prayer and meditation, which is a time to open my day with God and to be restful, right there in the moment. God is in me, and I am God's energy of love to serve my fellow human beings and to be one with the universe. In my restful state, I feel God's energy and know peace because I choose to believe. I feel comforted in never-ending Love.

My life rests in God, and I am restful in my activities. Grounded and centered in good-spirits, I continue to seek and savor the joys of living.

I don't have to be doing something or be busy because I am restful in stillness, silence, and peace. However, when I choose to do an activity, I try to do it in a restful state.

In time of troubles, I find it is restful to just take time and observe, let the process unfold, and welcome the positive energy and vibration to guide me. I trust my instinct and ask myself: what would a God-loving person do? I thank my higher source in advance for a solution. I accept the lessons and move on. I am no longer a basket case, but rather patient and restful writing about words that came out of a basket!

Have a restful day!

SAPIENT

Sapient is having and sharing great wisdom, sound judgment, insight, persistence, prudence, and discernment.

Sapient is living well as a result of taking time to study our life, improve our thinking skills, asking for guidance, and experiencing wisdom to move on. We become closer to living a sapient life when we understand our life with acceptance, willingness to learn our truths, and to shift our perspectives and perceptions. Then we make healthier decisions with improved behaviors and actions.

I really am enjoying living a sapient life with emotional well-being. I'm growing a little more each day and, hopefully, with growth, I become more knowledgeable, understanding, and sapient. Accepting my experiences each day opens my consciousness to a greater understanding of my beliefs. I maintain my soundness of mind by being responsible and disciplined.

My life has improved, and I am blessed each day as I live consciously, praying and mindfully meditating, reading spiritual books, and staying focused. These activities feed my mind with happy thoughts and my well-being, creating a sound mind that allows me to respond rather than react to life.

Have a day being sapient!

SPIRIT

Spirit is breath, soul, courage, a vigorous force, psyche, and soul in a person that gives one life, energy and power. Spirit, to me, is the inner quality of a person.

Wow, this is what I wanted in my life; having found my best spirit, I continue to live in good spirits. On April 10, 2001 I was in a serious car accident and found myself at home on a daily basis. My spirit felt broken, and I was faced with many changes to rebuild myself.

On April 11, 2003, a little baby sheltie dog was born and, weeks later, she came home to live with me. I named her Spirit Gracey. She gave me the courage to live as best I could each day. She became my baby, and I loved her to the moon and back. We traveled together and grew each day with unconditional love.

She lived up to her name: she was my breath and my courage. She lifted my spirits and taught me grace. My psyche changed, my inner soul grew, and she brought me unconditional love, which opened my heart to grow out of turmoil and chaos in my troubled times. We loved each other: walked, played, and comforted each other. Best of all, we shared our love every day wherever we traveled. She enhanced my spirit with her joy and love.

March 18, 2015, our journey ended on this earth. I was shaken, but I was not broken; I acknowledged that my heart ached and wept like a baby. I embraced all our good times and grieved my dog. Then I used all my tools to maintain soundness of mind. I said goodbye and asked God to give me a sign; fifteen minutes later I experienced a blessed sign. Thank you, Spirit Gracey, for all your love. You will live in my heart forever. My spirit is better for having you in my life. RIP Spirit Gracey, enjoy the rainbow crossover.

Have a day of good spirit!

Spiritual is relating to spirit, being closely connected to God, my true self, and others with interests, attitudes, and sharing similar views on moral living.

Spiritual to me is to be in relationships based on communication about experiences and hope. I become God's agent by living my life in goodness, gentleness, patience, love, kindness, faithfulness, and self-control. My daily practices keep my heart open to allow me to deal with my issues, and acknowledgement allows me to heal. Being spiritually fit, I face the truth and communicate immediately: screaming, weeping, and accepting the emotional pain, dealing with the issue, and releasing negative emotions of anger, blame, and guilt. I stay true to myself spiritually, and I feel the emotions of sadness, loss, and grief. Feeling the feelings and accepting the signs of peace, I am consistent in my journey and comforted in my grieving, knowing my dog Spirit and I loved; we shared our trust in each other.

Blessed with unconditional love, we shared growing, and my spiritual life bloomed; I became whole. In my spiritual conditioning, adventures, and enlightenment, I have learned the power of accepting life on life's terms, the gift of forgiveness, and freedom. Our love was strong, Spirit; you opened my heart, gave love and received love. You were my link to wellness in my heart, forever with good thoughts. Be a free Spirit and move forward in trust.

Have a spiritual day!

GOOD-HEARTED

Good-hearted is to have a kind and generous spirit, to be sympathetic, tender, compassionate, kind-hearted, soft-hearted, and benevolent.

Time is the greatest gift. In my high school years, I would go after school to the Bethany convent as a volunteer. I developed a compassion for caring for the elderly. I realized that the nuns, these wonderful women, simply wanted my time. They were so grateful for my time; I would take some for walks, write letters for others, and just be present with others. I think these later ones knew I needed their prayers!

My journey brought me down some colorful roads, but at the bottom of my heart I attempted to be good-hearted. Eventually, I returned to a healthier lifestyle, accepted my God, and found my good-hearted spirit. My Aunt Louise was a good-hearted woman, gracious and placid, who had the key to happiness and shared her journey with me. We prayed together; she encouraged me to sing, play my guitar, fiddle, and even play a bit of mandolin.

Today, I feel confidence and, as a result, I have grown to be a compassionate, good-hearted woman and love to share my time, love, and light.

Have a good-hearted day!

LISTENING

Listening is the ability to pay attention and process what I am hearing: to decipher, interpret, understand and concentrate on another while encompassing comprehension, retaining, and responding. It requires that I pay attention, focus and process, or not, and analyze with perspective.

The art of listening has done wonders for my serenity this weekend. I was listening to music: bluegrass, country, and Gypsy Jazz. Listening to such wonderful music activated my brain cells, and the brain circuits were able to mend. Jean Paul and I spent the weekend at a Hotel where we listened to, and played, music. Then we enjoyed an evening out at the local club and listened to the band "Christine Tassen et les Imposteures." So much great listening!

Now, how is this word "listening" spiritual?

I have learned that praying is talking to God, my energy source, and meditation is listening to God. My gut feels good when I practise sitting back and listening, as well as observing. My energy replenishes and my life overflows with courage to use my talents. My life is filled with infinite possibilities because I am willing to listen to wellness and follow through with healthy choices for the most part. However, I am human, and I do falter. The blessing is to get back up and thrive for improvement. I must stay awake and keep listening for the next lesson.

Have a day of listening!

VALIANT

Valiant is to be great-hearted, bold, undaunted, dauntless, fearless, and to possess bravery, courage, and determination. To be valiant requires us to be joyful, loving, kind, patient, strong, caring, and sharing.

The gifts of my spirituality allow me to share and to be good to others, follow the Golden Rule, learn to live and let live, and live a better life in humility, soundness of mind, and wisdom.

Last night, we listened to the band "Christine Tassen et Les Imposteures," who presented themselves as four valiant female musicians. They played Gypsy Jazz and Swing music that was traditionally only presented by men. They excelled in their valiant, undaunted, fearless, joyful, and strong presentation with a fabulous show.
I went online and bought some of their CDs so that I could listen to these four women, who are energizing and amazing. I would say they are the best in the universe; my ears and inner spirit give thanks. I am thankful for the four valiant ladies. Listening to their music is the best medicine, so soothing and healing.

Have a day being valiant!

FABULOUS

Fabulous is to be really good, incredible, fabled, successful, pleasing, astonishing, and to express a good time.

Today I celebrate my birthday, along with my aunt Edna. We enjoyed a conversation on the phone, and it was fabulous to share part of my day with her. Then I went out to supper with Jean Paul; it was especially fabulous to eat Chinese food. Nonetheless, the absolute most fabulous surprise was receiving a video from my little friend Gus Babineaux from Louisiana, who sang me happy birthday, and his older sister Gracie speaking French to me.

Fabulous is a great word, and it is so fabulous to share each day and develop serenity and hope. Living by the sea is a fabulous place to live, to meditate and watch sunsets that are so full of colors that light up the sky.
It's fabulous to have new technology so that we can share and reach so many more folks. We share and support each other in good days, as well as sad days. I am grateful to have so much support and encouragement to be the best me. I am blessed with a fabulous sense of peace, soundness of mind, and joy of life.

Have a fabulous day!

Musical is a word that comes from music. It is an inner voice and universal language of the soul.

As a child, my first memory of experiencing musical bliss was in church; I loved to hear all the lovely worshipping songs and especially the organ. Another space of musical bliss was out in nature, with the birds singing and the river rippling. Then it came from listening to the radio and watching TV, which amazed me, and made me feel happy, connected, and aligned in my heart and soul.

I have learned to feed my soul with music, hearing, listening, and playing; these activities have kept me connected over the years. When I hear music and feed my soul with pleasant sounds, my brain cells spark and ignite to soothe my soul. Musical friends are living in the moment, producing music together, and being present in the creative moment. Playing music takes me on a journey out of myself and divinely inspires musical arrangements to flow freely.

When I am relaxed into my music, I feel good and am spiritually uplifted. Listening and playing music instills an attitude of gratitude for my abilities and talent. My heart responds to music; I feel creative, compassionate, and at peace.

Spending the weekend with friends and playing music was a very spiritual time because we were in the flow. We were so uplifted and rocking, I even created a song in the moment! This feeds my spiritual wellness. I look forward to weekend jamming parties, retreats, and festivals, because they are places full of happy and loving musical folks. To be musical is one of my sacred blessings. Turn up the music and enjoy a musical experience!

Have a musical day!

SPLENDID

Splendid is to be very beautiful, brilliant, excellent, glorious, magnificent, majestic, impressive, and good.

Splendid, in the spiritual sense, is when I am beaming, brilliant, glowing, luminous, clear, and radiant. When I am living well, I feel splendid. Life is good, and I can share my experiences with my splendid friends and family. One night, it was awesome, fabulous, and great, spending an evening with a van load of friends. We went for a splendid ride and attended a birthday party, where we ate splendid food and then had a splendid drive back home.

My most splendid experiences occur while out walking and sitting in nature. Before the car accident, I hiked, biked, and camped along rivers where I felt safe and secure. All the voices and noises would disappear, and I would welcome the peaceful energy and open myself to God. I would pray and then listen. Sometimes God would send a deer along my trail to greet me; other times, it would be a partridge to wake me up to be more aware of my profound, splendid inner peace and calmness.

Have a splendid day!

Neat is to be graceful, elegant, efficient, cool, great, orderly, well-groomed, and tremendous, to name a few. Neat is a big word in the sense that it has many reference points. It is neat to find peace and love within and to live well in positive character attributes.

Writing is a neat experience for me, because it focuses my thoughts on one word a day. It is neat to realize that life is simply about love, the love of God within, the love of self, and the love of others. It is neat to believe that I am divinely guided, directed and protected when I open myself to the well-being of all humankind.

It is neat to live in good spirits in this awesome universe and to know that I am never alone. I am part of the whole that makes me happy and free to move forward, capable and willing to do for others with gratitude.

Finding my core self, and growing to be a neat gal, partner, aunt, sister, daughter, and friend, has been quite a journey. Today, my life is about people and unconditional love. I am grateful to have a neat life of love in action by being the best I can be each day.

Have a day being neat!

FLEXIBILITY

Flexibility is when you are willing to change and do things differently, such as adapting and being open to modification. Flexible means to be able to bend. I have been bent and twisted; I guess I have extreme flexibility.

Living in flexibility opened me up to a more balanced life because I was able to heal from stress and release my tensions; I grew flexible to strengthen my character to live better. Being pliable opened my heart to improved relationships.

I came to realize that I have a journey to live while on this earth in my physical, mental, and spiritual state; I am better equipped if I live with flexibility. My journey has been colorful and challenging, but my spiritual perspectives have guided, directed, and protected me. These perspectives include being honest, open-minded, and willing to accept changes along my path.

Living with the serenity prayer opens my mind to flexibility. Each day, I offer myself to be teachable, accepting, and full of gratitude for all that life offers me. I am open to healthy feelings and emotions, flexible to take time for grieving, celebrating and moving on in life. My flexibility allows me to enjoy living with peace of mind, joy, love, compassion, and serenity.

Have a day of flexibility!

ENHANCING

Enhancing is to improve the quality, intensity, strength; to elevate, increase, amplify, magnify, and complement.

I have come to practise the magnificent benefits of daily prayer and meditation, which are comforting and enhance my ability to live a balanced life. This conscious contact is enhancing my spiritual growth and inner peace.

Spending time outdoors and enjoying nature are crucial to enhancing my connectedness. There is great peace sitting near a bonfire, playing guitar and singing, and the feeling of peace enhances my well-being. Listening to the birds, the leaves of the trees, and the fire crackling is very peaceful. The energy is great for enhancing my brain cells to spark with joy, compassion, and love. Enhancing good thoughts allows me to learn to love myself and others unconditionally, which opens my heart and sense of well-being. As a result, I feel secure, confident, trusting and content with life.

God enhances my life every day; I live an inspired life in the Light, and I am so grateful for all my adventures and wonders of the universe. I'm enjoying life through my music, sewing, art, painting, travel, and spiritual books, enhancing each day with a bit more wakefulness.

Have an enhancing day!

Talents are the natural gifts of a person. They are special abilities, aptitudes, successes, capabilities, and genius.

I especially enjoyed my weekend with friends playing music, and I even played my bass. It is a slow process to learn to play that big doghouse bass, but I am patient and willing. We were well entertained and blessed to attend the Fanfare concert at the Saulnierville church. It was a real community showcase of the excellent talent of many folks singing and playing instruments.

I find the biggest talent in my life is the ability to share my talents. Many enjoy the benefits of natural talents, but it is the sharing of them that makes them real. When I am around musical talents, there is usually a great feeling of joy and happiness. At festivals, I feel the happy energy, the love, and the respect. There is lots of talent in building camps and little villages, sharing food, and helping each other.
Talents are gifts from my genes and God. There is great glory in experiencing and expressing my talents among friends and family. I will continue sharing my talents with all my heart.

Have a day of talents!

MODESTY

Modesty is the state of living humbly, being meek, down-to-earth, and unassuming in my abilities.

If we behave properly, quietly, humbly, harmoniously, and without vanity, then we have modesty. It is displayed in people who love themselves, love others, and take care of themselves without bragging or arrogance; showing gratitude, sharing their creativity, they are real and consistent.

Modesty is a characteristic that I witnessed in my mother and three sisters; they all knit socks in their meekness. They are grateful to get out for a ride, especially to the wool factory. They are all down-to-earth and soul sisters; all sharing their love, gratitude, and humbleness – the best examples of true modesty I have witnessed. For me, it's a work in progress!

Have a day of modesty!

Harmony is having the quality of being in tune, in balance, and melodious in producing music. Having compatibility and coordination, harmony creates pleasant music. Harmony also refers to having agreement, understanding, fellowship, friendship, peace, unity, and like-mindedness.

Living mellifluously is a blessing, which progresses a little more each day due to living on the beam with positive character attributes. Harmony in our life is a result of accepting positive ways of living in the moment, changing negative behaviors into positive actions and habits, opening our heart, mind and soul, creating positive intentions, and continuously reading positive affirmations and literature. Harmony is a gift and is best shared with others.

Daily prayer and meditation bring harmony into our life. Harmoniously living in fellowship with friends and family allows us to grow together in unity. Suiting up and showing up for life while sharing our talents produces harmony and connects us with good vibes. Connecting with like-minded people brings harmony to relationships, friendships, and fellowships. Most of all, the best harmony is when we get together with God's divine inspirations and play music together.

Have a day of harmony!

EMOTIONAL

Emotional is when one has intense feelings, and the subjective experience reflects psychological changes, thinking processes, and behavioral expression.

Emotional might be characterized as heart-warming, heart rendering, dramatic, affecting, haunting, moving, and sentimental. When a person expresses their emotions, they may be displayed as melodramatic, excitable, temperamental, sentimental, sensitive, responsive, tender, and loving.

A few weeks ago, I was emotional at the loss of my dog Spirit. This experience was dramatic in the moment; then I was faced with my thinking process, and I was able to express my feelings. I cried and talked with my partner Jean Paul; we focused on the positives and grounded ourselves. We played cribbage, and I cried and felt all the emotional feelings.

With my spiritual practice, I was comforted in prayer and meditation. I was emotionally traumatized but emotionally stable enough to respond in a healthy state rather than reacting. Thank you, my God.

Have an emotional day!

WORSHIPFUL

Worshipful is to feel and show reverence, honor, respect, and adoration.

When we meditate and pray, we grow spiritually in our worshipful state. We are divinely inspired in our attitudes and actions when we are being worshipful. We become closer through our words and thoughts to our Higher Power; emotional well-being manifests through inner peace, and we are divinely guided and protected.

It has been my personal experience to become energized and serene by being worshipful. My brain cells are nourished, relaxed, illuminated, and inspired. I am comforted in knowing that, together with God's help, I can resolve any problems that I am faced with in this life. Yes, problems help us to grow; in growing, I have developed a stronger connection through patience, tolerance, discipline, simplicity, and restraint.

Have a worshipful day!

TENACITY

Tenacity is the quality of determination, persistence, perseverance, purposefulness, tirelessness, staying power, endurance, patience, and stubbornness.

A person who hangs in there, and just won't quit, has tenacity. I went back to grade twelve three times until I had good enough marks to go to university. With my tenacity, I attended Dalhousie, Nova Scotia Teachers College, Saint Mary's University, Alliance Française in Paris, St. Anne's University, University of Chicoutimi, University of Jonquiere, and Acadia. Although I did not finish my thesis, I completed twelve of the fourteen credits at Acadia in my Master of Education program. Due to a brain injury as the result of a car accident, it was best to let it go.

This project of writing has fulfilled my aching heart, because it gives me a purpose to keep going in a positive direction. My new struggles called for my tenacity in recovering my life because it had changed. With a great medical team and support team, I am now functioning well in the moment, one day at a time. I have discovered that writing a page a day works my brain, and it is fun to journal. Also, sewing quilt pieces each day sparks colorful creations and, eventually, they become nice gifts. The trick is that just a little effort adds up over time. I am blessed with tenacity to live in the now!

Have a day of tenacity!

FEARLESS

Fearless is to lack fear, to be brave, daring, courageous, bold, audacious, valiant, strong willed, beautiful, independent, and intrepid.

As a child I was fearless; I would roam outdoors and wander away from home. I was fearless of heights, the dark, and trying new things. As I grew older, I became fearful; the fears grew until one day my heart broke. I realized that I had become fearful and felt emotionally dead.

I began my journey and regained my power through acceptance of my Higher Power, which rooted me in feeling the fear and rising up; by moving forward with God's comfort, I became fearless. In strengthening my spiritual awareness and practices, I became awake, which is now a daily journey of living in love and action.

Today, I enjoy fearless living, as I have let go of the wreckage of the past and learned to trust a loving God; this energy force of goodness empowers me to go forth to help others. Fearless living is peaceful, passionate, and all loving. Living on the beam of inspiration each day, growing in serenity, understanding my journey, and being positive with an attitude of gratitude; these qualities of living develop my sense of wholeness and belonging. Thus, I choose fearless freedom rather than the fearful prison of my mind.

So it is! I have cleaned up my life, learned to love God, and trust the process. I embrace love, peace, compassion, and acceptance of myself and others, while fearlessly living the good life.

Have a fearless day!

CELEBRATED

Celebrated comes from the word celebrate, which means to glorify, praise, magnify, perform, exalt, honor, mark, or observe. People are celebrated when they are greatly admired and renowned.

Special occasions are celebrated with ceremonies and festivals. We enjoyed an Easter celebration with the Comeau's family dinner; 23 of us sitting down to a pot-luck meal. Besides the Easter eggs, we celebrated each other with conversations. Later that evening, Jean Paul and I visited friends and celebrated our music talents singing and playing instruments.

Today is a day of prayer, meditation, and rest. I am on a spiritual journey where my goodness is celebrated in the light. Life is celebrated every morning as I start my day. I am so grateful for every breath and my days are celebrated with gratitude. I am reborn to live in the Light, which I embrace with an open heart, mind, and soul to the joys of living happily, contented, and inspired. Life is good.

Have a celebrated day!

HONESTY

Honesty is the quality of being honest with uprightness, fairness, right-mindedness, truthfulness, reliability, integrity, morality, and dependability. Honesty is when you live free from fraud and deceit. Honesty is the principle of being in a state of acceptance of pure, candid, trustworthy, and just character.

Honesty is choosing to live in the Light, with an open heart, pure intentions, and a way of life that is positive; we are able to manage life in a state of pleasantness, happiness, and joyfulness. Honesty opens our hearts to see the good in ourselves and others.

Living life in honesty allows me to accept God, good orderly direction, and to live a spiritual life. I came to realize that I know very little and that God has been carrying me, so I opened my heart to forgiveness; I have learned to live in peace. I have been blessed with love, and I am now able to move forward to be there for others. The more I share my gentleness, dependability, and uprightness, the more I receive.

Today is celebrated in being true to me, living in the Light, the truth, honestly, and with integrity. My world and word are good, and it is vital to be honest and accept the universal vibrations of love – God's love. Honesty is essential to my spiritual life and a progress in action; each day brings new beginnings with an abundance of blessings.

Have a day of honesty!

BROAD-MINDED

Broad-minded is to be open to accept views and behaviors different from our own, while being nonconventional, nontraditional, progressive, radical, and open-minded.

Being spiritual is having our own experience in following our heart and living fearlessly. We may be afraid, but we feel the fear and move on; being broad-minded we know how to respond in love rather than fear. In spirituality, we grow to live a progressive life, where our happiness is found in our broad-minded, open-minded, and honest acceptance of the divinity in us. We are God's agents, living in the Light, and sharing love.

Living broad-mindedly, walking the walk of good living, and discovering the truth, frees us from living in fear. Personal growth and enlightenment are the keys to living a lovely, truthful life. The Golden Rule is a broad-minded concept of accepting and respecting open-mindedly in unity. Regardless of our differences and beliefs, we are to be broad-minded to see the divine message of truth, love, and worship in all of them.

We need to believe in our own truth through our own perception of our heart and shared broad-minded peace; the world will be one in peace, love, and freedom.

Have a broad-minded day!

ADVENTURE

Adventure is an exciting, bold, risk taking, and unusual experience that starts with one step and can take us to meaningful insights.

A spiritual adventure opens us to connect in community, to a journey to find ourselves in the basic truth of who we are, what we have become, and to more adventures into new growth.

As a child, I would adventure down to the brook. There, I would feel the energy and the spirits talk to me. I could feel the peace in nature. As a young adult, I hiked along rivers because this is where I felt safe. My adventures allowed me to know stillness, quietness, and peace within.

My teaching career was an adventure. Every day was a new adventure, a natural progression of learning and sharing, behaviors and actions, and general and academic growth.

Lately, my adventures have been in writing, sewing, and learning to play a new instrument, the bass guitar. The past few years, Jean Paul and I have bravely adventured to many places. Life is an adventure; trusting the process is a lifelong adventure to share my love, my community, and my world with you.

Have a day of adventure!

NICE

Nice is to be kind, pleasant, delightful, and agreeable. It is characterized by showing skill, tack, accuracy, care, and precision. A nice person is friendly. Nice guitar playing is delicate and particular. A nice day is any day we wake up on this side of the sod.

Living in spiritual practices, one can learn to be nice, to find the good in people, places, and things, and to encourage wellness. Keeping a healthy, joyful mind and living in harmony with our friends and family are activities that make a nice life.

Today is a nice day, rain showers and overcast. Pretty flowers are smiling at me as I walk by my gardens. It's a lovely nice spring day with warmer air and chirping birds.

It's nice to be able to sew with a Saphire Husqvarna quilting machine. It's nice to choose a recipient, then create a quilt, and give it to the person. Today I will sew a nice red binding to complete another nice project.

Nice is well accepted behavior and actions, which includes doing nice things for people to create good energy and blessings. It's nice to be able to share my gifts each day. I have a nice list of one hundred family and friends from which I choose to receive my quilts. This brings me nice feelings and a pleasant life.

Have a nice day!

APRIL 11
SHARING

Sharing involves enjoying people, places and things jointly with others. Sharing communication of thoughts and feelings with others is a social skill. When we take part in sharing it's an act of generosity: unselfish, giving and gifting. It is the act of gratitude in action and participation to be willing to share our gifts and blessings.

Sharing your time with others is one of the greatest gifts for both parties involved. It is healthy to share our feelings and thoughts, to become grounded, and express ourselves. Holding in garbage (negative thinking) stinks up our mind, attitude, and perspectives. Sharing enriches our lives with healed thoughts and healthier feelings.

We are not alone in this world when we rejoice in unity with our God, Higher Power, Creator, and we feel peace and love. Being human, we understand that we all make mistakes; with faith, we share our experiences to heal and grow. It takes courage to open our hearts and share personal and sensitive issues, but we must do so in order to let go and move forward. We are blessed with being guided and protected under our creator, if we choose to stop and listen.

Today, I am sharing my confidence and serenity as a result of growing with others on the journey. I recognize that I am not perfect, only the best me I can offer; yet, I understand that I am an excellent being with gifts and talents to share. When I share, I feel God is working through me and communicates through others to help me. I am not perfect, but I am perfectly imperfect and on a path of progress!

Have a sharing day!

WISDOM

Wisdom to understand people, places, things, and situations, with the willingness to deal with truth, perception, and insight, is a virtue. Wisdom comes from knowledge through many lifetime experiences. It is rooted in good sense and sound judgment in what is reasonable. It also involves a wise attitude and proper course of action.

Wisdom is a great word and a great gift from God. When we embrace ourselves in God's love and direction, we learn to know the difference between right and wrong actions. Hopefully, we have the wisdom to know the difference and act accordingly.

We learn wisdom, which is to have insight, perception, sapience, and sagacity. I have found the Serenity Prayer to be helpful and comforting over the years. Learning to understand people, places, things, and accepting experiences with their uncertainties has developed my life to be one of balance. Seeing the big picture and stepping out of the box to live life on life's terms each day has been a slow but steady process.

My dear friend Luther told me that, to be wise, I must share my positive growth and know that my optimism and wisdom in sharing about life's problems will help others. I followed his advice and have grown to be a solution-based participant in life. Together in unity, we can solve anything that comes our way. This became my introduction to wisdom.

Have a day of wisdom!

REASONABLE

Reasonable is to be sensible, fair, logical, fair-minded, levelheaded, credible, just, appropriate, and practical.

Reasonable is being able to accept a higher power, knowing there is an energy beyond each one of us that guides us in direction, care, and protection. The more we give our lives over to the flow of energy in the universe, the more we receive our independence and freedom. It's reasonable to accept peace in our lives.

Living in a reasonably sound state of mind, I feel serenity, peace, and comfort. I use the Serenity Prayer because it helps me to be reasonable in situations that might cause me indecision and emotional turmoil. It keeps me out of trouble and focused on a positive response.

The result of being reasonable has brought me many gifts to enjoy my life today. I keep the faith, practise being reasonable, live in the moment, as well as the Light, and worship the Creator each day as best I can. It works for me!

Have a reasonable day!

OMNIPOTENT

Omnipotent is all powerful, almighty, and one who has all unlimited power with the ability to be almighty to handle situations and or matters.

If we use omnipotent to describe an individual who can do just about anything, we could say they are omnipotent. However, I can only see an infant as being omnipotent because at that time of their age they have the power to draw you to their every need.

As adults, we should learn that we are part of the universe. There is one God and Creator, and we are not it; however, we are God-like. We learn that we are well nourished when we rely on the power to guide us to be the best we can be on this earth. In our surrender, we progress in our love for ourselves and others as we grow in unity.

Love is omnipotent, when we live with love in our heart and are well enough to share with others. My life and communication are guided through prayer, meditation, drumming, and being open for the blessings from the omnipotent God in my life. I let go of all faults, pains, and sorrows to rise up living protected in love.

Have an omnipotent day!

EMPATHETIC

Empathetic comes from the word empathy which means to understand others' feelings. Empathetic is when you identify with others' feelings, thoughts, and attitudes. An empathetic person offers understanding.

Empathetic is when you feel the pain of someone else. An empathetic person is usually very sensitive, feeling your pain as their own sometimes. It is the compassion within our hearts for sharing our gifts with nonjudgmental and graceful responses.

When we realize that we are empathetic and understand the process of feelings, we are wise to take care of ourselves.

To be empathetic means having attitudes and actions where we feel the mental and emotional energy guiding us to be moral and behave in a self-enhancing manner, rather than being mean-spirited and cruel.

Being mindful opens our hearts to have empathy, which is spirited, intellectual and practical. With these virtues, we can improve our behavior and be open to be present for others.

Since I opened my heart to God's guidance, direction, and care, I have become an empathetic person. Sometimes I feel too much energy and have to retreat to nature to ground myself. I come back with kindness, caring, and compassion.

Have an empathetic day!

WELL-INTENTIONED

Well-intentioned is to be well-meaning with good intentions; being agreeable, positive, supportive, amicable, benevolent, and complimentary, but sometimes with unfortunate results.

When somebody is well-intentioned, they are trying to be helpful and kind, but sometimes they are unsuccessful or rejected and might cause problems.

Last week, I was well-intentioned when I reached under the cupboard door but hitting my head when I got up caused me to bang my head. Ouch! One sore head, bright stars, and pain were my results. I was well-intentioned to help a friend, and I had offered my van to help her move, but then I could not drive. I have the well-intentioned idea to perhaps drive in the morning, but the feeling and assessment of my improvement will decide at that time.

Sometimes when I visit the shut-ins, I am well-intentioned to spend an hour; yet I usually take longer because I have come to know the residents, and they all want my time. So I oblige them and take my time to visit. It takes about a half an hour just to reach the room where I am going to spend time with my dear friend.

Have a well-intentioned day!

NEIGHBORLY

Neighborly is to be kind, sociable, civil, helpful, considerate, and friendly. To be neighborly helps build safer communities; the unity among neighbors makes a strong and vibrant place to live.

As a child, I grew up in a small community just a few miles from town. We had the 4-H club and, using our head, health, hands, and heart, we strengthened our character. We made projects and presented them in our little community. Then we went to the municipal, provincial, and federal fairs. I enjoyed winning the top prize of being the member to go to the Royal Winter Fair in Toronto.

Living in a small community, everyone knows each other. I missed the neighborly community when I lived in cities. I was happy to move back to the countryside where I could be part of a community, knowing and becoming friends with so many folks. I am especially content here because I now get to speak my French in this wonderful Acadian community, where everyone is pleasantly neighborly. All in all, it is the best way to live neighborly, where we look out for each other and help each other out. I go for a wee walk with my senior neighbor Mariette around my home on our paved driveway and chat about what's new. We enjoy each other's company.

Have a day being neighborly!

IDENTIFY

Identify means to specify, attest to, illustrate, establish and/or indicate who or what something is, and to closely associate with them in name, interest, feelings, and actions.

Learning to identify with folks, rather than comparing, is a spiritual gift of decency. It is positive to identify with others and together share and understand each other. Identifying opens our hearts to help each other live in the truth, the Light, and to journey forward empowering each other. When we identify, we are sharing our understanding and exactly how we associate with people, places and things, as well as situations.

Today, when my neighbor and I were walking, we shared the difficulty we experienced washing our floors. She shared her solution to have someone come in to wash her floor, and I believe I will do the same as I wait for shoulder surgery. This will save my shoulder from the pain being aggravated and strained.

Spring has arrived! Today, Jean Paul and I were able to identify many birds in our backyard, such as: crows, cowbirds, cardinals, chickadees, mourning doves, blackbirds, goldfinches, warblers, grosbeaks, blue jays, bunting bluebirds, redwing blackbirds, and even a seagull.

Have a day of identifying!

POLITE

Polite means to show behavior that is decent, considerate, respectful, and being well-mannered, gracious, civil, and courteous. It is being socially correct and proper and relates to being sophisticated and courtly in your community and society.

How do we recognize polite people?

First, the polite people maintain eye contact in a conversation and make people feel relaxed and at ease in talking. Secondly, they work at positive relationships, accepting the other person for who they are and what they value, encouraging them to be the best they can. They also identify with understanding and compassion. Thirdly, polite people have the attribute of being gentle and are not too insistent. Fourthly, they are kind, nice, graceful, calm, courteous, and they make everyone feel good. Finally, they have good etiquette.

Politeness is to good-natured with an attitude of gratitude towards all creations. My journey on this earth used to feel never-ending, but now I realize it is very short. I believe politeness is very important, and our world could use a good dose. We are all connected in this universe; our spiritual wellness is empowered by politeness. Choose love, to be at peace, and to be polite each day. Politeness is peaceful and maintains serenity.

Have a polite day!

VIGILANT

Vigilant means to be attentive, alert, observing, on the look-out for possible difficulties and/or danger, and being able to recognize problems and signs of danger.

It is important to stay awake in life, to be sober in our thoughts, to be vigilant and pay attention to our surroundings and folks. I believe waking up each day is a gift to be cherished in wellness, but we still have to build our guard to be safe.

I am vigilant when I travel. There are cautions to take care of my travel documents and bags, as well as to be on the look-out for any abnormalities in airports, bus stations, and train stations. When I lived in Paris, France, I had to be vigilant as I travelled in the city because there were thieves looking for the opportunity to snatch my bag or even reach in my pockets.

It is my experience that we are cautioned to watch out for ourselves, to be aware of our daily living behaviors, actions, and communications. I am not disillusioned and distracted as much these days, because I am improving my conscious contact and living with good orderly direction. I am living in the moment and shining my light while being vigilant.

Have a vigilant day!

Bravery is having the quality of nerve, spunk, courage, valor, prowess, boldness, audacity, spirit, and magnificence while being brave, daring, and fearless.

Moral courage to change things that I can involves bravery because I risk being shunned, shamed, or disappointed for doing the right thing. When I am authentic in facing daily challenges, I display bravery in telling the truth, being honest, facing my defects of character, and being willing to grow spiritually, rising above them in love and joy. Yes, it is right to be brave and courageous to stand for our truth. Bravery involves risks, but living in the truth firmly, with patience, kindness, and gentleness, is worth it.

Bravery to share our experiences means taking the risk of being exposed, but the truth sets us free. Facing adversity can make or break a human being, but faith, hope, and love can heal the spirit within. I am enjoying my journey being brave, risking, clothing myself in compassion, and enjoying the joy of living.

Have a day of bravery!

UNCOMPLICATED

Uncomplicated is basic, simple, straightforward, clear, easy, painless, and apparent. The essence of life is uncomplicated; living with trust, honesty, love, forgiveness, unity, and being generous is fairly simple.

I was once living a complicated life, in a controlled, dark, dysfunctional relationship. I had to clear out the negativity and the emotional abuse. I chose to get back up and put myself on the beam to live in wellness. I opened my heart to experience, letting go and loving myself back to sanity. Practising a clear-cut, uncomplicated, and simple program of believing in myself, accepting my mistakes, feeling the hope with friends, and having faith in my God gave me the courage to take care of myself.

I participate in a community group where we live in the warmth of God's love, practising goodness and continuously growing to improve our understanding in a safe environment. My journey progresses each day with more love, peace, and joy. I feel like a kid again – full of basic, simple, clear, painless, uncomplicated love, honesty, and forgiveness, and living in unity with my family, friends and society.

Have an uncomplicated day!

MEEKNESS

Meekness is to be submissive, to be unwilling to fight or argue. Meekness is when you are compliant, obeying, deficient in courage, and docile.

Spiritual meekness is when you are having a hard time, carrying stress and a heavy burden as you succumb to endure others' pain. However, we must stand up for ourselves if we are being manipulated, shaped, managed, lied to, or misled. The problem is in recognizing when these things are occurring. Sometimes we are blind and lose sight.

In manipulation, we are not able to make sound decisions because we survive by trying to please the abuser. Once we recognize that we have been railroaded, beaten down, and taken away from our beliefs, honesty and faith by a loved one, we try to take back our life.

I had to lay my life down by the cold, hard truth and facts to see that I had become poor in spirit; I became ready for spiritual meekness in the positive sense of being gracefully healed. I recovered from a broken heart, and I surrendered to God, humbly, meekly, and gently. I found hope in my renewed faith. I am awake and now enjoy living a healthy life of wellness.

Have a day of meekness!

APRIL 24
LIKE-MINDED

Like-minded is when you think similar thoughts, enjoy similar tastes, colors, styles, and share similar opinions or ideas.

Like-minded people are usually comfortable with each other because they understand and share similar solutions to grow closer. When we find like-minded people with whom to share our experiences, they listen, identify and understand why we are the way we are. Being like-minded, we accept, encourage, and travel the journey along a spiritual path of wellness together.

Like-minded groups of people share similar tastes, like my group of bluegrass friends. I don't feel lonely when I have friends playing music together because we are connected, playing in unity with trust and confidence. Some share ways to improve my playing as I learn to play my bass. Hopefully, one day I will play well.

Living at festivals with like-minded friends is a spiritual experience of love, caring, sharing compassion, peace, and serenity. Being reunited year after year is such a lovely stream of energy, as is meeting weekly with friends. It keeps the mind tuned into happiness, joy, and contentment. Stick together in unity with family and friends and share your like-minded Light and inspirations.

Have a like-minded day!

Usefulness is serving some purpose, being helpful to someone in need, doing something that serves peoples' needs, or being of use to something or someone. Usefulness is from the word useful which means that some person, place, or thing can be used advantageously for beneficial purposes.

I am contributing to the world by sharing my word of the day, which makes me feel like I have usefulness. Some days I attempt to make quilts, which provides usefulness to the people who receive them; this activity also fulfills my feelings of usefulness and purpose. Other days, I share my time with neighbors, friends and family; being useful blesses me with feelings of usefulness.

Usefulness is a commitment to make the world a better place to live in as we are meant to live – loving and laughing together, while sharing our gifts. My heart-felt gratitude for God, living with good orderly direction in compassion and love, is a gift to me and guides me to serve others. This may mean getting out of my comfort zone, but it is usefulness at its best.

Have a day of usefulness!

CREATIVITY

Creativity is the ability to create something new, original, and unique. It is a form of intelligence from within our souls. Being in touch with our creator, and having an awareness of our creativity, is a gift from God; using our gifts with an attitude of gratitude is our gift to God.

Creativity provides fun and enjoyment as we let our soul bathe in positive creations, giving us a sense of meaningfulness and a feeling of connectedness. Spending time in creativity is sacred time, because we are divinely in tune to love, pray, and create.

I choose to give life to my creativity through my living, writing, sewing, and music, to name a few. Being motivated to give back in life to the best of my ability is my gratitude in action.

Spiritual creativity guides me in awareness as I sew, creating patterns and producing colorful quilts. In this activity, it is the process rather than the product that gives me the most joy, fun, and fulfillment in my heart. It provides me time to live in the moment, being present and focused. The same happens when I'm making music with friends. So get in touch with your creator and creativity to create.

Have a day of creativity!

RECONSTRUCTION

Reconstruction is to rebuild, rehabilitate, reorganize, repair, restore, remake, and/or reset.

Many human beings lose their faith in God, themselves, and their fellow beings when they are devalued, degraded, and destructed. Once this tragedy occurs in a human being's life, it may cause an emotional turmoil, with negativity, pain, suffering, unmanageability, possibly insanity, and loss of trust.

Reconstruction happened to me when I found my spiritual essence. I was guided by divine intervention to accept my destroyed life and spirit. With recognition and acceptance that there was a problem, I could begin to heal and grow towards the Light. Reconstruction, through learning healthy principles and a positive way of living, opened my life to infinite possibilities. Slowly, I was paroled from a mental prison and insanity.

Reconstruction of honesty, integrity, service, and charity are built through courageous, vital, and active participation in the process. A spiritual foundation and soundness of mind is reconstructed to comply to the law of absolute love. God is love, and I feel love's energy guide, direct, and protect me in my recovered life of well-being. Faith is restored; freedom is the gift.

Have a day of reconstruction!

PERSEVERANCE

Perseverance is when you are willing to continue trying to do something, despite the difficulty or opposition. Perseverance is the ability to maintain staying power, determination, absolute assurance, strength of character, and tenacity.

Life can present difficulties, roadblocks, and turmoil, but perseverance will see me through. My strength is in my Higher Power, my God, my creator. When I am mindful and take positive action to keep emotionally well balanced and live as God's will guides me, I find my direction to live with happiness, joy, and feel freedom. I am spiritually fit and living with God's conscience.

Perseverance is the quality of living to change for the better, for progress in connectedness, and being awake. Yes, awake, living in the now in this moment, in the perseverance to be God's agent of love, peace, and serenity

I have made mistakes and sometime journey down dark paths, but I rejoice in surrendering to God. I get back up, on the Light path, living honestly with hope, faith, courage, and truth. I reconstruct my life with integrity, willingness, humility, and love. I forgive myself and others and persevere in spiritual service. Now I go forth and live in good conscience, in unity with all. I am strong, in faith I am stable.

Have a day of perseverance!

GLEAMING

Gleaming is to share brightly, luminously, brilliantly, and radiantly. Gleaming eyes are sparkling and shine with inner light.

As children, we are born with positive energy, free from worldly thought, having a clear conscience and gleaming with abundance of love. Life is innocent; there is peace in the moment. Children are gleaming human beings. However, life for some is darkened and the gleam fades.

When people learn to live in the now, being persistent and consistent in living in the Light, they love and grow to be gleaming human beings. I have found that we vibrate in our healthy wellness and put out good energy of affection, grace, self-discipline, self-control, appreciation, compassion, generosity, and gratitude. Having had a spiritual awakening, my strength comes in my belief and faith of a loving God. I have the courage to transform, letting go of ego and spiritual maladies.

I have grown to be strong and live an effective life of happiness and to be gleaming in the Light. I am gleaming in spiritual consciousness and creating positive energy as I get out into nature to keep myself grounded. I love feeling the peacefulness, shining and gleaming with God's love in my heart. I am a kind soul, healed and blessed in my love of life today!

Have a gleaming day!

OPTIMISTIC

Optimistic comes from the word optimism, which means to have a positive attitude and outlook in situations and events, and also when you have faith for acceptable and favorable outcomes.

To be an optimistic person, you see the best and expect the best in people and situations. An optimistic person is hopeful and positive, brings encouragement, goodness, cheerfulness, and reassurance to light.

No situation is too big that God, you, and I together can't handle. That's right, we are optimistic keeping our faith, trusting, confident, on top of the world with a ray of sunshine gleaming in our optimism.

Life is happier with an optimistic personality and outlook, which we all have in us, but only experience when we are connected with our faith. Acceptance of living in the moment, just for today, as best we can in faith and trust, we are nourished in spiritual happiness, joy, and live an optimistic life.

We are not doormats or naïve, but we maintain an optimistic attitude and live in positive solutions with gratitude.

Have an optimistic day!

MAGNIFICENT

Magnificent is when a thing, place, or person is extravagant, awesome, inspiring, impressively drop-dead beautiful or handsome, and majestic. Magnificent is also when things are done skillfully, brilliantly, and with excellence.

Today is a magnificent day; I started with a morning stroll in my little woods, listening and greeted by the birds, and it was especially magnificent to see a redwing blackbird gliding to the feeder. It is about 9 degrees Celsius or 50 degrees Fahrenheit and lovely for being outdoors, absolutely magnificent after a long winter. The journey so far today is magnificent in that it is spiritually peaceful and serene. Walking in our little woods, there are many garlic plants and, when you move them as you pass by, they send magnificent fragrances to my nostrils where I am conscious of this pleasing scent.

Living in the moment in nature and listening to God through meditation is magnificent. Praying to God is talking to God; I talk to God, but I also sit or lean on a tree and listen to God. Keeping my mind in tune is the best thing I can do for my well-being. A strong, healthy mind need not wander, because it is safe, grounded and at peace with all creations and, thus, the journey is filled with Love, Light and Laughter. Life is magnificent.

Have a magnificent day!

THOROUGH

Thorough is taking great care to do something, completely, meticulously, painstakingly, carefully, conscientiously, and diligently.

It's a good practice to take a thorough look at one's life regularly. We stay awake and conscious of our being and tune up our connectedness as human beings. We are wise to work to share our thorough inventory with God and another human being, like confession. We thank God that we do not have to be perfect, but we are willing to strive for improvement and a better life in peace, serenity, and faith. We are thorough in our journey to become healthier, and we volunteer to give back and be of service to help others; in helping, we have thoroughness in living well.

It has been a blessing to write a thorough description of what this word means to me. If I am thorough in positive living, I become stronger, courageous and able to live in the moment. I am not to judge, dictate or impose my beliefs on others; I am to accept God and all the people as they have been created. I am busy enough living my own journey and learning the lessons so that I can be thorough in living life on life's terms. Life is a joy today, serene, and lovely. I aim to live, love and laugh thoroughly each day.

Have a thorough day!

MAY 3
INTEGRATION

Integration is the act of being grounded in your integrated whole personality when we live in harmony and cooperative behaviors. When healed, we are free to love and accept ourselves and our world.

Life trauma, abuse, and accidents may cause dissociation in extreme forms. We all experience dissociation at some level. For example, you may say, "I lost myself" or "I lost my mind for a moment," but PTSD (Post Traumatic Stress Disorder) folks move toward a deeper level of dissociation. DID (Dissociative Identity Disorder) people move to the extreme form and, thus, may experience depression, anxiety, suicidal, auditory, hallucinations, phobias, and impulsivity. There is a greater need for integration of the many aspects of the person so they can be healthy, balanced, accepted, loved, and have improved stability.

Integration may occur once the perceptions of internal personalities are united with all parts, and new awareness heals the trauma. Integration involves learning to accept and love all of us, living in the moment, and in our core personality. We no longer feel the need to dissociate and live in victim or survival mode, but rather rejoice as a thriving human-being.

Integration involves learning to be aware and awake in consciousness, free from the grips of trauma. We are paroled from being trapped in our negative, limited perspectives, and we learn to be honest, open-minded, and willing to live as best we can. We manage our core personality and deal with frustrating people, places, and things. We maintain our spiritual growth, living, loving and dancing to the beat of our recovered Spirit, integrated!

Have a day of integration!

RESPONSIBILITY

Responsibility is to behave in a morally right way, with trustworthiness and reliability while being responsible, which means to be able to deal with taking care of some person, place or thing, and doing what is right and required. I believe it's most important that you take care of yourself, which is not being selfish, because it is in being responsible to self that we then are able to be responsible for others.

We are born and raised, and then we must take responsibility for ourselves, to choose our own reality. Some of us get messed up and disconnect, making unfortunate choices, having reactions and numbing our feelings, dissociating and living in negativity. Others, free from trauma, are able to take responsibility and are able to connect with better choices, responses, and feelings of confidence.

Today, I choose to take responsibility for my life. It has not been an easy life, road or path but, holy Toledo, it has been eventful. With great tenacity, I have taken on an improved and enjoyable life, leaving behind all constraints.

Responsibility is looking at the whole picture of life: my higher power, God, my inner wisdom, nature, science, and my personal experiences. Letting go of past traumas and living in the moment, I take responsibility to own my decisions. I take responsibility to share my gifts of writing about my life's experiences; in sharing them, I may help another suffering human being to improve their life.

Have a day of responsibility!

ADAPTIVE

Adaptive is to have the ability to be flexible and capable of adjusting to life. Adapt means to change to deal with our life and to find solutions to improve our life.

An adaptable person is able to reconstruct their life, changing behaviors and beliefs so that positive change can manifest into a better life. When an adaptive person deals with life, they accommodate, conform, adjust, shape, edit, and reconcile with an open heart to be the best person they can be. Being adaptive leads to many opportunities and experiences of more love, peace, and joy in this life. Being honest and open-minded allows us to live our own lives in consciousness and oneness with the God of our understanding.

We are on an improved path when we are open and connected in our spirituality. When we live using our adaptive skills, we know our limits and move forward as best we can each day.

Adaptive skills have saved my life many times. When I deal with the sacred losses in my life, I become adaptive in coping and healing. I coped with depression and was adaptive in my consciousness. I grew strong, healing through having a spiritual experience and awakening my soul to rock on in a new chapter of life, which continues to heal with every new adventure.

Have an adaptive day!

EASYGOING

Easygoing is a tranquil and relaxed manner of living, being placid, unhurried, cool, calm, and collected.

Easygoing people are not critical and demanding. Rigidity is absent as they live in a casual manner, being serene. As children, we are pretty easygoing for the most part. As we grow, we develop our personality characteristics; some of us are gifted to be easygoing and live this way naturally, while others learn to be adaptive and mellow in life. Hopefully, we all learn the art of living well and become easygoing at some point.

Easygoing is a state of being happy, content, and free from living in structures, boxes, and critically demanding ways. Life is best lived connected to our spirit, being kind, loving, composed, giving, generous, tolerant and patient; thus, easygoing. Yes, living in the moment, today, now, minding one's own business, and being humble, make for an easygoing lifestyle. Contented people are easygoing, grounded in peace with all creation, filled with serenity, and happy with life. They are happy-go-lucky and compassionate, enjoying life as it presents itself one day at a time. They live in the now and do what's best for their health, living in goodness and sharing this goodness.

Have an easygoing day!

MAY 7
PROMISES

Promises are reasons to believe good things are coming your way. Promises are statements made telling someone that you are going to do something or receive something. They give people hope for improved conditions, a better lifestyle, and happiness.

Spiritual promises include grace, freedom, empowerment, peace, trust, love, serenity, and abundance. In order to transform to live a life filled with love, peace, and kindness, we need to know about these promises and understand what they are offering. Then, we need to do the work to walk the walk, responsibly in peaceful faith, accepting our new life and thriving in the blessings from our transformations. The experience of living with unfulfilled promises exhausted my well-being.

Changing my living conditions and transforming my lifestyle saved me from mental and emotional turmoil. I kept my dreams alive by healing and dealing with reality. I leaned on God's love and allowed God's promises to become my reality. My preservation depended on my willingness to turn my heart over to the care of God. I am living in serenity, free from broken promises, and nourished in daily promises coming to light in my life.

Have a day of promises!

EARTHY

Earthy is when a person is realistic and practical. An earthy person is direct, simple, and down-to-earth.

We call our planet Mother Earth, and we are all here to live earthy in our spiritual journey. Earthy people share their brotherly-sisterly love and respect of humanity. We are grounded and surround ourselves with positive energies, and we bring light and love of our contented journey to all, while respecting all whom we meet. We allow our friends, family, and others to learn for themselves and figure out their own issues. Nonetheless, we are willing to share our hope, encouragement, and mellifluous life with anyone, anywhere; we are sharing our gifts from God and how we come to live in a contented, happy, and abundant lifestyle.

I can attest to running from my life as an earthy person and living a drifter lifestyle. Always on the run, looking for quick fixes, until one day I hit a desperate bottom, too sick to carry on. After a 17-day hospital stay, I had to do some work to find my way back to my life and to purify my thoughts with healthier decisions and actions. I became reconnected to God, and I began to live with my happy earthy Spirit. I found my voice: honesty, feeling grounded, and an earthy spirituality of living well, are my rewards. Just like a good Garden, we need to prepare ourselves for success. Throughout life, we need to read, nourish, and cultivate with our God. Keep a healthy garden and a healthy life.

Have an earthy day!

PEACE OF MIND

Peace of mind is living in the absence of anxiety and mental and emotional turmoil, but rather in a state of peace, serenity, and tranquility. For me, living with peace of mind is the result of learning to live as one with mother-nature, the spirits, and God's love.

Life has its challenges; sometimes people exist in chaos with distorted thinking, insecurity, fear, disconnection, being alone, and dissatisfied with the noise and clutter in their minds. However, healing can change the situation, and, with growth, we will feel peace of mind and feel more connected, trusting, belonging; we will have positive thinking, security, and feel like we are part of the universe. It is a promise of knowledge and clear understanding that we will learn to be strong in all aspects of our life; when life's chaos might come our way, it does not rattle our peace of mind.

Peace of mind is the result of acceptance, honesty, forgiveness, and love to live with an optimistic attitude, which grows from reading positive affirmations, living on life's terms, directing my thoughts, and navigating to healthier decisions. Using visualization, I bring consciousness to my happy place and keep a balanced perspective while inducing a feeling of calmer energy that allows me to live in compassion and kindness. Learning the art of living in the now, and being well-adjusted, thinking sanely and fruitfully, has given me my life back. Finally, I have found peace of mind and live with contentment.

Have a peace-of-mind day!

Curiosity is having a strong desire to know, learn, and inquire about something. The gift of desire is to be an adventurer, to satisfy your curiosity to make better connections for better health. There is also the curiosity of "nosiness," which can be for positive or negative reasons.

Today, I am focused on the benefits of curiosity, such as in social relationships, where we are curious and open to learn about another. We seek healthy communication skills to show our interest through inquiry; it is intelligent to be inquisitive and seek the truth.

Curiosity motivates us to learn the meaning of our life, to find a healthy perspective, and discover a simple and playful spirit within us. We might feel uncomfortable in our curiosity with the unfamiliar, but we grow in our open-mindedness and, hopefully, become willing to experience new things. It is good to give up judging, labeling, and having expectations.

I have grown to see life and its many opportunities as a gift. I am awakened and healed through the curiosity to explore and increase my sensitivity, consideration, and acceptance. Change is daily, and I grow stronger in faith each day, equipped to deal with uncertainty. I am grounded in energy vibrating in connection with God and the Creator. My curiosity is alive and well.

Have a day of curiosity!

FAITH

Faith is having a belief in something beyond self, like a belief in God, the Creator, the truth, the promises, or in a set of principles. Faith is living honestly in sincerity and confidence. It is an act of faith to live with a grateful attitude, with awareness that there is something, some energy or force, even though we can't see it.

Life's challenges occur sometimes with doubt, shame, blame and guilt. We become disconnected from our authentic path and lose our faith and hope. However, by divine intervention, some of us find our way back and surrender to God, the life force, and come to realize that we need to change our thoughts and patterns of living. Taking stock of our personal development, we learn about ourselves and others. We acknowledge that we have been on vacation from our true purpose and accept God's and others' help. We grow in faith, seeing that we feel better knowing we are not alone and have been carried for a while.

I had to let go of my fears and doubts, to live in faith with a loving understanding of life and all its challenges. I learned that all experiences were lessons and that it is part of living with all the ups and downs. I grew in faith that I was just where I was supposed to be on my journey and that all is well. So I live in the now, rejoicing in my new confidence and bloom in deeper faith. I am able to move forward in living in the positive and am thankful for this day.

Have a day of faith!

Rational is having the sense to be agreeable to reason, being able to make sound decisions and living in a state of sanity. Rational includes being wise, intelligent, and enlightened. Rational people use reason and logic to think out their problems using a sound mind to find solutions and then follow through with action.

Living a rational life includes having the intent to live as a real person and being true to your authentic self. We are all individually unique and search for our happy place in life to achieve contentment. It's important to take our own personal inventory of our thoughts, beliefs, and actions, and ask ourselves if we are being rational; if not, we become willing to change for the better. Learning to be rational requires honesty, respect, strength, and effective navigation skills to work through troubles until we find a solution. Rational people understand the benefits of being inquisitive and are mature enough to have faith in improving their reality each day. Life is ongoing, and change is reasonably consistent.

Irrational, negative-self-talking people create havoc and unhappy minds. The cure is to have rational self-talk, which empowers them to grow and to stand assertively, navigating into positive outlooks. Rational people manage to be generally happy and easy-going, enjoying successes, and have figured out how to manage their life's journey to find contentment and peace of mind.

Have a rational day!

JUSTICE

Justice is the rationality and fairness, mutual agreement of everyone concerned. It is right to give to another human being what belongs to them because this is the moral principle and spiritual virtue of living in just conduct. Justice is also a form of punishment for wrongdoing. To give justice to a good song is to appreciate it and listen to it, play it, and enjoy it over and over again.

Justice is demonstrating just behaviors: honestly, morally, fair-mindedly, objectively, naturally, and with impartiality. However, we are not perfect and strive for progress, because we all fall short at some point in our humanness. This is when we should look at our lives and see where we made mistakes and take action to correct our wrongdoing; thus, we have justice.

When we recognize anger, resentment, shame, blame, guilt, and being unable to forgive in our lives, we are then required to recover and heal ourselves to restore peace of mind. Our amends allow us to move forward, restore our dignity and serenity. We become charged with new energy and strength to live in kindness, compassion, and acceptance.

My life has improved, and I can now live in peace with positive opportunities and possibilities in a state of good judgment, courage, and prudence. I trust God and live with an orderly life, free to help others and know restorative justice. The truth set me free!

Have a day of justice!

MAY 14
SILENCE

Silence is the state of being silent; being mute in an absence of communication, not hearing audible sounds and noise.

Silence has not always been a very comfortable place for me, but, over the years, the chatter has settled, and my life has mellowed out. Today, I have found peace and am blessed to be comfortable in silence. I enjoy silence out in the woods, camping, and being outdoors. I enjoy silence as much as possible because it is good for my brain.

Silence is a spiritual blessing and great for meditation and prayer, an act of living faith, which is a skill achieved through practice. Learning to be still and comfortable teaches me to be patient and have courage and perseverance in willingness and tenacity.

Have a day in silence!

SUPPORTIVE

Supportive is when someone provides understanding, is helpful, and shares kind encouragement and emotional support.

To be supportive is an act of creating hope in troubled minds and helps build confidence. Supportive psychotherapy and group therapy provide a healthy safe place to learn adaptive thinking patterns to deal with our issues, understand conflicts and behaviors, and learn new ways of living.

Learning to trust the process, and accept supportive love in guidance and direction, is a miracle for me. Sharing this understanding of deep peace and feeling of love is supportive to live a serene life of contentment. My goodness has developed and become a way of life, and I feel the peace deep within, doing good deeds and being supportive to others.

I am inspired to be creative and helpful in all I do, to be supportive, and positive. I have learned to trust God, which keeps my mind open and free from emotional and worldly clutter. I take care of me, minding my own business, and being responsible for my life. The gift of being content in one's own skin is a beautiful healthy gift of living well with peace of mind.

I had to learn to love myself in a positive sense, free from my twisted ego, and know that supportive love of my Creator is a blessing of happiness and a joyful life. So I rejoice in my healing and wholeness of feeling complete and belonging. I am not alone; I am living in a supportive community of unity, and life is good.

Have a supportive day!

"Aces" is when a person displays good behaviors and excels in an activity, and describes someone who is very skilled, adept, excellent, outstanding, decent, pleasant and generous. Aces people feel social connectedness, emotional strength, and are capable to be supportive in community unity and wellness.

Developing "aces" characteristics involves learning how to positively interact and attain better health and well-being. As we grow, we develop character attributes such as goodness, peace, and serenity, a sense of faith, a positive identity, and personal competency in life skills. We feel the blessings of love, peace, and joy, and grow to be decent, generous folks – an aces character.

An aces person learns skills and is considerate in dealing with life, being patient and kind, free from judgment and criticism, displays a decent presence in their demeanor, and is grounded in open-mindedness and acceptance. Aces folks are comfortable and contented in their life and shine with happy hearts and soul energies. They are positively blessed and excited for the next adventure in life and authentically true to themselves in honesty and respect.

Have a day of being aces!

REWARDING

Rewarding is something that is satisfying, fulfilling, and pleasing. It's rewarding to experience satisfaction after completing a good job, singing a good song, and any activity that makes you feel gratification.

Many lessons in life have troubles, friction, trials, and turmoil. It is rewarding to know that we are not alone, and our faith will see us through. Sometimes our thinking needs to be fine-tuned so that we may clearly see the truth and reality of our perceptions, habits, and discipline.

Learning to be joyful in very difficult times is rewarding, because we learn confidence and are able to endure problems and discipline ourselves to find solutions. It is rewarding to know that we need not strive for perfection, but rather progress. It's rewarding to know that we simply have to be mindful and maintain our integrity.

My integrity has grown from living in the truth with honesty. Once I got a grip on life and my responsibility to take care of myself, I became connected, staying awake, conscious, and grounded. I found glory and now rejoice, having peace of mind and an improved way of living. I have developed my discipline and exchanged my dysfunctional habits for healthier, positive ones that enable me to live a serene life, which is very rewarding.

Have a rewarding day!

ADMISSION

Admission is the act of acknowledging the truth, admitting that some person, place or thing in your life needs attention and to change for the better. Admission is when we are allowed entrance into something or someplace.

Admission can be a growing point in our life. When we accept that we need to change our thinking and do the work to grow, we become more conscious in our daily life. We are in a state of admission, which then allows us to give ourselves permission to be courageous and take risks, to improve our coping skills, and find a balance. Admission of our mistakes and making amends heals our uneasy, shameful, or guilty conscience.

For me, admission of faith in God was the gateway to a strong and peaceful life. Acknowledging I had character defects released their negative hold on me, and I was free to then change my thinking, habits, and behaviors. The passport to my happiness was in admitting that my creator was guiding, directing, and protecting me.

Have a day of admission!

AMBITION

Ambition is when you have a strong determination to do something, such as achieve a goal, purpose, or dream. Adopting eagerness, motivation, and enthusiasm to achieve success, along with willingness and action to carry it out, is great ambition. A person with ambition will strive seriously, sincerely, soberly, and thoughtfully to achieve their dream.

We seek to find meaning in our lives and, once we do, we understand the meaning and what feeds it, then we know peace and balance. When we are content in our purpose and meaning, we know happiness.

The past few years, my friend Eleanor encouraged me to write a word a day. I thought about this idea last fall when I was staying with friends in North Carolina in a log cabin in the mountains, and I became motivated to write. Just how would I start? I thought about it because many folks often said, "Alison, you should write a book." So, I began thinking about the process. I decided to pick 365 words, wrote them on cards, and placed them in a basket.

On January 1st, I started by picking a word and writing a page, sharing its meaning to me. My ambition has served me well and created a commitment with discipline. I must say, after having a brain injury and dealing with brain fog, this is a challenge. However, I believe it has been good therapy for me.

Quilting is another ambition for which I became passionate. I am able to make baby quilts and lazy-boy throws using my sewing machine. It is a great project, and I enjoy working with the colors and designing. My most important ambition is to create and maintain a life of serenity. My ambition motivates me to pray, meditate, exercise, eat healthy, be good to myself and others, and to love life.

Have a day of ambition!

DEPENDABLE

Dependable is when you are trustworthy, loyal, faithful, and stable. A dependable person will continue in a commitment to see you through a tough time, even if they have to miss sleep or contribute in sharing expenses. They are respectful and take care of themselves to avoid personal burnout; they are grounded in their contentment and open to help others.

A dependable person is honest, with integrity and a grateful attitude, which are wonderful characteristics that enable a person to develop a strong work ethic, whether on a job or volunteering. A positive attitude keeps a person open-minded, enthusiastic to live in the moment and to find solutions. A dependable person will usually go the extra mile to help when possible. They learn to be responsible for their actions and behave in a mature manner, taking full responsibility for their commitments, one day at a time and with peace and contentment.

I have learned the importance of taking care of myself. I find support to maintain my wellness by having faith in God the Creator, who is dependable in providing me with comfort.

Have a dependable day!

KINDNESS

Kindness is the quality of being kind, caring, generous, considerate, and having gentle behavior. Kindness is a good quality and way of life, and, hopefully, more folks choose to develop this ongoing spirit of kindness.

We learn to be kind, and we are blessed with peace and serenity. Kindness involves being connected in your love for life and others. It is a learned behavior and includes gaining wisdom and insight to become thoughtful, respectful, and empathetic. When we are grounded, we are stable enough to listen without interrupting, identify rather than compare, and to be understanding and comforting, showing kindness to others.

I find that kindness is a wonderful quality, especially when we can make time for sick family and friends in time of need and support, which is appreciated with a phone call or a visit to a shut-in. A fundamental attitude of kindness is a great spiritual practice. I have learned, and intend to share, kindness, and it has become a way of life for me. It is important for me to stay connected to positive actions, to be easy-going, think simply, and to be able to help out when possible. My kindness enriches my life each day, and I am blessed to share this kindness with others.

Have a day of kindness!

MEMBER

Member means to be part of a group, family, friends, party, community, and society.

To be a member in an organization or association, we sign up for membership, becoming part of a group and, as a result, enjoy a feeling of belonging. As a member, we are unique, individual, and a distinct part of the whole. We become united and connected with a common concern, and we work together for progress. Each member brings their gifts to the group, and we grow in acceptance and tolerance. We gain a universal understanding while working together.

Being a member has many benefits, such as gaining positive feedback and encouragement. Sometimes we are challenged and forced to look at our perceptions on life. As a member of a group, with honesty and respect we learn to accept others' opinions and suggestions without judging; we learn to identify and adjust accordingly. We learn to focus in a healthier direction and strive to resolve conflicts, as we learn the gift of tolerance and patience. Together, we share common concerns in our quest for understanding to make better sense of our lives, their meaning and purpose.

Each group I joined over my years had a purpose; I have learned that success is dependent upon nourishing and maintaining the group focus. The first group I remember joining was 4-H; I loved it and eventually became a leader. As a member of any group, it is my responsibility to participate, to learn what is good for me, to take what is good for improving my life, and to apply the benefits to excel. It's important that I participate and follow through with healthy actions for the group to benefit from my presence. My commitment as a member is the key to my belonging and thriving in happiness as a contented member.

Have a day as a member!

MAY 23
LIGHT

Light is the absence of darkness; light requires an illumination source, such as the sun, a lamp, candle, or fire. Light makes things visible, radiant, and bright. Light is a way of describing someone; for example, she is the light of the party, she lights up the room with her radiance and brightens up the mood with her peaceful and joyous spirit.

Light reflects a person's ideas and the ability to be awake, conscious, understanding, and knowledgeable. A person with a bright idea brings wisdom to a problem and helps us see the light of a situation. Light as a form of wisdom helps guide us out of despair, depression, and troubles. Some of us need support at times, and we may seek to talk with someone or a therapist to see the light.

Learning to live in the light, the truth, and the way of peace, joy, happiness, love, and confidence, is a wonderful journey and experience. Living well in faith with God blesses me with kindness, compassion, forgiveness, healing, love, and healthy perspectives. I have become lighthearted, living in goodness with healthy direction.

Acceptance of life, people, and situations opened me to this love, the Light, and brought me through to better days. I have grown from having a dark perspective into the light and am able to see the light of situations that come my way. Love conquers all. Being honest and respectful to myself are the two keys to my growth in acceptance; whether I choose to continue is my choice, but I must be willing to accept the consequences. I have learned to choose to live in the Light.

Have a day living in the Light!

Rugged means to have great determination, requiring a person to be tough, rigorous, strong, robust, and resilient. A rugged person has strength to deal with difficult people, places and things.

Some folks are challenged in life. They develop rugged endurance to live positively, on the beam, with determination to grow in honesty and become open-minded and willing to change for the better. A rugged person may help themselves by freeing themselves from negative thinking, self-deception, disconnectedness, criticizing, and ostracizing. They rebuild their character attributes to include the truth, improved thinking, connecting, supporting, encouraging, motivating, and being responsible in their choices and consequences. Rugged people are tough enough to free themselves from anger, resentment, shame, and guilt.

I guess I'm a rugged person because I can now look back and say, "Wow, how I have grown." I know how to reach out and get my garbage out, no more recycling that old past. I have given up self-reliance, self-will, and chaotic tendencies, and turn to God for direction, the most rugged creator of our universe. I love the powerful energy from living a good life. Positive direction and having a rugged soul bring purpose and meaning to my life, and the reward is contentment and happiness.

Have a day being rugged!

UNASSUMING

Unassuming is to be modest, lacking pretension and arrogance, a state of being meek, humble, unobtrusive, low-key, natural, and reserved. It's a gift of pleasantness, politeness, and delightfulness to be unassuming. To assume means that you suppose and take it as granted without proof. Some say to assume is to make an "ass" out of "u" and "me," which is the result of you making assumptions and conclusions that you shouldn't.

Unassuming folks are secure and mature. They do not possess false pride, but rather are humble solid characters living in the truth and reality of the day with no need to boost their ego to almighty significance, importance, or power. Being unassuming, we are stable, can read between the lines, and are intuitive and agreeable, knowing the facts.

Unassuming people stand firm in their grounded spirit and are not intimidated, bulldozed, or railroaded by others who are manifesting negativity. I believe these folks are devotional, spiritual, and emotionally stable, humbly living a modest lifestyle minding their own business. Being unassuming and living a serene life is a path of serenity. There is no need to boast once we've learned the skill of letting go of our assuming; our maturing tames the ego and we live humbly, becoming unassuming to enjoy life in peace and love.

I get a kick out of people who call me on the phone, and they start assuming that I just woke up, or whatever. I am quick to say, "Why are you assuming and trying to guess what or how I'm doing? How about, 'Hello, how are you?'"

Have an unassuming day!

MATURITY

Maturity is having the ability to act, live, and respond in an appropriate manner at the correct time and place. A mature person has developed a sense of purpose in life with a clear comprehension, direction, and confidence of understanding one's meaningfulness.

We are meant to take responsibility to create meaningful relationships, experiences, and adventures in our lives. Some people take longer to mature than others and some never grow up. Maturity comes when we let go of our childish behaviors and reactions, and we become independent and responsible adults.

Emotionally immature people damage themselves and others because of their insecurities. The road to change and grow mature includes letting go of raw emotions, hurts, pains, manipulative and self-absorbed behaviors, and moodiness. Maturity is the reward and comfort to live well in peace and serenity.

Let's look at a spiritually mature person. I believe they are consistent and persistent in living in disciplines of goodness, kindness, respect, and honesty. Their maturity might be seen in their graceful conduct, confidence, contentment, and self-control. A person with maturity shares their love and peace, fellowship, prayer, and gives their time to serve and help others.

Have a day of maturity!

TRUTHFUL

Truthful means being honest, true, factual, open, genuine, candid, forthright, and straight-shooting.

To be truthful to oneself is to give your life total attention, to live honestly, and to be willing to live in the moment, which will result in contentment, serenity, and a fulfilling life. Truthful living is having the ability to live in the Light and Love with God-consciousness, grounded and spiritual in divine living with knowledge and forgiveness. Truthful living allows us to let go of our fearlessness, and we know a new freedom. Our truthful journey encourages us to mind our own business and live our own lives in positive joy, purpose, meaning, and contentment. We rejoice in truthful living in the here and now. This is it, the reality of enjoying life one day at a time.

Truthful living harmonizes my life with a positive, strong, and hopeful attitude. I have found my peace and become willing to share my experience with others. My willingness to find my passion, meaning, and purpose is revealed in my daily actions and service to help others. Today, I am blessed with a truthful life, a miraculous transformation.

Have a truthful day!

MEDITATIVE

Meditative is to be contemplative, thoughtful, pensive, studious, reflective, and awake in consciousness. To be able to meditate in is to be able to practise calmness and relaxation of the mind, which promotes better health, improves concentration, inspires creativity, consciousness, and universal love. Being meditative leads us to god-centered living in harmony with all creation.

Taking part in meditative practice helps remove negative conditioning from people that might feed stress and materialism. Learning to let go becomes natural as we transform and live positively in gratitude and peace of mind. Meditative practice enhances our spiritual progress and helps us tune into our reality.

A meditative environment is quiet, peaceful, and calming. Water sounds or spa music can help relax our mind. Remaining conscious throughout the practice is necessary for growth and spiritual progress. Meditative activities direct energy in your mental and emotional and spiritual self to happiness and love. Now, in total consciousness, relaxed and with an open heart, we are ready to share in the well-being of all family, friends, and society.

Have a meditative day!

EPIGRAMMATIC

Epigrammatic is to be concise, clever, and sharp with witty humor. Epigrammatic comes from the word epigram which is to have the ability to make a quick, memorable, brief, surprising, or shocking witty statement.

An epigrammatic person has the gift to be funny, comical, and entertaining. They have the intuition to share creatively, based on their recollections and readiness. They are very particular and capable of sharing their emotional feelings and cleverly expressing their perceptions in a precise, brief, and funny way.

Epigrammatic examples:

Oscar Wilde

> "Fashion is a form of ugliness so intolerable we are compelled to alter it every 6 months."
> "Some cause happiness wherever they go, others whenever they go."
> "I have simple tastes; I am always satisfied with the best."

Mark Twain

> "Denial ain't just a river in Egypt."
> "Always do right. That will gratify some people and astonish others."

Have an epigrammatic day!

Sanity is to be of sound mind, saneness, stability, reasonableness, and rational in the state of being emotionally grounded in awareness, feeling personal freedom, and having healthy perspectives in a mental state of living in love, abundance, security, compassion, understanding, and forgiveness.

Life can affect people in many ways that develop into insanity, which is a disability to remain mentally well. The focus on reality can become lost in the trauma or in distorted thinking, which can cause dissociation from reality; we then go to another place in our mind, where we create a safe way of dealing with the fear and pain. Delusions, hearing voices, and lacking healthy distinctions diverts us from healthy critical thinking. Denial allows us to block out awareness of the pain, fear, shame, and helplessness. These unconscious perceptions become ways to deal with and tolerate life. Rationalization becomes the norm and a way of hiding one's hopelessness, fears, and insecurities.

Restoring ourselves to sanity involves dealing with the trauma and becoming grounded and in touch with reality. Cultivating and weeding out the voices, and developing healthy critical thinking, is essential to become well. We learn to feel the fear and pain, and then work it out to rebuild sane, enjoyable, and reasonable coping skills with confidence and manageability. Sanity is the integrated ability to be present, honest, conscious, and disciplined to be a critical thinker with soundness of mind. I am grateful to be restored and recovered from insanity.

Have a day of sanity!

NURTURING

Nurturing is the act of providing food and protection to another, especially infants, children, and seniors. Nurturing is rearing, teaching, training, educating, nourishing, and aiding in development. To nurture a broken soul involves careful, comforting, supporting, dignifying, helpful, humanizing, and inspirational encouragement.

The number one principle in a spiritual life is to surrender, to look at our life honestly, and to nurture ourselves. I believe my surrendering to God has nurtured my soul. I am no longer feeling alone; I have grown strong in belief and am now living awake in a new freedom and awareness, having nurtured soundness of mind.

I nurtured my spirit by accepting a happier spirit, the result of surrendering my life to the energy force of a loving God. My faith nurtures my spirit, which I share with my family and friends through volunteering, complementing others and living in goodness. The gift of maintaining consistent and persistent conscious contact with God is the best way for me to nurture myself.

Have a nurturing day!

DEPENDABILITY

Dependability is the ability to be trustworthy and reliable and having the quality of perseverance, devotion, endurance, and faith in doing a great job. Dependability involves showing up, on time, and being capable, sober, stable, rational, honest, and faithful. Sometimes we need to put aside our own agenda and convenience to be there, available to help someone.

Dependability in relationships includes loyalty, trustworthiness, consistency, persistence, and steadiness in promises to care for each other. Each person is true to their word, no matter the inconvenience or sacrifice. Dependability states: "I will develop an attitude of gratitude and step up to the plate or challenge; share my experiences, strengths and hopes, correct my mistakes, and share my time to follow through with my promises. I will maintain my integrity and encourage others, keep confidences, and live in solutions."

I have learned that my spiritual progress is a daily effort to live in goodness and dependability. My contentment is dependable on my willingness to live in the Light, love and peace; depending on the God of my understanding; respecting the Golden Rule; and being a sane person. My happiness comes from within; I have learned that God lives in me and, being awake to hear the sound guidance, allows me to live a sane life. My dependability on God is a blessing and has healed me to live a contented life.

Have a day of dependability!

TRAILBLAZING

Trailblazing is to be a pioneer at blazing a trail in a new way in a park or forest, or using a new technique, theme, or subject. A trailblazing person takes the lead and creates, develops, explores, instigates, opens up, spearheads, and shows the way by being innovative, radical, trendsetting, and having a leading edge.

Trailblazing is the ability to develop new ideas to improve life skills. Trailblazers connect to the Creator's divine love, inspired with a sense of connectedness both out in nature and in their creative zone. The soul is nourished and transformed to a new and deeper level of peace and freedom. Trailblazing is a spiritual practice enjoyed in the moment, being totally conscious and present to receive God's love, guidance, direction, and protection.

I love trailblazing because it is a great way of meditation while I am hiking in nature. It helps me to balance as I hike along the trail, dealing peacefully with the forest debris. I may trim back some of the debris to help my path be more open and comfortable to hike, similar to when I have to cut back and clean up the debris in my life. Cleaning along the way creates a balance both in my hike and my life. Trailblazing opens spaces for others to enjoy, leaves signs to help others find their way, and creates places to rest in peace and serenity.

Have a trailblazing day!

JUNE 3
INFORMED

Informed is having knowledge, information, and insights on a subject. An informed person is educated in their thinking; based on this knowledge, they are capable of being level-headed, reasonable, sensible, logical, firm, and rational.

An uninformed person may suffer from impairments to reasoning skills, and this impairment may lead to intellectual and emotional uncertainty. However, becoming informed and growing to a state of maturity might heal us to want to make reasonable decisions, restoring us to soundness of mind and a healthy mental state of living well.

Feeling free comes from changing and accepting my life patterns after becoming informed of my chaotic and dysfunctional behaviors. Time, effort, and energy have shown me how to be informed and, as a result, becoming wise to know the difference between healthy and dysfunctional behaviors. I am now open to transform my living situations, being connected in love and peace within and growing into healthier perspectives.

However, choosing to mature is optional because some people remain in their self-willed and chaotic ways of living. I choose to benefit from being informed and embrace change daily. I am blessed to choose to live in a God-centered way because I have felt the love. Today, being informed in this way, I accept that God is good, and life is good.

Have an informed day!

RESILIENT

Resilient is the ability to willingly heal from depression, illness, or adversity. A resilient person is buoyant and will thrive to spring back and rebound to be well.

A traumatized individual has suffered at the hands of someone with sick behaviors, which might lead to despair and hopelessness. It may be catastrophic because an individual may get numbed out of life, lose their joy of living and become victimized in their thinking. Recovery is possible with resilient people.

A resilient person will bounce back with knowledge and understanding of the past under the guidance of a good therapist, programs, education, and by having a willingness to move forward. With tenacity, and hard work on ourselves, we move out of victimhood and survive to be healthy and thriving in life, accepting reality, knowing that we are a changed person, and that everything's okay. As a resilient person, I found peace within and dealt with these life challenges slowly, but surely, one day at a time. I found meaning in my life and am healthy to live in my core personality. I grew to be responsible, grounded, and peaceful within; consequently, I live in the now, which has empowered me to be healthy, stable, and reconnected.

Have a resilient day!

JUNE 5
PURPOSEFUL

Purposeful is to have a useful purpose, a reason, an intended aim, a desired goal, and rationale.

Starting our day with purposeful prayer and meditation helps to recognize pure goodness and love. Finding meaning and purpose in our life encourages healthy physical, emotional, and spiritual wellness to go deeper in spirit and experience the love of God.

A purposeful person has determination to understand and accept their thoughts and behaviors, and they have clear perspectives on living well. They live their journey with integrity, honesty, and being accountable to themselves to be their best person each day. Self-actualization and wholeness are the result of purposeful studying to find our dignity and wellness.

My purpose in life is to learn the lessons and find contentment so that I may experience happiness. I have found that it is in giving that I receive. Learning and practising living in the now, being compassionate, and purposeful in helping others, blesses me with opportunities for personal growth, self-improvement, and a purposeful life.

Have a purposeful day!

METAPHYSICAL

Metaphysical relates to learning about the physical nature of the human mind, a step above to the mystical, supernatural, and spirituality of life. It is the science to accept various notions of understanding the nature of being who we are and understanding our world.

As we learn about the power of a belief in a god, we regain faith, which is a highly abstract conceptual and theoretical notion. We come to trust God and be blessed with developing knowledge to understand the world and its ways. Now we are metaphysically engaged with the ability to relate to the unseen. Metaphysical studies might involve gaining insight into the dynamics of the universe and its nature. We can live well, one day at a time, in metaphysical spirituality, knowing we will continue our journey in the eternal world.

As I sought a God of love, I found spiritual truths of inner peace, and I realized serenity. My spirit has healed, and I am open to live a metaphysical, spiritual journey.

Have a metaphysical day!

WELL-GROUNDED

Well-grounded is having the ability to live disciplined, healthy, vibrant, and balanced. We base our living on a valid, coherent, rational, reasonable, sensible, good, and firm foundation and experience being well-grounded. We live in a state of conscious contact with God, our source, and others.

Life is full of challenges, and our response to it is based on self-esteem. Living a fragmented, dissociated life with low self-esteem can be healed in time as we learn to let go of our self-defeating, negative thinking.

Once I was able to surrender my dysfunctional lifestyle of living off the rails, I grew in faith. I changed my attitude by rebuilding myself and being honest with cold hard truths; these changes resulted in serenity, and I was able to become well-grounded with soundness of mind. I now live mindfully in integrity and work to be the best that I can be each day. It has been a journey of self-discovery and acceptance.

I am able to enjoy peace of mind. As I shared my secrets, I weeded out my delusional thinking and was able to fertilize my mind to grow and live in the sacred truth of respect and honesty. I continue to progress each day, blessed to be well-grounded. I am now able to practice mindfulness and rejoice living in love, kindness, generosity, and balance with a positive self-esteem. I thank God and my changed perceptions because now I am able to be healthy, stable, and well-grounded.

Have a well-grounded day!

COURAGE

Courage is the ability to persevere in dealing with difficult situations in life. Courage is a state of humility and becomes second nature in self-affirmation.

Courage is a virtue of choice and the willingness to deal with pain, suffering, and uncertainty in times of trouble, such as addiction, abuse, mental illness, death, and dying. Moral courage is to deal with what is right and just in the instance of shame, opposition, and discouraged self-esteem.

I have developed my courage by surrendering, trusting my instincts, and persevering through difficulties life presented me, with faith, hope, and love. I grew with the powerful source of God's energy, which has blessed me with courage to have the nerve, bravery, and daring to open my heart fearlessly to deal and cope with life.

My life challenges opened me up to question who I was and where I was going with my life. Having courage allowed me to heal. I have dealt with my personal truth, and I was able to heal my anger, resentments, false pride, fears, and negative thinking. I now have the courage to share this journey with you, the readers. As I took responsibility to deal with my dysfunctional thinking and behaviors, I experienced freedom and peace to live life courageously in release, forgiveness, tolerance, pity, and patience. I am now free to live my life with a healed heart and soundness of mind.

Have a day of courage!

JUNE 9
ENERGY

Energy is having the strength to carry out mental, spiritual, and physical activities with vitality, vigor, zest, spark, buoyancy, enthusiasm, and liveliness. Energy is a source that empowers us to have dynamic power to help self and others complete tasks, projects, and services.

Living with harmonized energy comes from personal development and transformation on a daily basis through prayer and meditation. We learn to let go of our debilitating self and self-importance, and we become humble. We accept our awesomeness and enhance our self-acceptance with gratitude for our awakened state of sanity. Spiritual energy raises our consciousness, and we grow to be better people – stable, grounded, and well-nourished.

I have learned to stop contradicting people with negativity, anger, resentments, fears, and revenge if and when they seem to suck out my positive energy. I have learned that I need to stay conscious and alert, so that I may resist falling into old dysfunctional ways and maintain my personal energy for goodness. I have learned to pray for harmful, negative people, and let them go. I must stay strong to keep myself balanced, living in the now, awesomely present, funny, peaceful, and joyous. I am comforted with spiritual energy and stay tuned by surrounding myself with positive people, music, prayer, meditation, art, and creations; I serve and love others with compassion and the grace of God!

Have a day of energy!

ORDERLINESS

Orderliness is the quality of keeping things neat, clean, well arranged, and orderly. Orderliness is a system, order, pattern, and organization to live a healthy lifestyle.

To live with God is my good orderly direction in my life, which has resulted in my growing to be peaceful and contented. Staying awake and in tune, I keep myself free from my disorders and chaos. I am not without problems, but I do apply problem-solving and find solutions.

I am living better by keeping a daily practice of faith, rather than reacting in a state of confusion and uneasiness. I practise being grounded and living efficiently in proper moral conduct in a healthy functional manner. I maintain my orderliness by cleaning out negative ways and surrounding myself with the higher healing energy of encouraging folks.

Orderliness has served me well mentally and emotionally. I am now able to make the best of most with living in the now in good faith. I start my day gratefully, asking for guidance to serve in peace. I maintain a routine of cleanliness with things in order, keeping the clutter down and living in harmony with God the Creator and the universe. Trusting my journey to unfold as it will, living in good orderly direction, and being blessed is a sound life of orderliness which results in me being stable, peaceful, and contented. I am as I believe I am, and so it is!

Have a day of orderliness!

ACTION

Action is taking charge and doing something to achieve results through organizing and holding an exciting event, such as a party, celebration, or wedding; or, unfortunately, it may be action to cope with a tragic event, such as a devastating illness, trauma, abuse, warfare, or death.

Healthy action comes from my heart with my love and inspiration to serve others. Believing in goodness, trusting God, and in keeping the faith with which I am blessed, I make informed choices in a state of reasonableness and confidence, which enables me to take action to overcome chaos, confusion, disillusionment, and obstacles that arise on my journey. Letting go of past mistakes, learning to practise integrity, and being true to my word with positive action and honesty, have rewarded me with peace of mind and heart.

I am now healed and living in the present moment with healthy connections and joyful living skills. My action is in my daily practice of obedience to be the best person I can be, to share my well-being, and to make positive contributions. Having restored my dignity and self-esteem, I am able to embrace mindfulness and be considerate of others' feelings. I listen to my instincts, live in unity, and act in a healthier manner by responding rather than reacting. I change my perspectives, become adaptive, understanding, and live in peaceful resolutions, which has brought my life full circle.

Have a day of action!

REDIVIVUS

Redivivus means to come back to life, to wake up from existing, to be reborn, and to be revived.

When we are railroaded in our beliefs and lose faith, we suffer from a spiritual malady because our spirit is broken, harmed, or hurt. Some of us will fight to gain control of our journey; others of us become chaotic, trudging through life as lost souls in a seemingly hopeless state, bouncing from pillar to post. It is a fortunate day when a spiritual experience occurs, and we are touched with the grace of God. We learn that God is good, and we receive an awareness and understanding of unconditional love. Good is God and God is good; as we change our way of thinking and believing, we are able to seek truth and trust God. We accept the responsibility to live a life of gratitude and appreciation.

When I became willing to change, opened my mind to let go of the past, and invited God into my life, I experienced being reborn as I woke up. It was a miracle for me to trust again, to forgive, and to become kind and compassionate. Being revived involved connecting with healthier perspectives and accepting God's guidance. My God is love, energy, good vibrations, nature, "four directions," forgiveness, and unconditional love. I feel this love in the guidance and direction for my daily actions. I feel the presence in my meditation, and I am blessed to continue to grow each day.

Have a day of redivivus action!

DEVOTIONAL

Devotional is a feeling of love in quiet loyalty listening to God. Devoting time and energy to God in prayer is a devotional act. The benefits are spiritual growth, peace, and strength.

Learning to trust God is a wonderful gift and enhances the joy of living each day. Our ability to practice our daily devotional connection allows us to feel higher energy and nearness to God. We grow in love, kindness, awareness, caring, compassion, and forgiveness – shining with peace!

We practice devotional time to enter into the world of the spirit. We cease fighting, and we live and react sanely. We persevere in our devotional practice to be open to serve others and sharing our love of God. Our spiritual devotional practice includes asking God to direct our thoughts and behaviors, so we may retrain our brains to do God's will.

Being mad at God did not serve me well, but then I learned that was not God with whom I was angry. I embraced God to be relieved of my selfishness and to be filled with inspiration in positive, intuitive thoughts, and better decision-making skills. My devotional practice became my state of consciousness to be well. I now thrive in the love, happy and content being blessed with God's grace. Maintaining daily devotional practices keeps me emotionally well. My energy is vibrant, and I am a free spirit.

Have a devotional day!

GUARDIAN ANGEL

Guardian angel is an angel who looks out for you throughout your life, whereas a spirit guide is a loved one who passed away.

We are wise to call upon our guardian angel for assistance in troubled times because they will assist, protect, and comfort us. Having mindfulness to be grateful for their good energy, and to reach out, insures we maintain soundness of mind and the ability to cope with our lives and all that it brings. This journey is challenging, and it's comforting to know that, if I ask, my guardian angel will help.

I guess my guardian angel is the positive voice I hear telling me to rejoice in my daily living, to transform my thoughts, and to improve my character. My guardian angel sparks my intuition and motivates me to excel and keep my dreams alive. Although sometimes circumstances change our dreams, like being in a major car accident; when it happened to me, I had to create new dreams. Such is life on life's terms; so I picked up and recreated my life to find alternate passions, such as painting. I'm sure it is my guardian angel that guides my brush.

I often sense my guardian angel and have become sensitive to the energy, feeling like someone is carrying me. I am grateful for this enlightenment and respect this experience when I sense it in my heart. I have had many experiences throughout my life journey; for example, when I walk in the forest, I am most in tune with my guardian angel and feel rejuvenated in happiness and joy.

Have a day with your guardian angel!

CENTERED

Centered is being in the middle – balanced, emotionally healthy, and calm. A centered person is grounded and balanced in my thinking and perspectives. I guess I'm centered because I was the middle kid of thirteen!

Centered people have learned the art of surrendering, letting go, and being open to help with positive energy. When we are centered, we have learned to let go so that we are open to infinite possibilities and personal freedom. Accepting life and allowing the process to direct things; whether life is what we perceive it should be, or what it may be, is not our business. Accepting life is freeing in that we learn that we do not have to carry the world but, rather, live our part to share the experience. I trust the process rather than forcing things to go my way.

To be centered, I have learned that all people have their own personal journey to live, as they develop and grow; so, I must not paralyze myself in another person's business. I must stay centered in my spirit, free from illusions, chaos, and conflict. To stay centered, I must speak my truth, live in unity with society, know what I stand for, and accept that other people have their own minds. Living centered involves being capable of accepting life as it is and living in solutions.

Have a centered day!

COPING

Coping is the ability to deal with people and life circumstances and making a conscious effort to solve personal and interpersonal problems. Being mindful to cope accepting what one can, taking action to change what one can and growing in wisdom to minimize, tolerate and let go of stress and conflict.

Life has many challenges and I have learned the Serenity Prayer, which guides, directs, and protects me from all kinds of trouble. My biggest growth in learning coping skills came from learning healthy strategies and adopting new outlooks on life. Once I modified my views and perceptions from negative, fearful, and unhealthy ways of thinking, I was able to focus on positive, fearless, and healthy coping skills.

My emotions were stuck, disconnected, distracted, and festering hostile feelings until I learned positive coping strategies. I used several social support groups and therapy to gain acceptance and positive thoughts. I learned to value myself and build positive self-esteem to cope with life on life's terms. Developing communication skills, the art of letting go, and forgiving has blessed me with the great gift of peace of mind and the ability to thrive in the joy of living.

Have a day of coping!

REALISTIC

Realistic is when we see things as true and real, and we are able to be down to earth, sensible, rational, level-headed, and use common sense.

A realistic person sees the truth as it presents itself in the now, lives in the present moment and in positive mindfulness. They cope with the real, hard, sober truth with God's will, surrendering to peace. Our human existence is imperfect because we all make mistakes from time to time. Hopefully, we clean up the wreckage of our past and find faith to live maturely and peacefully as we move forward on our journey. If we are lacking trust in our faith, we will get more of the same old patterns that keep us in a spin and paralyze us in unrealistic thinking.

Realistic coping skills keep me focused on better outcomes with open-mindedness and non-judgmental attitudes. I gain peace through honesty, opening my heart, and being willing to accept things as they are, just for today, with positive communications. Realistic thinking is crucial to my mental health because it allows me to manage my thoughts, composure, and behaviors in times of troubled situations. My coping skills now include filtering out the negative and focusing on what is good and positive, avoiding all or nothing thinking, and staying focused on my own life and journey. I live in a realistic soundness of mind with principles such as acceptance, mindfulness, faith, hope, concentration, and with an effort to stay awake, conscious of God's will, not mine!

Have a realistic day!

GRACE

Grace enables a pleasant way of conduct, behaving gently, smoothly, and calmly while being mindful, thoughtful, and considerate. Grace is a virtue to act with encouragement, connection, flexibility, freedom, and divine love. Grace is a prayer at the beginning of a meal. Grace is having a time period free from consequences.

My life's challenges sometimes have led me to in live dark experiences and thoughts. My journey included hard, ugly, rough, and dysfunctional ways of behaving. Yet, with the grace of God and maturity, I grew to become responsible, loving, beautiful, smooth, and functional in my well-being.

Through divine love, I experienced harmonious healing, integrating myself in spirituality and grace. Living in grace, I feel love, compassion, and serenity so I'm able to radiate a vibrant energy of peace. I accept the grace of God, trusting the direction toward positive realistic thoughts to go with the flow. With stability, I stay balanced in my trust, gracefully accepting, giving, and taking. I feel my feelings, acknowledge my fears, and, most often maintain myself in times of uncertainty.

However, I do falter because I am human, but the progress is amazing. I continue to grow as God's grace fills me with mercy, empathy, forgiveness, and the ability to practise unconditional love.

Have a day of Grace!

WELCOMING

Welcoming is to be friendly, pleasant, and graciously polite with responsiveness. Welcoming is a positive exercise in hospitality and helps your guests feel a sense of belonging, which opens doors to well-being and healthy relationships.

Welcoming people create healthy relationships by greeting people with love, openness, and acceptance. Kindness and welcoming bring people closer, which enables better understanding and opens dialogue for dealing with reality. Because we are all on our own journeys to learn about life and each other's journey, honesty is vital for growing towards positive strategies and healthy solutions for living. We are not aiming for perfection but, rather, progress in healthy dialogue to be welcoming in settling our disputes.

I welcome my Higher Power into my day and trust that I am guided to be welcoming, to live in progressive growth, and also help others to live in this light of love. Welcoming is a core value that helps me to develop a healthier respect for my relationships. It is welcoming for me to be attentive to learn about others, to have proper perspectives, and to remain flexible in my attitude for maintaining my peace and serenity with love.

Have a welcoming day!

JUNE 20
LIBERATED

Liberated is to be set free, to be released, discharged, detached, unshackled, and saved. Liberated is to feel connected and complete, content with our life, and to experience oneness with the Creator. To be liberated in one's mind is to live with a clear conscience.

Life is about learning and self-realization, growing to be the best you can be, and to cope with the lessons along the path. We are not doormats and are not to be used; rather, we are to be respected and conscientious to help nourish, guide, protect, and help others, while at the same time keeping healthy boundaries so we do not wear ourselves out. We are liberated and free to share from the heart and must maintain a healthy balance. We are liberated to live, learning to love unconditionally and peacefully.

I became liberated when I found peace within and learned to live beyond the negative by staying focused in positive energy. As a liberated person, I feel the strength to be open and accepting of myself and others. I'm conscious of being creative and resourceful, having a focus on solutions, finding answers, or just letting go. I have learned that I must do the work to be able to cope with danger, fears, anxiety, and depression. The greatest gift of liberation is learning to stay awake, in tune with knowledge of God's will and the universe's energy and love.

Have a liberated day!

DELIGHT

Delight is a pleasurable experience of glee, satisfaction, contentment, and a strong feeling of happiness.

Delight is having soundness of mind to live in the moment, to be conscious and awake in your life, making healthy decisions and choices. Letting go of past and future living allows one to delight in the now, being present in the joy of living. Life is impermanent, and changes are inevitable; going with the flow, and accepting life on life's terms, opens opportunities for delight.

I must be vigilant to take stock off my life and thinking patterns and be conscious to live in light, which brings me delight. I must use my talents and share my delight. I have grown to appreciate life, to believe in myself, and embrace positive self-affirmations. I take responsibility to care for myself and to rejoice in my progress. I have learned to let go of resentments and aggressiveness in exchange for assertive living with boundaries; oh, what a great delight my life has become. I am so grateful for the delight in my life, and I am confidently living with contentment. I am now true to myself and free – living in delight.

Have a day of delight!

BEAUTY

Beauty is the quality of loveliness, attractiveness, and satisfaction. When we look at something or someone with beauty, we feel pleasure.

Spiritual beauty is deep within, divinely growing in kindness, humility, compassion, and faithfulness. I am attracted to peacefulness, which is beauty. I am connected with an understanding of God and have been blessed with healing, which is the deepest beauty. I am blessed with being mindful, loving, and tolerant. Beauty is within, deep to the roots; I am living each day to the fullest and being nourished in divine goodness. The real beauty is in my presentation and actions in daily living because God prompts me to share my experiences with love from my heart.

Beauty is both within and outside each of us. It is good to take care of ourselves to look good both outwardly and inwardly. It is a pleasure to present myself with a quiet and peaceful heart and spirit. Beauty is being able to love God, others, and self. Praying and meditating helps to nourish my spiritual beauty.

Have a day of beauty!

Quiet is to be silent, still, and calm, making no noise, and being tranquil. Quiet is a great gift of personal strength.

Walking in quiet tranquility in the woods is very powerful; such activity allows the mind to rest and enjoy life's calmness. Finding inner stillness is important for nourishing our mental, emotional, spiritual, and physical health. When we retreat in a quiet walk, we are empowered in God's creation and feel renewed.

Sailing is a quiet boat trip, free from noisy motors. We are quietly practising sitting, relaxing and breathing fresh air. When the lake is still, we sit quietly by a bonfire and listen to the crackle. Being tranquil and quiet folks, we enjoy the serenity.

I have learned to be quiet, letting go of the chaos from past trauma, negative thinking, and living a dysfunctional lifestyle. I now find peace in quietness. I learn to quiet my spirit through prayer and meditation. Starting my day in quiet prayer, I prepare to head in a positive direction for a quiet, peaceful, and loving day. Taking short walks in the woods, and walking my labyrinth in quiet prayer, is comforting and feeds me to be a gentle spirit. Meditating while sitting on my park bench, I listen in quiet serenity. Each night, I give thanks for my day and accept God's protection for a quiet sleep.

Have a quiet day!

THANKFUL

Thankful is showing gratitude, appreciation, and relief with a positive attitude. Life is meant to be an expression of our love for our time here on earth. Living a thankful life is good for our mental, emotional, physical, and spiritual health. When we are thankful and mature, we are content, satisfied, and accepting with the outcome of our living conditions.

Sometimes our living conditions are unsatisfactory. We learn that we can reach out, get help, and change, knowing that there are solutions for all circumstances. We recognize that our life is a mess, and we take a turn on the road, changing our thoughts and path. We surrender to our Higher Power, trusting that we will have a renewal in our strength to move on and make the best of our lives. We change our consciousness to one of faith, and we are thankful to have a second chance for an improved and good life, which is emotional and healing.

Today, I am very thankful each morning for waking up in a safe and peaceful place, full of love, understanding, and acceptance. I thank God for a good night's sleep, and I am thankful for all my blessings: God's love, a good partner, family and friends, our home, and my talents. I use my talents and show my thankfulness by being the best person I can be with kindness, caring, love, patience, helpfulness, gentleness, and generosity. I focus on the good and engage in living fully.

Have a thankful day!

TEACHABLE

Teachable is to be educable, trainable, and capable of being taught while, at the same time, having the gift of wonder, being open to discovery, adventure, and growth. Teachable is being able and willing to learn.

Creating teachable circumstances involves timing, respect, attention, and then simple, direct, and precise communication with focus on a topic. Tone is very important because it affects whether we tune in or out. A positive tone of voice creates an interest to listen and, possibly, the ability to learn. We maintain a teachable Spirit by being open, accepting, trusting, willing, observing, and by developing our skills to change, adapt, admit, and ask questions. Our confidence grows, and we learn to humble ourselves; we know that, the more we learn, the more we need to learn and, therefore, remain teachable.

I have learned that being teachable is to live in a positive way that empowers us to grow in respect and opens us to help others along the path. Being teachable has enabled me to be a problem-solver. I now have the confidence to confront and resolve anything that comes my way. The benefits of being teachable are grace and humbleness to listen, learn, practice, repeat, learn, and master new things each day. I am blessed with opportunities every day, as long as I stay teachable.

Have a teachable day!

INSTRUMENTAL

Instrumental is to be helpful and influential to cause something to manifest. Instrumental is also a piece of music composed for instruments.

Instrumental pieces of music are lovely and have no singing. Bluegrass and Old-time music instrumentals are appreciated because the focus is on different instruments throughout the performance. In some instrumental pieces, a musician takes a break, and their instrument playing is highlighted. Instrumental interludes sometimes occur in the middle of songs, when the singer takes a break and the musicians continue to play instrumentals.

To be an instrumental person in helping and influencing things to happen can be a gift. We take charge to be awake and mindful, to be instrumental in sharing solutions. Living consciously allows us to be instrumental in our own and others' spiritual growth and well-being.

I have grown to be open to share my experience so I may be instrumental in helping other people feel the love and peace of my presence. I practise doing good things, and I feel purposeful, which brings contentment. Being instrumental in sharing God's love nourishes my mental health; I manifest good thoughts, and I am loved.

Have an instrumental day!

SOLICITOUS

Solicitous is showing concern, care, interest, and compassion for the health and welfare of another human being. A solicitous person is kind, thoughtful, attentive, and considerate.

Life is sacred, fragile, and precious from the beginning until the end. There are no guarantees in life; it is wise to learn that there is a Higher Power, and we are here to serve in the spirit of love. It is a gift to be able to be solicitous and serve others, especially with folks in illness, sickness, and the final stages of dying. It is true that the more we give of ourselves, the more we receive. Being solicitous is our chance to share our time and true goodness, to help as best we can.

I have experienced great sickness, illness and "dis-ease" in my life; with the help from solicitous folks along my journey, I have healed. They planted the seeds of compassion and love in my heart with their sharing and caring. It is by the grace of God that I have developed a healthier character and am a solicitous person. It is with great gratitude that I have become able to understand others' needs, share my time, bring joy and laughter, and do fun activities as the situation permits. Understanding others' attitudes and beliefs helps me to be compassionate, patient, and kind, serving others with grace and dignity.

Have a solicitous day!

INTUITIVE

Intuitive is having the ability to be insightful, quick-witted, sharp, intense, and sensitive, and knowing true and factual things beyond reason, time, and space.

Often, traumatized people recover and realize that they are intuitive. These intuitive people grow to experience a conscious awakening and high levels of peace, love, joy, and healing. I was one of these folks who, upon awakening, adapted to a new way of life, surrendered to God, and made a commitment to maintain conscious contact with God for guidance and direction. Spiritually intuitive living includes praying, meditating, being present in the here and now, and feeling peaceful and healing energy. Faithful practice results in feeling good, being compassionate, and being in tune with divine love.

An intuitive person has a healthy connection with their gut feelings. They are blessed with the language of the soul and know what is wrong or right. Through their meditation, they slow down, know silence and stillness, and listen to their inner voice. Their intuitive senses are sharpened, becoming spontaneous, hardwired, and innate. Intuitive people trust their hearts and believe in themselves, accept and acknowledge their intuition, and have courage to let it guide them to make better decisions during their journey.

Have an intuitive day!

GENTLENESS

Gentleness is having the ability to be meek, mild, calm, sweet, kind, and careful. Gentleness is displayed with a humble attitude, a kind and forgiving spirit, and a caring manner.

Gentleness is a desirable characteristic of being considerate, well-mannered, and demonstrated with the acceptance of love for oneself and others. People with gentleness are caring and nurturing; because of these qualities, they are able to help others work through and solve their problems. They possess good listening skills and are there for you, helping you to grow through your pain and trauma.

As we grow on our journey, we realize that love is gentle. We mature to learn self-control and behave with gentleness. The more we learn to behave with a loving heart, gentleness, and think positive thoughts, the more we are able to be gentle with others. We learn to do so one day at a time, and we progress a little bit each day. Our gentleness grows as we let go of our hurts and traumas, and we begin to celebrate life. We practise gentleness each day, and we continue to progress a little each day until gentleness becomes a habit.

I am blessed to know gentleness and to celebrate life as best I can. Some days are harder than others, and there is nothing that I cannot handle with the love of God. I am strong, empowered in gentleness.

Have a day of gentleness!

PRIVILEGED

Privileged is to have special opportunities and advantages in life to be fortunate, prosperous, and lucky. The best privileged life is one of good health.

Along my journey, I have been privileged to meet many good folks, who have given me great opportunities to better myself. I was privileged to attend grade twelve three times before I managed to graduate. Then I was privileged to join the armed forces in a communications trade and also to start studying at university. Then, I was privileged to move to Paris, France to study French, my heritage language. I was privileged to find a great host family. I taught English to their child Delphine. Next, I returned to Canada to complete my studies and become a grade-eight teacher. I was privileged to study at University St. Anne, Dalhousie, NSTC, St Mary's University, University of Chicoutimi and Jonquiere, and Acadia University. I was privileged to use my education and enjoyed teaching for ten years. Unfortunately, my life changed when I was injured in a vehicle accident; however, I was privileged to have a great support team for my recovery.

On a beautiful summer day, I set up a tent at the Clare bluegrass festival, and, *voila*, a handsome man, full of gentleness and tranquility, was camping just across the path. We were privileged to meet each other, and we developed a pleasant and enjoyable lifestyle together. On our journey together, we have met many wonderful folks who have privileged us with hospitality and kindness.

Have a privileged day!

JULY 1
RADIANT

Radiant is to be brightly shining, vibrant, full of energy, and self-confident, while expressing happiness, joy and freedom.

Today is a day with radiant faces celebrating Canada Day. Musicians are shining brightly and presenting their music; also, there will be fireworks, radiant in the dark skies. The energy is vibrating and radiating unity in our community. Being radiant is a state of gratitude, where we are carefree and shine at our best. We have learned to live one day at a time and in the moment. We are living mindfully and become radiant with love shining in our eyes. We are peaceful, in unity in our world.

My journey is a blessing; I have found God and am blessed with God's grace. I have grown radiant through wellness, gleaming with positivity, gentleness, kindness and peacefulness. I am in tune with nature and know stillness. I enjoy my quiet time in prayer and meditation, which fills me with the joy of living. I'm grateful to be radiant, sharing my joy with gratitude and action.

Have a radiant day!

FORTUNATE

Fortunate is to have good luck, to be blessed, to have an opportune, favorable advantageous life, and to be humble, kind, patient, tolerant, and loving. To be fortunate is to have good health and a healthy lifestyle.

I am fortunate in having learned that faith, accompanied by self-sacrifice and unselfish constructive action, feeds a healthy lifestyle. By watching others, I am fortunate with the gift of learning and knowing that the more we give, the more we receive. On my journey, I am fortunate in having met good people, who shared a healthier way of living with me.

In surrendering my dysfunctional thinking, I am fortunate to have found peace in my mind and soul. My heart has mended through the spirit of divine love. I have been fortunate on my journey despite the different traumas that I survived. I now thrive blessed in wellness of mind. I am fortunate to be able to live in a relationship with a wonderful man, who happens to be a retired cook and steward. In the past few weeks, I've been unfortunate to experience pneumonia, but I was fortunate to have the care of Jean Paul, who has been so kind to make sure I had good food for healing. I am fortunate that he is so loving and kind.

Have a fortunate day!

FORTITUDE

Fortitude is being courageous in dealing with life's challenges, being strong mentally and emotionally. Fortitude includes bravery, courage, determination, tenacity, staying power, backbone, spunk, guts, and constancy.

Fortitude is a virtue that helps us stand strong in facing obstacles during our journey. The struggles are opportunities for growth and overcoming fear. A person with fortitude will go to any length to move through their struggles. They are fearless and have the nerve to be honest and standing up for justice. They endure difficulty courageously, and their fortitude sees them through.

I am fortunate to have found fortitude, courage, strength, open-mindedness, and wisdom on my journey. My spiritual serenity comes from becoming willing to let go, to love God and myself. My Creator continues to give me opportunities to develop fortitude with healed mental and emotional states to be strong, faithful, loving, and kind and to share my experience and be of service when I can!

Have a day of fortitude!

WARM-HEARTED

Warm-hearted is to be loving, compassionate, humane, sympathetic, unselfish, and understanding.

A warm-hearted person is radiant and pleasant. They walk quietly, but they are intense with generosity, inspiration and joy. I have met many warm-hearted folks along my journey. I love camping, festivals, and travelling; I find people are relaxed and tend to be warm-hearted. I look forward to festivals because I am sure to be surrounded by warm-hearted folks as we sing, play, eat, and sleep.

This morning, I received a warm-hearted telephone call from my dear sister Elizabeth, sharing unconditional love. She informed me that she missed me, and she loved me. She is authentic and graciously affectionate because this is the language from the heart of a mentally challenged human being.

She is a great teacher and an example of warm-hearted living. She reminded me that her birthday was July 31st. Then she said, "I love you; please come get me; take me camping, and we will have a bonfire. You can bring me a new guitar, a black one like Johnny Cash's with a button and a strap, and don't forget a bag!"

Warm-hearted at its best! I am blessed to be able to fulfill her wish and to see her joy! Although she will never actually play it, she will have the joy of having and holding it as she sings her favorite song, "Livin' on Love" by Alan Jackson.

Have a warm-hearted day!

JULY 5
HAPPINESS

Happiness is an inside job, which comes from being mentally and emotionally content in a state of peace, loving kindness, and compassion.

Happiness is the result of enjoying the moment and living in reality with positive behaviors and actions. Happiness develops when we are in tune with an attitude of gratitude. Happiness comes from respecting oneself and others and enjoying life on life's terms. Sharing your talent, projects, and accomplishments keeps you involved, which also brings happiness.

Acceptance and positive relationships are necessary to experience happiness. It helped me to accept a Higher Power to direct, guide, and protect me. We pray and experience the joy of life and know that we are not alone in this universe. This practice gives us a whole feeling, a stable mind, and self-confidence. We find happiness and pleasure from good behavior, acts of kindness, singing joyfully, and bringing moments of love to those we meet on our journey. Experiences bring opportunities for happiness, so we live awake and conscious of the blessings in the moment.

Have a day of happiness!

CONSIDERATE

Considerate it is to be kind, caring, respectful, and compassionate regarding the feelings of others.

Living a life with soundness of mind, stability and, a sense of having a universal connection allows people to be considerate. They see the world beyond their egos, are thoughtful of other people's feelings, and have good manners. They understand the Golden Rule to respect all religions, because we are all one, and we are considerate in doing good deeds unto others.

Learning to be considerate comes from positive living and being responsible to ourselves and others. When we make a mistake, we are considerate to apologize so that we may continue to live in peace. We must live in gratitude, willing to sacrifice in the moment and to help others in time of need; being considerate, we will both reap the benefits. We learn to manage our lives so that we live in peace. Our baseline for being considerate comes from living in connection with a loving God, consciously thinking of goodness and acting as an agent of love.

Have a considerate day!

DELIGHTFUL

Delightful is pleasant, pleasing, pretty, palatable, and pleasurable to experience; something that is amusing, captivating, entertaining, and satisfying.

To live in a state of wellness, being mentally emotionally and spiritually fit, is delightful. Being capable of identifying personal qualities, through self-examination, enhances self-awareness to improve good mental health, which allows us to live with stable vibrations, emotions, actions, understanding, and inner contentment.

Changes in life are constant. Healthy prayers, such as the "Serenity Prayer" and "Lord, make me a channel of Thy peace," are great comforts for serenity and peace of mind, while dealing with life on life's terms. Nurturing the mind with positive habits of prayer, meditation, sharing, and singing, enjoying nature, and reading positive literature, have contributed to my new delightful transformation. It was hard getting used to this delightful transformation, because the feeling of things going too well was scary and overwhelming. Eventually, my mind settled into soundness, ease, comfort, and delightful inner contentment. I am passionately grateful and thankful to know God and to be delightful.

Have a delightful day!

COMMUNICATIVE

Communicative means we are ready and willing to talk. Communicative people are open, forthcoming, reserved, and frank in sharing their thoughts and feelings. Healthy communication skills include speaking calmly in a kind, caring, loving, clear, and precise manner.

Life's challenges sometimes lack positive experiences and healthy communicative skills; the result is lost souls. Resentments, anger, jealousy, low self-esteem, lack of confidence, false pride, and fear set in. People sometimes become anxious, obnoxious, and threatened because they have lost faith and are overcome by negativity, becoming dysfunctional and desperate characters. To regain emotional and mental stability, a positive interaction with healthy communicative skills is necessary for growth beyond this negativity. It is wise to strive for progress and learn to reach out in a positive communicative way.

The language of love is communicated in healthy communicative interactions and embraces the following qualities: honesty, open mindedness, focusing on who is speaking, engaging in listening, sharing positive feedback, understanding body language, and having willingness to learn. We may develop the skills by nourishing our minds through starting our day in prayer to be balanced for the day, reading and telling ourselves positive self-affirmations, accepting our goodness, and living in the "now" with peace, love, joy, and contentment.

Have a communicative day!

Play is to engage in an activity for fun, enjoyment, and entertainment. Play is also the act of participating in a game or sport. Play is a spiritual discipline.

We connect spiritually with life and, in doing so, we humble ourselves by learning to change, getting in touch with our childlike feelings, and discovering the fun of play. We let go and enjoy being carefree, trusting, and worry-free. Play is essential for a balance in life. Play replenishes our spirits.

This weekend, I am going to play with my friends. We will play our instruments and make music, go for walks, and just hang out. While we play, we'll enjoy laughter, tell jokes, sing songs, and maybe even eat some junk food.

Some forms of play include walking in the woods, playing in the garden, swinging in the hammock, and riding a bicycle. Play releases stress and allows us to feel alive. Play wakes up our spirits and nourishes our souls. Play releases endorphins and heals us so we can connect with happiness, joy, bliss, and good feelings.

Have a day of play!

AWARENESS

Awareness is the ability to perceive and feel the reality of emotions, senses, life, people, places, and things. Awareness is the state of being awake, trusting in the universe and our creator, and feeling whole and contented.

Events such as childhood trauma, addictions, death, job loss, injury, and divorce can be overcome with awareness and realization that we have been affected and how. We learn to adapt and refocus. We have the awareness we need to make some positive changes in our routines and rebuild our lives. Awareness and acceptance come from an honest communication with self and others. Some of us need therapy, programs, and interventions to help us through our troubles and move on.

Awareness that I have a problem is my first step, and my integrity to speak my truth is my saving grace. Sharing my perspective helps me to hear myself and stimulates desire for more growth each day. This awareness allows me to change for the better, a little each day, and I humbly thank God for positive direction and guidance. This divine presence and inspiration nourish my soul.

Prayer and meditation open my heart and soul to understand the importance of living in a state of awareness. Following my intuition, heart, and good senses helps me to grow and discover my talents, which I share through my creations of quilting, music, art, ideas, writing, gardening, and adventures in nature. Being open to develop new relationships inspires me to appreciate my journey and to recognize experiences as strengths. My enjoyment and contentment are in sharing my awareness of my experience.

Have a day of awareness!

Enrich is to enhance, improve, upgrade, supplement, polish, reinforce, compliment, deepen, elevate, and raise the quality or value of someone or something.

I took a good look at my life when I found myself asking: "What is the meaning and purpose of living? Who am I? How can I improve? What are my patterns? Why am I so confused? What is this depression? What are my distractions? What am I contributing?" These questions lead me to study my values, beliefs, and direction. I was seeking to enrich my life.

I began to enrich my life through thinking differently and positively. This healthy thinking enriched me. Needing help with this process, I reached out to a therapist to assist with my cognitive issues. I have learned to be an observer, look deeply, talk about my journey, travel, read, and meditate; these activities enrich my level of serenity. Setting goals, finding harmony, freeing my mind, and using and sharing my gifts ensures that I enrich my life.

Have a day of enrichment!

IMITATE

Imitate is to follow, emulate, and copy a person's speech or behavior as a role model, example or pattern.

The ability to imitate starts when we are babies. We learn speech and behaviors from our family, both the good and the bad. Sometimes we learn to imitate bad behaviors that block our growth. When we have low self-esteem, we often use negative and unbecoming behaviors to impress others. When this happens, we are living in the fog and are no longer are in a state of awareness. We lose ourselves and our conscious contact with the God of our understanding, and we lack the sense of being loved.

When we find help, we begin to grow aware and straighten out our thinking and behaviors. We develop new behaviors by imitating positive role models. The aim of imitating a healthier person is to develop a positive, improved, and enriched life. We look for people with qualities that we admire. We imitate their patterns, and we slowly accept the changes we need to make to shine our light. These new behaviors are empowering because they allow us to grow; our self-esteem increases, and we grow in confidence. Our new patterns of speech, habits, love, compassion, and faith are welcomed.

Have a day to imitate something positive!

MEMORABLE

Memorable is when some person, place, or thing is worth remembering. Memorable is unforgettable, significant, remarkable, impressive, and glorious.

I think of an amazing day, years ago, as I headed out on my bicycle with 60 pounds of food, clothes, and bedding. I enjoyed the lovely scenery, the smell of fresh-cut hay, and the ocean smell of saltwater air as I pedaled along my route. I was peacefully singing, coasting on the hills, pedaling along and waving to people I saw in the countryside, and was having a memorable time. Then the "OH NO" feeling came as it started to cloud over. I was about five minutes from my friend's camp, so I pedaled faster and felt content as I came off the road down the steep bank, relieved that I would get in before the rain. Surprise! Yes, I was surprised because my friend's camp was all boarded up, due to vandalism. The secret hidden key was no longer any good.

As I pushed my bike back up the hill, I was soon drenched, cold, shivering, and tired. I had traveled about 30 miles in the heat and 10 more in the cold rain. I recall a memorable moment of sanity when I accepted a ride and put my bike in the back of a truck, driving the remaining 10 miles on a cold, dark night on that lonely, old, crooked countryside road. I will never forget the two extremes of hot and cold in one day; today, I regard that experience as one of my most memorable biking days.

Have a memorable day!

UNIQUE

Unique is being one of a kind, particular, individual, uncommon, rare, and exclusive.

As we grow each day, we realize that each individual on this earth is unique in their own way. Through our growth and personal development, we discover our own unique personhood. We take stock of all our good and bad habits, and, hopefully, we are willing to improve our unique character. Acceptance of self and others helps us to enjoy others' unique ways. There is no competition; we are all unique.

Choices are instrumental in the way we live. Becoming comfortable and confident with ourselves, we accept spiritual growth, which has many benefits for better ways of living. As we surrender to find our uniqueness in our talents, gifts, and blessings, we enjoy our lives more each day. When we choose to share with others, we are bringing our unique gifts to them. It is through identifying with others that we grow and strengthen our uniqueness and gain confidence.

I am grateful to have moved out of my egomania; I am good enough in my own authentic uniqueness. I love living in togetherness, connected and sharing the joys of life. My spirit is content and free, and I am humbled to be part of this universe.

Have a unique day!

SOULFUL

Soulful is expressing sincere, passionate, meaningful, heartfelt, and deep emotional feelings.

Living in unity with God, self, and others in healthy relationships, and being the best soulful human, is a recipe for contentment. Personal development through prayer, meditation, sharing, communication, self-actualization, and acceptance of our unique soulful spirit and energy, is a process in action. When we surrender to God, our blessings and abundance of gratitude grows; we become soulful, agreeable, harmonious, and uplifting. We become more and more mellifluous and sweet sounding in our assertive daily living. We are humbled by the grace of God and love.

My journey has brought me down many different roads, and I certainly dance to the beat of my own drum. Sometimes this dance brought me to my knees; yet, today, I am blessed with a soulful feeling of living as I express my feelings in songs, writing, and poetry. My soulful living is the result of surrendering to God, becoming aware and grateful for my blessings, being open to new ideas, having a sense of wonder and adventure, creating my own reality, being present in my daily living, and accepting my uniqueness. Life is like music: harmonious, soulful, and pleasing.

Have a day of soulful living!

POWERFUL

Powerful is having great strength and competence. Being powerful is commanding, compelling, capable, and almighty. Powerful people have the ability to influence people and things in their favor. They have a strong effect, and some people are also able to share guidance and direction.

As my journey progressed over the years, I met some powerful friends and therapists along my path. They were powerful in sharing their experiences to help me find a way back to my inner core personality, peace, and serenity. We gathered and communicated, sharing our stories to find out that, in the end, we are all one. We respect each other's individual concept of a Higher Power, the most almighty, powerful Creator of our universe. We empower and encourage each other to do our best.

I found that I was capable of being a powerful positive thinker through letting go of all past frustrations, disappointments, and fears. Today, I feel my compassion through prayer, meditation, and being consciously aware of my behaviors and actions. The secret is to strive for progress each day and to forgive myself and others. I strive to carry only positive healing love, energy, and joy to those I meet throughout my day. This is a very powerful way of living in peace, joy, happiness, and contentment.

Have a powerful day!

SPONTANEITY

Spontaneity is the quality of being unrestrained and unconstrained, with the ability to be at peace and to act uninhibited and naturally.

Spontaneity is one of the most positive characteristics I enjoy. I have learned to make general plans but not to plan outcomes. I turn my life over to God each morning, and I spontaneously find freedom by giving up my control. That's right, I'm not in control; I can live spontaneously going with the flow and enjoying God's will for me.

My guardian angel guides me and allows me to be flexible and confidently enjoy spontaneity. It is amazing to finally connect and live in the moment, open for change and abundance to live naturally, at ease and in tune with the Holy Spirit that promotes spontaneous spiritual experiences.

Sometimes I spontaneously invite friends over to my home, and we have a wonderful time. With spontaneity and great joy, I share my blessings with my guests. We all need community in our lives: for personal well-being, company, and to be respectable citizens. I am glad to live in a community with so much life and vigor. There are many activities in which to take part, and it is good to have the opportunity and freedom to be spontaneous.

Have a day of spontaneity!

BIRTH

Birth is the beginning of a new life, when a baby comes into the world, out from its mother's womb. Birth is also to bring forth.

Spiritual birth is a concept that involves waking up to our senses and living consciously. It is letting go of old ideas and living in unity with God, others, and self. Some of us wake up to realize that we have merely existed through life; in a spiritual awakening, we accept a new birth and renewal.

It's a good day when we accept ourselves, dedicate our time to making changes, and carry on. It is a great relief to let go of holding on to hurts and pain. Talking and identifying with others allows us to grow stronger and, eventually, we begin to rejoice contentedly as we heal. We grow out of being stuck, and we live with integrity. Happiness is an inside job.

It is wonderful that, in happiness, we can live peacefully. I choose to make the best of my days, and my responsibility is to maintain my connection with reality. I am responsible for the birth of each new day, so I must cherish the gift.

Have a day of birth!

PROMPT

Being prompt is to be quick, on time, without delay, quick, speedy, punctual, and timely. To prompt someone is to assist or encourage someone to say or do something.

Over the years, folks prompted me to write a book by folks because they enjoy my way of expression. While visiting friends in the North Carolina Mountains, I was inspired to write. I felt the quiet peace in the log cabin as I looked out at the mountains; I heard the calling that it was time. I came back to Nova Scotia and thought, "Where do I start?"

Then, my dear friend Eleanor prompted me to write one positive word a day. I decided to write 365 words on slips of paper and placed them in a basket. Each day, I would pick one and write what it has meant in my growth journey. I was on my journey, one day at a time, to write a book. This book was meant to be a practice run, but sharing with my friends prompted me to publish my reflections on these words.

It is a pleasure to write, but it takes much effort on my part because of the brain injury from a car accident. The process to write each day begins with me picking a word from my basket. Then, after breakfast, I meditate on what the word means to me. Next, I brainstorm on a sheet of paper, rest, and then write my one page. This process usually takes me a few hours. This practice is a healthy focus for me each day, because it helps me to exercise my brain processing and has the beneficial side effects of giving me a daily purpose. I have grown in self-confidence by seeing how far I have come in my healing journey. I can attest that you can heal from trauma if you are willing to look at yourself honestly!

Have a prompt day!

RESOLVED

Resolved means to be intent on, insistent on, committed, and strongly determined to do or achieve something.

After living in chaos for many years in dysfunctional living, I resolved to find my voice and strength to heal. My journey to wellness opened my mind, body, and soul to let go of the dysfunction so that I could move on. I am now resolved to living my life in love, respect, honesty, faith, courage, and compassion, as well as justice and service.

Changes in my consciousness to be focused, grounded, and centered came from years of changing my ways and habits. I am pleased to feel the growth each day, and I am growing stronger in confidence and self-esteem every day. Writing helps me in my awareness of living, I have resolved to living my life peacefully and sharing my experiences to help others have hope and find their courage.

Living in solutions, staying awake and committed to using my voice, speaking my truth, respecting my intuition and gut instincts, and helping others, are my resolutions. I am open to helping others; I am not a doormat but, rather, a welcome mat!

Have a resolved day!

WANTED

Wanted is to wish to feel accepted and loved by others.

Dysfunctional existing does not permit us to feel wanted and loved because our spirits are broken. In our minds, we feel rejected and unloved, which beats us down and sometimes breaks us; we might turn to addictions and dependency. Healthy living builds character and teaches us self-worth and esteem; we feel wanted.

Feeling accepted, wanted, and loved, heals our broken spirits. When we find support, we feel unconditionally loved and wanted, and we feel a sense of belonging. As we reach out to maintain help with support, we grow to believe we are wanted, respected, and valued. Being part of a healthy group, family, or community, rewards us with being part of something greater and knowing that we matter. This involvement instills us with a sense of connectivity, comfort, and confidence. Accepting help allows us to awaken to live in harmony and find our own wanted self. We are enough!

Have a wanted day!

MENDING

Mending means to set right, fix things, repair, restore, make better, and improve matters. When we act by mending, we renew our usefulness and become whole in our mind, body, and soul.

Mending is a process in our universal school of continual growth through releasing, receiving, and renewing our faith in ourselves and others. By the grace of God, I am capable of mending. The first step was to find a support system and team to help me become willing to be honest and respectful. The second step was to learn to listen and to listen to learn. Finally, the third step was to participate in the work, to take actions, and to run with them.

In renewed faith, mending became possible as I took the action to get to the root of my trauma and subsequent problems. I became passionate to wake up and learned many healing tools to improve my circumstances and mindset. These tools included letting go of the past, healing toxic relationships, and surrendering expectations. Having expectations set me up for disappointments; I choose not to let myself experience the stress.

Have a mending day!

REJUVENATED

Rejuvenated means to re-energize, refresh, reawaken, restore, and recover.

To mend our mind, body and soul, we may become rejuvenated by participating in journal writing. This exercise allows us to recognize our insanity and sort out our problems by taking action to look at solutions and try new ways. We maintain unity through social connections and by being involved with a support group where we feel welcome. We slowly gain new perspectives with new ideas, which rejuvenates and nourishes our spiritual growth. We learn to think positive thoughts, be centered, and ground ourselves to experience serenity in our new attitude of living.

To be rejuvenated and take care of our well-being, we also go out in nature and walk in the woods, on beaches, and Labyrinths. We take care of our spirits to receive blessings. We listen to peaceful music and surround ourselves with healthy environments.

I plan goals but not the outcomes, because having expectations sets me up for emotional disappointments. It is important for me not to stress myself. This is a process of learning to live in peace with acceptance. The progress is welcomed, and I'm rejuvenated each day. I am now living awakened and rejuvenated, feeling useful and whole. Each day, I'm rejuvenated with the love of my God and have another day to express myself.

Have a rejuvenated day!

THOUGHTFULNESS

Thoughtfulness is an act of kindness, consideration, and compassion.

Being authentic and real as we learn to be true to ourselves, we learn to be thoughtful to keep our spirit and soul nourished. I did not conform to the world, and I sadly strayed down a lonely path of destruction, denying my spirit the joys of life. Fortunately, I found my way back and it has been an ongoing process to rejuvenate myself. It gives me strength to have recovered from the effects of not being thoughtful and dragging myself through life bouncing from pillar to post. Hurt, pain, betrayal, and rejection allowed me to falter.

Here I am, today, transformed by renewing my mind and learning to have thoughtfulness, which is good and acceptable. I am by no means perfect, but I'm willing to grow and learn. I have learned to be a helpful citizen and to share my progress with others in need. Taking time to be of service to others, without expectations, is thoughtfulness in action. Writing snail mail letters is very thoughtful, loving and kind, as is making a phone call out of the blue, hosting a party, and making homemade gifts. It is a blessing to be awake, sharing consciousness with an open heart, a healed spirit, and peaceful mind; I move forward to live the will of God in the grace of thoughtfulness.

Have a day of thoughtfulness!

Tremendous means to be marvelous, fantastic, wonderful, and doing something that is very good. It also means to be huge, massive, enormous, gigantic, mighty, and monumental.

Life is beautiful and tremendous when we open our hearts to accept people and life as it presents itself. Sometimes, we need to heal to arrive at this point in our lives. It's crucial to trust the process as we grow to be sane and stable and to have good direction in our lives. We grow and change to be tremendous in our ability to carry on in our lives without regret and bitterness. It's a tremendous feeling to be part of a healthy lifestyle living with solutions and reaping the benefits of doing wonderful deeds. Our body, mind, and soul feel tremendous love and healing. Living among tremendously healthy people brings out our light and love of life, and we regain faith to enjoy the blessings of love.

One of my favorite things to do is go to festivals where the music is tremendous. The people, food, and environment are tremendous. It's wonderful to be able to share in this tremendous experience in a place full of love and joy. Celebrating our appreciation for each other's talents is fulfilling. Our hearts are open, and, in the moment, we feel the spirit of God among us in love and respect, a tremendous gift of living well. My life is tremendous today because I rest my care in God's hands and enjoy the guidance to keep up the good work living my best.

Have a tremendous day!

NOTED

Noted is to be well known, famous, famed, great, celebrated, and acclaimed. It also means that someone has noticed something that we have done and admires it.

Life will challenge us all in one way or another. Let it be noted that there are always solutions. Together, with unity, we can achieve our dreams through manageability, creativity, communications, and spirituality. Manageability of a healthy lifestyle includes learning, through fact-finding, our personal strengths and, then, using them to change our behaviors so that we may experience the blessings of living in the now.

My personal manageability includes being connected with self through good orderly direction focused on wellness. My Higher power is my guardian and as long as I'm willing to pray and stay awake, I feel blessed with the courage to continue living my life.

My creativity helps me to learn how to broaden my understanding through writing, changing perspectives, painting, quilting, making music, singing, and playing instruments. It is through these activities that new visions are understood and my understanding reveals clarity. Let it be noted that I am, in my mind, enough and have regained my sense of confidence. In communicating clearly and precisely through speaking and writing, my confidence grows. I have a voice, noted to be heard in the name of justice. My confidence is the result of interacting with several groups. It is important to be noted for open-mindedness and willingness to live in solutions; each day is a new chance of celebration.

Have a noted day!

WELL-LIKED

Well-liked is to be loved, accepted, esteemed, cherished, respected, and popular.

When spirits are lost to addictions, abuse, neglect, and trauma, they lose their confidence and choices are diminished, if not totally numbed. There is no serenity, and the person's spirit feels unaccepted, rejected, and shamed. The good news is that there are solutions to overcome feeling defeated. For a chance to recover, we need to be open to a psychic change, have the willingness to act, and make time to grow to accept oneself. It is good to have a support team and the love of family and friends.

In severe cases, medical help may be needed. This is possible with acceptance to change; we learn to regroup our thoughts in a constructive way to find a balanced lifestyle. We may have felt like an unloved and unwanted weed, but now we can plant a new seed and grow to be the person we are meant to be. If we keep a seed in a bag lacking earth, water, and love, it cannot grow. It is the same for humans. Once you take the seed out of the bag and tend to it, the results are amazing. When you water it and keep the weeds away, it flourishes. And so it is with humans; when we are confined in mental illness and boxed in, we are stuck; yet, like a seed, we can come out to recover and heal, grow, and reap the benefits.

We grow in confidence, and we learn to like ourselves. As our skin thickens, we learn to laugh at ourselves and begin to shine. Healing allows us to become more focused on a positive, productive, and healthy reality. If we are persistent and consistent, we will feel ongoing change happening, and we will become content in our living situation. We will feel well-liked and accepted as we are integrated back into society.

Have a day well-liked!

IDEALISM

Idealism is to have wishful thinking, fantasizing, daydreaming, and having unrealistic belief or pursuit of perfection. Idealism involves people believing that they can live up to high standards and honesty ALL the time.

This idealism belief of perfect visions and right conduct can set us up for disappointments; while realism, on the other hand, is to plan goals but not the outcomes. When we expect perfection, we get trapped in negativity and frustration; but when we accept what is, as it is, in the moment, we can feel positive and hopeful. We learn that our idealism keeps us stuck because we keep doing the same thing and expecting different results, which is total insanity. Our minds are closed and resistant, blocking our growth.

Trauma, addictions, and abuse can alter our psyche, leaving us vulnerable to negativity. The good news is that we can heal ourselves back to our natural state of being free spirits. We learn to breathe and sigh with relief, as we transform from idealism to realism in the hopes of growing and nourishing our spirit. We focus on progress not perfection, as we take on a new way of living. We do this by letting go of our past troubles, and we get busy improving our psyche toward a balanced way of thinking and living. As we confront ourselves and our behaviors, we take personal stock of just who we think we are, and then open our heart to heal, to receive blessings with gratitude. Humbled, we feel healed and move forward, continuously growing graciously each day, feeling a wee bit better. We understand idealism, and we know we must strive for progress.

Have a day free from idealism!

NEUTRAL

Neutral is to be out of gear, sitting idly, and doing absolutely nothing to get out of turmoil. Living in neutral is to exist in a disconnected sense, not living fully awake, not being able to be helpful, and not supporting ourselves or anyone else.

Mental illness and spiritual malady bring some of us to this point. The detachment from reality, and being stuck in dysfunctional thinking, make for a shaded life, blocking brightness and hope. Living on neutral ground in this sense is a dangerous existence of loneliness, isolation, frustration, and negative coping. Guilt and shame are debilitating, unless we reach out and take steps to open our hearts to new ways of living.

The first gear is to act, honestly admitting and sharing the reality that we cannot heal alone. In reaching out, we have a chance to recover and progress as we slowly carve out our pain, let go of shame and blame, and replace it with unconditional love for ourselves. Mending our spirits through the power of prayer, meditation, support teams, and self-help groups is a process for wellness. The action is in the participation. Having taken responsibility to progress and learning that happiness is an inside journey, we come to realize that we can live with ourselves and be content. Life is an adventure, so shift your gears and enjoy the ride.

Get out of neutral and have a great day!

CONSCIOUS

Conscious is the state of being awake, aware, alert, responsive, and mindful. Conscious people are aware and sensitive to their own reality.

Living life in a state of healing and wellness becomes possible when we wake up to different ways of coping with our own existence, ideas, and feelings. We can progress to this state and way of being, if we are open-minded and desire to take the steps to experience this new path of freedom. Conscious people have an attitude of gratitude once they take back their life and act for their well-being.

When I was ill, I was stuck in a state of existence, going from pillar to post. My attitude was stuck in shame and blame. Changing my negative thinking came as a result of healing and believing in myself. Changing my conscious contact with myself allowed me to transform and believe in a Higher Power, which opened new doors for me so I could learn to live a contented life. When I am at my best, I am capable of cooperation rather than competition. Most days, I feel that I'm in a conscious state – content, healed, and radiating wellness. I am truly blessed.

Have a conscious day!

ENJOYABLE

Enjoyable means experiencing pleasure, gratitude, and contentment while being agreeable, delightful, and divinely living in God-consciousness.

Positive energy is an enjoyable force, which we create in our own reality. Energy is a force, revealed when we are mindful in meditation, that opens us to experience divine consciousness and live with a powerful sense of well-being. Consciousness is being aware of our beliefs, thoughts, emotions, and intentions. In our conscious contact with our God, we feel the energy force and receive positive energy, empowering us to accept, change, and recreate our beliefs for the better. Life is more enjoyable when we are open to change, guidance, and redirection.

Certainly, I have recreated my life through positive cognitive modifications and rewired my brain to practise healthy living skills with the help of many people. Today, I am mindful to appreciate all enjoyable experiences with love. I am mindful, living in the moment and in a state of balance equipped to handle life on life's terms. My transformation to live in healthy consciousness rewards me with an enjoyable and contented life.

Have an enjoyable day!

REHABILITATION

Rehabilitation is a process to restore, mend, and heal from trauma, disease, illness, and injury. Rehabilitation involves recovery from spiritual, mental, emotional, psychological, physical, and environmental effects and dysfunction.

Rehabilitation involves many stages, such as: acceptance of the shock and denial, then the pain, shame and guilt that brings us into the anger and bargaining. Why me? The depression, isolation, and loneliness stages are challenging. We may need some major help to work through the sad reflections that have an emotional and mental hold on our thinking. Hopefully, we see the devastation this has on our life; a psychic change enables rehabilitation. Rebuilding the physical body is a work in progress and, with tenacity and time, improvements and rehabilitation occur.

Now, we are ready to complete our rehabilitation with acceptance, respect, and integrity to be healed, to be the best person we can be in our rehabilitated humanness. We grow with a new awareness in our consciously awakened state and live with realistic solutions. No problem is too big for you, me, and the universe. We live in the now and move forward in honesty, being open-minded and having willingness to grow each day with our fellow humans in unity. Rehabilitation is an experience and journey to a state of contentment with an attitude of gratitude!

Have a day of rehabilitation!

CONCENTRATION

Concentration is the ability to focus on a person, place, or thing with full attention. Concentration involves focused thoughts, whether good or bad.

Many distractions can lead to poor concentration, such as trauma, injury, and illnesses. It is healthy to surrender to these distractions with courage, faith, hope, and willingness to develop positive concentration focused on goodness. To rehabilitate to better concentration we must change, grow, and learn to practise techniques to overcome bad habits.

Concentration, prayer, meditation, mindfulness, and doing good deeds, is the recipe for soundness of mind. Concentration on daily conscious contact with God, and being awake, aware, and open to the creator, stimulates powerful energy. Then, add dedication, discipline, determination, and perseverance to be at one with the universe; sharing your positive vibrations and shining your authentic spirit each day is a gift. Be grateful and experience the wonderful side effect of being at peace. Find your happy spot, practise relaxation exercises, focus on positive thoughts and concentrate on God's Will. Visualize the new you, happy and content. Think good thoughts; you are what you think!

Have a day of concentration!

LIKEABLE

Likeable is to be friendly, considerate, appealing, truthful, enchanting, and approachable.

A likeable person is one who treats people with respect and kindness. They are open-minded, free from judging others, forgiving, and complimenting. They say less, as they have learned the gift of listening. They have learned to listen, and they listen to learn, which expands the capacity for understanding. Having paid attention to others, they are open to encourage and identify, speaking slowly and confidently.

Learning to be likeable has been a journey of changing behaviors one day at a time. Because we are all living the experience of being human, we are not perfect but, rather, working towards progress. Being likeable allows us to show our own vulnerabilities because of confidence and optimism, and, thus, able to offer help to others, while carrying the message of hope!

Have a likeable day!

GENTLE

Gentle is to have a blessed character with a meek, graceful, and pleasing spirit. A gentle person has an inner beauty that radiates calmness and shines with strength and confidence.

Life can harden a person's character, diverting us to negative, hateful, and unkind behaviors. Hope can motivate us to have the courage to change. Until we recognize that we have lost our authentic spirit, things stay the same, and we become the walking dead, stuck in rough, obnoxious, angry manners; gentleness has been lost.

There is hope! When we open our hearts and minds to different ways of being, we wake up and choose to change for the better, living in God-consciousness. Our perspectives change, and we become loving, patient, and kind folks. Our life becomes magical, and we grow to have hearts of humility. But for the grace of God, there go I in a gentle spirit! Yes, go forth and kill them with kindness, being gentle.

Have a gentle day!

AUGUST 5
EAGER

Eager is to be gung-ho, excited, interested, pumped, anxious, impatient, and enthusiastic for something or to do something.

Learning the joy of living is an action in progress. One day at a time, we become eager to accept, believe, and trust life. We are eager to live in honesty, open to change, and willing to move forward just a little more serenely each day. One big thing about living in serenity is the gift of learning tolerance and letting go of all negative thoughts about people, places, and things. We learn to be eager to identify rather than compare.

Today, I am eager to get up each day to go meditate on my path, breathe in the fresh salt-water air, and to smell the garlic aroma in my little park. I'm eager to expand my spiritual, psychological, and relational health each day, with an attitude of gratitude. My perspective is to live grounded, so that I am eager to continue growing in love, peace, and compassion. I am eager to go on vacation soon. I am eager to have friends from Montreal come visit soon, and I am eager to share my experience, strength, and hope on my journey.

Have an eager day!

AUGUST 6
MESSENGER

A messenger is one who carries a message, which can be either positive or negative.

An open-heart messenger will share in an understanding and connected manner, bringing a balance to others. A messenger might carry a positive message of hope, with honesty and integrity, is inspirational. A strong-minded messenger with intuitive perspectives carries a message in a sensitive, gentle, insightful, and guiding way as they share their experience, strength, hope, and knowledge. They inspire others through sharing their journey of personal human experiences and how they have grown to be emotionally healthy, through identifying rather than comparing experiences. When we identify, we might inspire others and bring peace.

It's a work in progress to be a stable, healthy human being and messenger. My realities have varied throughout my life and my messengers have come from various places, with both good and bad news. Having recognized and accepted God within is the true healing power. We stay spiritually and emotionally fit by living open-mindedly and being creative, using our God-directed skills and talents, and maintaining conscious contact with God in an attitude of gratitude.

Messenger blessings!

ZEAL

Zeal is living in a state of enthusiasm and dedication.

My zeal was dampened by many people who tried to tame me from my "wild and crazy" ways of living. As far back as I can remember, I never felt like I fit in; I always felt detached and different. Then, one day, I woke up to create my experience, strength, and hope towards maturing and zealously changing my way of thinking. Slowly, my brain matter changed. I began to make better decisions and found courage in practising zeal, devotion to God, and becoming a missionary to help others.

It was my zeal for participating in programs of healing that brought me into this state of mind. I am happy to have found my zeal for living "One Day at a Time!" Zeal, which includes diligence, urgency, sincerity, gusto, determination, and willingness to be open, honest, and live a solution-based life, has rewarded me with health, happiness, and contentment. With the guidance of my Higher Power and love, this zeal stirs my creativity and rewards me in all that I do.

Have a day of zeal!

WORTHY

Worthy is to have, or to show, qualities with merit, to be able to forgive yourself and others, and to connect ourselves to others with a teachable heart.

Feeling hateful, valueless, disrespected, and dishonorable, instill unworthiness. Having our spirit tampered with could create low feelings of self-esteem. For many years, I tried to build myself up with alcohol, which destroyed my feelings of worthiness. But by the grace of God, I found help in waking up, becoming capable of rebuilding my broken spirit, and learned the walk of life. I slowly "walk the walk," one step at a time.

Walking in a worthy way of living includes having a God-oriented life, with belief in God and myself, and living with sound principles. Being awake, with gratitude and self-confidence, allows my gifts to excel. Participating in family, community, and programs gives me a sense of belonging. I am rewarded with living in a state of caring, generosity, tolerance, and the ability to carry out acts of decency. Being worthy is a work of progress, not perfection, but we must always aim to be our best and know that we are already perfect in God's eyes because God doesn't create junk!

Have a worthy day!

DRIVEN

Driven means to be motivated, forced, hell-bent, guided, directed, and consumed by a source greater than ourselves.

Spiritual maladies occur when we are not driven by the God of our understanding, and we become absorbed in shame, blame, and guilt. Recognizing the pain, and becoming willing to change, drives us to look at our symptoms of distress, anxiety, panic attacks, flashbacks, nightmares, dissociations, and rejection. When we become responsible to act and live in the solution, we are driven to rejuvenate our soundness of mind, and we take positive action to change and grow spiritually.

Being driven to live one day at a time has rewarded me with the ability to mend and rejuvenate to experience a state of serenity. Daily prayer and meditation give me courage, strength, and hope. Letting go of toxic relationships is like weeding a garden. Waking up our spirits to be driven to live in healthy relationships and participate in social groups, support groups, labyrinth societies, and music groups is my solution. My blessings come from living one day at a time in an attitude of gratitude, with willingness to nourish my spirit to be strong. The breath of life is fragile; let it be driven in love and compassion.

Have a driven day!

GIFTED

Gifted is to have exceptional ability. To be gifted is to be talented, skilled, capable, and apt. Gifted people have intense passion, sensitivity, and unusual levels of perception.

Gifted living may involve being very critical of oneself with high expectations, which may lead to frustrations, addictions, and despair. Fitting into life is difficult for a gifted person; they are trying to belong and might feel like an outsider.

Learning to accept that you are gifted, and embracing your blessings, is the beginning of a more settled life. You realize you have problems choosing a direction because you have so many interests. Learning to cope with being gifted comes first with awareness, then acceptance and mindfulness. Once we can achieve a sense of peace in our lives, then we can learn to live with our gifted spirit. Prayers, meditation, relaxation exercises, making a priority list, and living in the moment, are essential to calm a gifted person. Today, just for today, I will live in the moment, the present; that is why we call it a gift.

Have a gifted day!

SELF-CONTROL

Self-control is the ability to control our emotions, feelings and desires, our behaviors and composure. Self-control involves self-discipline, firmness, and presence of mind.

Self-control gets lost in addictions, trauma, and unhealthy behaviors. Through healing and improved living conditions, we gain a healthier way of living. Self-control comes with the help of divine intervention. We surrender to our creator, turn our will over to the care of the universe, and, in doing so, we gain self-control. We live one day at a time in goodness: positive and encouraging each other.

Self-control is a state of doing what is right, not acting on impulses, and managing good behaviors. Self-control is a gift, a reward of living in soundness of mind. Living in a state of mindfulness, love, peace, and serenity feeds our emotional health and well-being. Prayer and meditation keep us fit with self-control. We are at peace and disciplined in our self-control. We enjoy the grace of God and know peace. Self-control is empowering and a life of godliness.

Have a day of self-control!

ENTHUSIASM

Enthusiasm is the intense excitement, energy, keenness, and interest we have about a person, place, or thing. Enthusiasm is the state of our mind, emotions, and feelings.

Enthusiasm is the result of getting our lives in order with divine intervention. When we live in honesty and integrity, we open our spirits and souls to know peace, love, and contentment. Acceptance, belief, and faith open our spirits and soul with enthusiasm to move forward and to change, to adapt our perceptions, and to enjoy the gift of serenity. To have enthusiasm is to have a healthy passion for living with oomph, eagerness, and joyfulness.

It is my great pleasure to experience enthusiasm in living well and being open-minded in God-consciousness. Inner peace comes from nourishing my spirit through prayer and meditation and being enthusiastic about sharing my experiences, strengths, and hopes. Each day is a blessing, and I am enthusiastic to write my word each day. I am pleased to be able to live in the moment and be blessed with better health, happiness, and enthusiasm for a long live.

Have a day of enthusiasm!

AUGUST 13
TASTEFUL

Tasteful is showing good taste of elegance, attractiveness, refined, and pleasing behaviors. To live choosing what is appropriate shows a tasteful character.

Some time ago, I realized life had to be lived in a tasteful manner in order to be truly enjoyed. I let go of my dysfunctional behaviors and, very slowly, I peeled away the layers of abuse, addictions, and shallow existing. Spiritual grace and the love of fellowship encouraged me to surrender to a Higher Power. My rough edges were smoothed and healed to a tasteful new level.

My spiritual journey began through surrendering to the help from others, one day at a time. By seeking change in life to feed my soul, I have learned the art of tasteful principles, such as: honesty, open-heartedness, forbearance, tenacity, teachability, and living on the beam. It is tasteful to be kind, caring, and compassionate in my daily living. By God's grace, I have learned to let go of my fears and anxieties for a tasteful life, blessed with happiness, joy, and freedom.

Have a tasteful day!

AUGUST 14
SELF-SACRIFICE

Self-sacrifice is to give up our own interests in order to be there for others and help others in their health and well-being. A person who is able to self-sacrifice is sweet, kind, lovely, pure, heavenly, good, and godly.

Hopefully, there comes a time in life when we let go of toxic living and are blessed with inspirational living. Our journey opens us to heal our body, mind, and soul. We choose to recover and rehabilitate through surrendering to our God-consciousness, and we are strengthened through faith, hope, and love. We learn to sacrifice our time to share our experience, strength, and hope with an attitude of gratitude to serve others. We give up short-term gratification for long-term rejuvenation. Our behaviors and actions are improved as we practise the art of giving unconditionally.

When we devote our lives to living well in trust with God, we are inspirational to others and enjoy sharing our gift of inner peace. We do so one day at a time. We take care of our personal growth so, when we are called upon, we have inner peace and the blessings of kindness, patience, generosity, and self-sacrifice.

Have a day of self-sacrifice!

AUGUST 15
EMPOWERED

Empowered is when someone is made stronger, more confident, and qualified in their being. Empowered is to have the power to do something, to take positive action and move forward.

Life challenges us with lessons of reality. Daily, we are given opportunities to be set free, liberated, and unshackled from negativity. In standing for what is right and just, we are empowered and gain our confidence. When we live in conscious contact with God and the universe, we are empowered. Together, with brotherly and sisterly love, we can move forward into positive living.

Becoming spiritually connected in gratitude has empowered me to live in happiness and abundance. I have learned to trust the process, feel the fear and do it anyways, live in the moment with commitment to being awake and fully aware. Aligning my mind, body, and soul required me to come forward in courage, strength, and hope. To remain empowered is to live fully today, one day at a time, without judgment of myself or others. Empowered living is nurturing, uplifting, encouraging, spiritual, supporting, and validating. A person with an attitude of gratitude is empowered in inner peace.

Have an empowered day!

GRACED

Graced is one who is blessed with kindness, love, forgiveness, and mercifulness. Graced is to have elegance, serenity, and charm of movement.

By living in soundness of mind, free from difficulties, troubles, trauma, addictions, and abuse, we are graced in peace, which gives us security. Life is a journey, and we change and grow, nourishing our souls in spiritually minded respect and honesty. Discovering mindfulness, with composure and soundness of mind, results in freedom from fears and acceptance of life as it is.

Graced by living in God-consciousness, awake and disciplined in faith, we know peace. Our souls are graced with beauty, and we shine with divine love in cheerfulness and contentedness. We are restored to sanity, graced by God, and live well. We walk the walk, thriving and flourishing one day at a time as graced spirits, with our hearts and minds connected and graced in positive wellness.

Have a graced day!

INSPIRATIONAL

Inspirational is a person, place or thing that motivates, encourages, and inspires us to want to experience, create, and manifest something for the good. To be inspirational is to share good thoughts and ideas.

Sometimes life deals rough, dysfunctional, and heartbreaking experiences, which may lead to distractions such as negativity, doubtfulness, and discomfort. Divine intervention guides inspirational people to us; hopefully, we mature and are open to renewing our spirits within and are awakened in strength, courage, and hope to move forward.

Our souls are ready for acceptance and positive energy. The inspirational experiences of meditation and prayer nourish us to grow and burn brightly in radiant love, as we are blessed with being one with the universe. We are open to inspirational living to know God and peace. We experience inner peace and become able to be in the midst of racket, chatter, and chaos while still being tranquil, quiet, and calm in our minds and hearts. We accept inspirational living and share our happiness of living well with love, grace, and gratitude.

Have an inspirational day!

COMFORTING

Comforting is the ability to serve, console, support, calm, cheer, as well as uplift a person's sense of wellness and well-being.

It is comforting to surrender to a Higher Power and to know love. We find it comforting to turn our will and our life over to the care of a loving God of our understanding. We weep no more; sadness, loneliness, aloneness, anger, and depression are lessened, and we move forward with courage, strength, hope, and faith. We build our self-confidence and grow with the comforting support of our new-found spiritual family.

Oh, how wonderful and comforting is our new life living in the now. We spend time in nature and nourish our souls, being grounded in the moment, and we connect with the universal energy of wellness. We weep with the joy of living in goodness, peacefulness, and serenity. It is comforting to share time with friends: travelling, enjoying concerts, hanging out on the beaches, in nature, around campfires, and camping. The most comforting for me is the smell of the ocean air and the sound of waves as I drift off into a comforting night of sleep.

Have a comforting day!

LEVEL-HEADED

Level-headed is the ability of sharing and feeling confident in oneself while being grounded, healthy, reasonable, sensible, rational, sober, sound, and right in the head. Living level-headed is an action in progress.

We choose to do the inner work to bring about personal growth as it empowers and grounds us in goodness. We give up comparing and judging as we learn the art of identifying. We accept and trust the process while taking ownership of our own actions and behaviors. It is important to humble ourselves and think good thoughts for acceptance and peace of mind.

In peacefulness, we live level-headed, minding our own business and getting on with nourishing our self-confidence. We become grateful, having no uncertainty regarding our personal growth, confidence, success, and many abilities. We rejoice in the beauty, love, wonder, and pleasure in our lives. Now, we are free to be open, grateful, and inspirationally level-headed in sharing our journey.

Have a level-headed day!

DILIGENCE

Diligence is to be careful, conscientious, meticulous, persevering, persistent, dedicated, and committed.

Improving personally is a process of hard work. We must be able to practise diligence at daybreak in our prayer and meditation to strengthen our spiritual development and maintain healthy living. Being spiritually diligent in practising goodness, integrity, confidence, values, patience, forgiveness, and level-headedness, we are able to live well. With our conscious, alert, and awakened mind, we are strong in faith to withstand pressures, difficulties, and temptations. We have learned the importance of daily discipline and positive living.

Our commitment to living in diligence is improved through good habits such as reading empowering books, attending retreats, listening, training, and studying the art of living with inner peace. As a result of due diligence in our lives, we find love, hope, happiness, and peace of mind. We become well and share our new joy of living through sharing our experiences, strengths, and hope. We live in gratitude and share life, living in the moment.

Have a day of diligence!

MANAGEABLE

Manageable means to able to be reasonable, controllable, managed, and handy at accomplishing healthy ways of living.

Life is not meant to be without trials and troubles, because we do not live in a bubble of constant happiness and contentment. Some days, we have to deal with circumstances beyond our control. However, being grounded, we are capable of coping in the moment in a manageable manner. There is no situation too big that, together, we can't find a solution and a manageable plan to sort things out. It is important to keep the faith and live in hope.

We are strong in solution-based living. Our lives are manageable with healthy boundaries, the power of focused breathing, eating healthy, dealing with pain and anger, and the healing benefits of spending time in nature. As we let go of worry, low self-esteem, and feeling that we are not good enough, we find our confidence to live in a healthier way. Our life is manageable as we work at communicating our faith, hope, and love. We take responsibility to take care of our own life; as a result, we grow to heal from feeling powerless. We feel empowered to get on with our life; manageable living becomes a way of living, and we are blessed with gratitude for our trust and faith in our Higher Power. It is important to pay it forward, encouraging others to find manageability in their lives, because it is through giving that we continue to grow.

Have a manageable day!

UNSELFISH

Unselfish is when we are willing to give our time, money, talents and serenity in brotherly and sisterly love for the well-being of others. It is unselfish to have and share concern for our fellow human beings.

As we learn to live at peace within ourselves, we develop unselfish habits to enrich our compassion, tender-heartedness, generosity, love, and trusting the process to live in an unselfish manner in service to others. In being unselfish, we align our energy with goodness, kindness, and patience.

In studying and taking steps necessary to grow in spirituality, we come to realize that we are all one, because we have all been created in goodness. We learn to appreciate the wonders of the universe. We are well: recovered, empowered, and rehabilitated to a place of peace and unselfishness. We are open to share without expectations of rewards or payback. Our blessing shows in our unselfish desire to help others out with valid concerns. Let's all join in the journey of unselfish living, giving of ourselves in sacred, sacrificial, and loving ways.

Have an unselfish day!

FORBEARANCE

Forbearance is having the ability to remain tolerant, patient, self-controlled, and good-natured in times of troubles, traumas, drama, and hardships.

Forbearance is a wonderful virtue and essential vital quality of a spiritual and divine life. We learn, over time, to grow and mature so we understand the importance of letting go of our attachments, hatred, anger, unhealthy and violent reactions, and dysfunctional behaviors. Our faith, inner peace, sources of joy, nonviolent responses, right conduct, and healthy behaviors, enable us to have forbearance. We learn to walk gently, letting go of our bullshit and truly being at peace no matter the situation. We demonstrate forbearance and are not affected by negativity, criticism, blame, shame, guilt, and praise. We rest humbly in our inner peace.

Forbearance is developed with an attitude of gratitude for our precious life. We are grounded in our daily living with mindfulness and faith. Being centered and focused in prayer and meditation, we nourish our capabilities of showing restraint, and we are strong in maintaining our inner peace and remaining undisturbed. We live being a faithful human forbearer of integrity, truth, and faith. Our faith gives us the gift of walking quietly, minding our own business, and becoming one with our Higher Power and the universe.

Have a day of forbearance!

LAUGH

To laugh is a way of expressing pleasure, fun and amusement by vocally producing sounds, such as a chuckle, giggle, roar, howl, and "cachinnate." Laughing can also be a way of expressing emotions such as being nervous.

Life can get us down if we are not engaged in prayer and meditation and living in the moment. It is not possible to laugh and express pleasure when we are in despair, darkness, and depression because we have lost ourselves to ill mental health. There is hope; we are all capable of recovery if we choose to open up. We find that we can laugh as we heal, and our body, mind, and soul transform with a psychic change. We come to realize that laughter is the best medicine.

The ability to laugh at ourselves is a blessing because it triggers the release of endorphins to reduce pain. We heal and learn to laugh, which is good medicine because it lowers our blood pressure, reduces stress hormone levels, and improves our cardiac health. Laughter becomes an expression of our improved health; it eliminates fears and blesses us with cheer. Laughter has healed and smoothed my rough edges. My laugh is the healthy expression of faith, hope, and love.

Have a day of laugh!

HOSPITABLE

Hospitable is the art of welcoming guests warmly and generously into our space, and making them feel welcomed, inspired, and uplifted.

Hospitable people are spirited, stimulating, and enthusiastic with a positive mindset toward sharing joyful experiences. They provide a pleasurable, peaceful, and powerful environment in which to question, seek, communicate, grow, and blossom. In our time, we share honestly and openly, feeling secure we are loving and enjoyable company. Our perspectives are respected in a safe place, and we know peace in a hospitable environment.

Hospitable is an art form of sharing our acceptance of life. We learn to be hospitable and welcome people through positive living, which allows us to interact comfortably in a peaceful, loving, and compassionate manner. We learn to give, which is as rewarding as receiving. We share our joyful unselfish life being hospitable, and we enjoy peaceful living. Our company feels the love and experiences joy when in our hospitable energy, feeling freedom like a butterfly and knowing they are important and loved.

Have a hospitable day!

SELF-ACCEPTANCE

Self-acceptance is to love yourself with all your deficiencies and your giftedness with an attitude of gratitude, knowing yourself, and journeying through the process of improving yourself daily.

Look in the mirror and ask yourself if you are doing all you can to live in self-acceptance, with positive self-esteem and contentment. We all need to take stock of where we are in our lives from time to time. I once realized that my fears, shame, blame, and guilt were holding me back in sadness, despair, and depression. It was my job to look at my character and to change by improving my thinking, my habits, and my understanding.

It was a hard job to look at myself and a long road to recover and rebuild myself to be a positive, peaceful, and pleasant person with self-acceptance. My emotionally ill health is healed through self-acceptance. I must say the journey was very slow but steady. Over time, I grew to trust and have compassion for myself. Today my self-acceptance keeps me in a state of love and peace with healthy emotions, thriving in well-being with a strong sense of feeling connected.

Have a day of self-acceptance!

SERVICE

Service is the blessing of helping or doing work for someone with kindness, assisting and doing good deeds, especially for someone in need.

Service work, which is a wonderful expression of love, is a great balancer because we get out of ourselves; yet, the more we give, the more we receive. Serving others is a great healer and brings pleasure to many other people. When we are well-grounded and centered on healthy living, we are capable of sharing our spirit of love, patience, kindness, and compassion.

How do we get to this point in our lives? Some of us just do it naturally. However, some of us have to learn this skill from divine intervention as we change our ways. We become awake and learn to live by principles and disciplines while living with a sound mind.

I have gratitude for a new way of living, and my mission is to pay it forward, because many people have helped me along the road to my present state of contentment. Service work brings the best out in me because I am looking outward. I am no longer high-strung, bouncing off the walls because I have changed, matured, and transformed from my egomania. I am well now, with values, appreciation, gratitude, and open-heartedness, ready to be of service to my fellow human beings. Life is good.

Have a day of service!

AUGUST 28
POTENTIAL

Potential is having the capability to make your dreams come true and having possibilities of developing your ideas into something positive.

Action steps are needed for living in the moment in faith, serenity, and peace of mind. We have potential, when we live in integrity with a conscious mind, to improve our state of living as we nourish and heal our souls; by dealing with reality, the truth, we take care of ourselves to maintain optimal progress in living spiritual lives. Our spiritual progress is fed by our potential to let go of fear, insecurity, anxiety, anger, and all negative aspects of personality. We rehabilitate our lives so that we may live in the Light.

Our potential for better living is determined by our willingness for prayer and meditation, armed with guidance to deal with life's challenges. Exercising positive character attributes and healthy actions in living strengthens our souls in humility; we will be able to fulfill our potential on a daily basis.

I have developed spiritually and continue to grow by encouraging others to experience their own potential. I am contented and living a purposeful life, mastering my mind, body, and soul in serenity.

Have a day of potential!

COMMUNICATION

Communication is when we share, talk, have conversation and discussion to exchange information, ideas, news, and our life stories. We communicate our message, disclosing information visually or through speaking, writing, listening, body language, and emotional awareness.

Being the middle kid of thirteen, my communication skills were weak as a child; I felt lost in the crowd. Barriers to communication included: differences in attitudes, perceptions, and viewpoints, taboos, and emotional issues of resentments, low self-esteem, embarrassment, shyness, and raging anger.

My healing journey taught me to communicate in healthier ways. By learning to respect myself and others, I am able be assertive, understand body language, and become open-minded. My speaking abilities came from sharing my experience, strength, and hope with confidence, clarity, empathy, friendliness, and positive persuasion. The most effective style of communication is assertiveness, a great balance and change from old passive-aggressive ways. With assertiveness, an improved self-esteem, self-worth, and self-confidence has developed with the guidance of good therapy and healing programs.

Have a day of assertive communication!

PROGRAM

Program means to have a planned schedule and order of events with a good design for living.

My program for manageable and healthy living was broken, dysfunctional, and hurting. I found myself sick, sad, and lonely and living every which way. I found healthy programs for healing that included living by the following principles: becoming honest, gaining hope, reconnecting with faith, having courage, learning and living with integrity, developing willingness to change, finding humility, love, justice, and perseverance, spiritually growing and becoming an inspiration in sharing my story, which has given me a life of abundance. I have benefited from recovery with better health, happiness, and joy. My gratitude is zealous, and I'm able to excel in my gifts because hidden talents keep oozing out of me.

I'm sometimes overwhelmed with my gifts, and I find it hard to focus. Meditation and prayer in the morning brings my creative forces to light. Having a priority program allows me to live in serenity. Having no expectations and accepting outcomes frees me from getting frustrated. I just pick a talent and go with it one day at a time with gratitude, open-mindedness, optimism, humility, patience, generosity, self-acceptance, and faith!

Have a day with a program!

ENDURANCE

Endurance is the power to withstand hardship, and enduring difficult situations without giving in. It is the act of doing difficult tasks, and having tenacity, stamina, perseverance, courage, patience, guts, and sufferance.

Life is a journey, an adventure, an experience, and sometimes an act of suffering; yet, with endurance, we can find a balance. I was fortunate to have found a balanced lifestyle before I was injured in a car crash. Fortunately, I was able to draw on my acceptance of people, places, and things to endure the drastic changes in my stability.

My endurance to be understanding and do my best each day to accept my losses and grieve the life I knew, as well as having the love to know that I create my own reality, kept me trudging forward. It was rough and shaky at times but, with my ability to reach out and continue communicating, I was able to process the feelings and keep moving each day. Endurance for progress was my goal and success. Persistence and tenacity were my greatest assets. Being broad-minded also opened my senses to new joys in life. I never made it back to work. With time, I have been able to let it go and spend my energy on keeping one foot in front of the other, although some days they just don't want to go too far. The secret is to make the best of each day.

Have a day of endurance!

SEPTEMBER 1
CHEERFULNESS

Cheerfulness is to exhibit the quality of being in high spirits, happy and optimistic. Cheerfulness leads to happiness.

There was a time in my life when I was depressed, discouraged, distressed, and unhappy. I was not able to be noticeably cheerful but, with the courage to accept and change my life, I learned new ways to live. Having found a program, therapist, and renewed faith, I was able to deal with my sadness and sorrows.

Some of the side effects of communicating and having a conscious contact with God, working a program and letting go, and surrendering include the following: positive thinking, attitude of gratitude, inner happiness, speaking peacefully, mindfulness, and doing good for others. Cheerfulness is contagious, so I try to "kill them with kindness" and laughter therapy. The power of God's love shines in cheerfulness, and the energy I spread comes back to me tenfold. Cheerfulness is fun; with it, I shine my light in good cheer, walk in lightheartedness, and live with uninhibited enjoyment, jocundity, hilarity, and zeal. This cheerfulness becomes a habit as a result of letting go of the wreckage of the past; I live one day at a time in peace, prayer, and meditation.

Have a day of cheerfulness!

Solutions are tools used to solve problems and a means to deal with difficult issues, situations, and people. Solutions allow you to find your way forward and to progress by living with a new vibration.

Feeling overwhelmed by problems, we often get stuck; we suffer, feel lonely and lash out. Isolation sets in until we have an epiphany: a realization and awareness that this too shall pass.

Opening up to God, living in faith, clarifying, communicating, journaling, exercising, praying, and meditating, contribute to love-based living. As we unravel and peel back our layers; crying, feeling the emotions, and wiping our tears, we begin to illuminate. We let go and accept God's guidance; we feel the love and serenity, and our days become more harmonious. We respond rather than react, because God empowers us to be kind to ourselves and others. We live in the solutions and watch our spirit shine with heightened imagination, creations, and talents. We thank God for the lessons, the epiphany, and the beautiful life.

The greatest gift is to have awakened, learned the gifts of solution-based living, and to have the ability to practice living in the light. We all have trials and difficulties, but they don't have to manifest into problems. So I deal with the emotions, feelings, and discover the deeper "me"!

Have a day of solutions!

MENTAL

Mental relates to our mind, intellect, and cognition, which include the ability to be reasonable, thoughtful, rational, and experience inner peace. Mental also relates to psychiatric and psychological disorders, such as: being unstable, delirious, disorderly, strange, manic, depressive, flakey, unbalanced, and manifesting overly sensitive states and behaviors.

Life can affect people in different ways, and we all deal in our own way with our thoughts, feelings, moods, and behaviors. Some of us are wired differently due to addictions, impaired neurotransmitters and nerve receptors, and traumatic brain injuries. Signs and symptoms appear that indicate physical, intellectual, emotional, and behavioral changes. Ongoing medical conditions, accidents, trauma, divorce, and death of family or friends can bring on mental stress and illness. Our lives are changed, leaving us questioning the value of living.

Restoring ourselves includes recognizing our low energy, tiredness, fears, guilt, confusion, racing thoughts, and feelings. With this recognition, knowledge, and acceptance, we may begin to create our own reality of wellness by reaching out, getting help, communicating, changing our routine, eating well, exercising, meditating, praying, and, in chronic situations, taking medication. We learn to have new perceptions; we stay awake while taking care to have gratitude for improved thoughts, mood, feelings, and behaviors.

Have day of mental wellness!

SEPTEMBER 4
VALUABLE

Valuable is some person or thing that has value, use, and worthy characteristics. Valuable means being of great service while being precious, prized, treasured, irreplaceable, and "like gold dust."

Valuable life skills are to have resilience in coping with emotions and stress. These skills include having empathy, assertiveness, tenacity, self-awareness, equanimity, creative and critical thinking, articulate communication, and problem-solving abilities.

These valuable life skills are not a given, but we can share our experience and hope with others and learn these skills on our journey. For example, I have learned these skills by becoming willing to change my life. Living with honesty and acceptance to deal with my trauma rewards me with a manageable life. Having hope with a belief in God gives me soundness of mind. Having faith allows me to surrender to God and experience reasonableness. Courage and fact-finding awards me with relief, tolerance and patience. Integrity brings humility and spiritual experiences. Willingness leads me to a state of growth and new character blessings. Humility aids character building with a change in attitude towards growing in positive attributes. Love allows me to forgive and experience good relations. Justice and apologies bring peace into my heart, knowing I've tried to make amends. Continuing to grow through perseverance to be spiritually fit keeps me living in God-consciousness. Living spiritually with prayer and meditation fulfills my desires. Service, through sharing my experiences, is valuable insurance for living a happier life with contentment.

Have a valuable day!

SEPTEMBER 5
STABLE

Stable has many meanings. Today I will talk about the stability of a person who exhibits a sane state of mind, being sensible, mentally healthy, and having the ability to have long-lasting relationships.

Addiction and trauma have no boundaries; they cause us to feel unstable, unbalanced, insecure, angry, and resentful, resulting in a spiritual malady of self-destruction. The skills to overcome instability, uncertainty, vulnerability, unpredictability, moodiness, and capriciousness require the following: getting help, progressing in a program, building a support team, changing life perspectives, learning to share emotions, and taking care of self.

I found myself in the "I love me jacket" at one point in my life; I needed to find a routine that allowed me to heal, respond rather than react, trust the creator and energy source God, and to move toward stable behaviors. I was then able to function in a loving way, sharing, caring, and blooming into a confident woman. To maintain living in a stable way, I had to get right in my head and become grounded and balanced.

Creating a new lifestyle is a work in progress. It takes mindfulness and a clear head to build new life skills; I needed to change my unstable mind from being crisis prone to be functional in a mentally healthy way. I surround myself with humble, growth-oriented, and honest folks. I take ownership of my living circumstances, deal with my issues, own my emotions, and feel the feelings with my heart open to God, while being patient, because everything improves in time. I go through roadblocks with the tools and skills I have learned, and I experience a stable state of serenity and love.

Have a stable day!

PASSIONATELY

Passionately is a way that expresses, shows, or causes strong feelings. We passionately express love, romance, and desires by admiring, being sentimental, wooing, and being turned-on and all-consuming.

When I reflected on my life and saw that I was growing cold, angry, and resentful, I did not like what I was seeing, especially that I was not capable of acting passionately. I was suffering from boredom, lacking in my trust of God, and living with unresolved conflict; I had lost my passion for life. I had some work to do if I was to learn how to live passionately. The first thing I had to do was acknowledge, deal with, and let go of the past. Acceptance allowed me to find the courage to passionately manifest courage, excitement, positivity, determination, fun, generosity, and open-mindedness. With motivation to grow and change, the blessings followed.

I became satisfied with my life and God; together we built character, and each day reveals new talents. My purpose in life is to channel God's love through my eyes. I have recovered, and I am passionately able to share this love. I am excited, devoted, and passionately express thoughts and behaviors that pave the way for better days. Staying awake in God's love feeds my passionate soul. I am grateful for the ability to be able to get upset, speak my voice, act moody, and emotional. It feels good to feel, and today I'm okay with feeling passionately. I speak passionately because I love to have a meaningful existence, and sharing it passionately with folks is the gravy!

Have a day living passionately!

SEPTEMBER 7
HAPPY-GO-LUCKY

Happy-go-lucky is to be cheerfully free, casual, playful, high-spirited, open-minded, understanding, emotionally healthy, stable, and enjoying the moment.

I remember being happy-go-lucky as a young child; I enjoyed being outdoors, wandering off down to the woods, along the pond and river (or perhaps I should say brook), away from our home of 13 kids. As I grew older, I found that I had lost my happy-go-lucky spirit; my spirit shifted as my self-esteem, self-worth, and joy of living became dysfunctional.

Subsequently, I became teachable; I began growing, accepting life's lessons, and became willing to let go of the wreckage of my past and a self-destructive lifestyle. I began learning to be respectful of my precious life with a nurtured mind, body, and soul, and I accepted the gifts of recovered wellness.

I am responsible for my wellness, keeping spiritually fit to live in the moment and being happy-go-lucky. My new life is well balanced, which allows me to be creative, stable, tolerant, understanding, non-judging, resourceful, down to earth, gentle, assertive, and emotionally healthy. My happy-go-lucky free spirit allows me to shine my light and live well, serving my community through volunteering and spreading cheerfulness wherever I journey. I love this balanced way of happy-go-lucky living.

Have a happy-go-lucky day!

SEPTEMBER 8
REASSURING

Reassuring is serving by helping another to remove doubts or fears, by encouraging, comforting, cheering on, restoring confidence, and being inspiring.

We may feel broken, experience grief, illness, dysfunction, mental fatigue, and question ourselves; then, we wake up to this pain, which is evident in our lives, and we feel better when reassuring folks help us heal. We open our hearts with restored confidence, letting go of our fears, losses, and worries, mourning our past, reassured that we are not alone and are worth it. We release our sorrows, slowly accepting new joy. Blessed, we dance in the light, enjoying the moment, continuing to open our hearts to let God carry us until we are happy-go-lucky. Love reassures our spirit with its cheerfulness.

Trusting this process and experiencing calmness, peace, and living in the light reassured me that everything I experience is part of my journey. Once I was reassured, I could open up to tackle, enjoy, create, and better deal with, my journey to wellness. To maintain my high spirits, kindheartedness, cheerfulness, and humanity, I accepted and trusted myself, being of good service and reassuring other folks. I walk in confidence, and I pray to God to feed my soul. I meditate to listen to God's directions, and I go forth reassuring those I meet along my path. I am now enjoying my journey!

Have a reassuring day!

SEPTEMBER 9
SURE

Sure is to be confident in what you think and know, having no doubt about being right, being of strong will, mind, and spirit.

Our journey sometimes leaves us unsure, shaken, and unsatisfied. After being around negativity and traumatic experiences, we recharge our spiritual mind and energy with quiet time and reflection. We look at our part or our lack of control over what has compromised our stability. We are challenged to deal with life, both the good and bad. We need to "pull the rip cord" to land with ease rather than "dis-ease."

The outcome of my coping and willingness to act allowed me to land on my feet: sure, confident, and blessed with the tools to deal with my life. To maintain my wellness, I am sure to keep spiritually fit, charging my thoughts with positive information, praying, meditating, and resting. Being secure, satisfied, disciplined, and uncompromising with my wellness is sure to improve each day, which prepares me for life events. So if I come across a roadblock, I have the ability to cope and roll forward ready for my next lesson.

Be sure to have a good day!

EXPANSION

Expansion is the quality of expanding, augmenting, increasing, and boosting growth.

Life with trauma closes us off, and we isolate, deprive, numb out, and self-destruct. Losing our control, we might feel vulnerable, betrayed, fearful, and confused. We might develop a sense of helplessness and low self-esteem. Recognizing emotions such as sadness, fear, shame, anger, and denial is paramount to begin recovery. We look at our behaviors such as outbursts, insomnia, nightmares, and hurting others so that we may change our ways. We need to be mindful of thoughts because we become what we think. Our untreated trauma might manifest as sleep problems, food disorders, and internal problems. Expansion of our perspectives is the gateway to healing and learning how to manage our self-care.

My journey of expansion has given me the ability to feel the feelings, learn to pace myself, change my negative patterns, reach out, transform, and grow healthier. I have grown to be open-minded, understanding, and trust the process of expanding. I have changed my internal dialogue; in my conscious awareness, I am awake to recognize narrow and foggy thinking. Expansion enables me to embrace change and accept the blessings to believe that I am good enough, I deserve happiness, I can have a good life, and I am alive and well. I can speak my voice now with confidence and healthy self-esteem. The work of expansion is intense, but the outcomes are extraordinary. Together with God, there are no limits on my journey of expansion. The blessings are mine to be realized!

Have a day of expansion!

PRODUCTION

Production is the action of producing, creating, making, building, manufacturing, and fabrication.

The process of healthy production in my wellness involves learning to identify with others rather than comparing, which leads to building healthy mental, emotional, spiritual, physical, and social wellness. In reflecting on issues with integrity, devotion, goodness, knowledge and Godliness, I am able to process letting go of the old and inviting in the new; I move forward, satisfied with the production of creating my own reality. I find my bliss and cheerfulness and harvest my wellness, growing mature as I continuously cultivate my high spirits, abundance, and healthy relationships.

I connect with God – my source, higher power, creator, positive vibration; I enjoy the energy as I change slowly through releasing, pausing, reflecting and opening my heart to freedom. As I continue to persevere, I am effectively maintaining my skills to produce love, peace, joy, kindness, faithfulness, self-confidence, self-esteem, self-acceptance, and patience. Today, I am a serene, patient soul who patiently enjoys maintaining my wellness with writing a page every day. Daily journaling keeps me in positive production.

Have a day of production!

SEPTEMBER 12
SENSITIVE

Being sensitive is to be quick to sense, feel, detect another's energy, and to have the ability to appreciate others' feelings. A sensitive person is mindful, attentive, conscientious, diligent, thorough, particular, alert, awake, intuitive, and unhurried.

When we feel affected by issues, criticism, or conflict, we may feel like we need to withdraw, cry, think obsessively, and become mentally and emotionally drained. Learning to change our perspective to deal with our sensitive personality, we become compassionate, understanding, and use our skills to cope rather than fall into negative thinking. We take time to rest, especially when we feel anxious. We become sensitive to see anxiety as a clue and reflect, so we can adjust our perspective on the issue. We recognize we are being mentally drained, and we take time out by stopping and, realizing we can't process others' conversations, we might change the subject or retreat to a safe place.

I have become extremely sensitive and have learned to be mindful so that I can maintain my stability and cope with people, places, and issues in a healthy way. Keeping nourished, pleasant, contented, and rested are good skills for feeding my sensitive soul. I nurture my sensitivities by being creative, painting, singing, playing music, and writing. I am sensitive to others' feelings and am aware of their cues: facial expressions, body language, and tone of voice. Being mindful, I choose to go through roadblocks, having faith to help myself to cope in healthier ways. When I have the energy to help others, I share my skills because I am sensitive in wanting to make our world a better place to enjoy.

Have a sensitive day!

CHOICE

Choice is when you have several options and you make a mental decision according to the option's merit.

Distraction, chatter, and brain clutter takes away the choice in making decisions, and choices get lost in the chaos. It's soul-soothing to make the choice to quiet the chatter and to learn to live in the moment, focused on wellness and growth. As I let go of my worries, fears, and stresses, I come to know peace. Ah, the serenity and joy of life becomes a way of life because I am willing to pray and meditate in a grounded and mindful state of soundness.

My journey started with the choice to move forward, to live and let live, with the grace of God each day. My ability to make a choice became possible as I woke up and began to transform my life. Simply existing became a way of the past. The choice to live my life to the fullest became my new attitude and letting go of the past became a regular practice. The choice to be a breathing, happy spirit, and sound soul has served me well.

I thank my Creator, who provides me with new experiences and strong desires to live well in unity with an attitude of gratitude. My choice to unite and grow together with the folks in my life has opened positive energy, and our vibrations become one. You, me, and our Creator now walk together, united in the joys of living in our highest energy of love.

Have a day of choice!

GOD-LIKE

God-like is to resemble the nature of God, the divine capacity for love, compassion, goodness, like the celestial and heavenly energy force.

Spirituality and inner soul-seeking are crucial to my wellness. Staying focused on God-like living, practising good behaviors, and journeying began for me after many years of living in "dis-ease." When I found myself uncomfortable with myself, I realized I was in bad company in my head and needed a change. I chose to turn my life around, dug in my heels, and the fun began.

It was a struggle but learning to live with God-like behaviors became easier with time. Today, I find myself at peace and living well, because my desire is to live in serenity. Trailblazing my new path is fulfilling and energizing. Living as a free spirit, I greet each morning and day in a God-like style, full of compassion, peace, strength, and wisdom. My spirit is blessed with kindness, hospitality, openness, creativity, and peacefulness. I am comfortable with myself today because I choose to live in a God-like way.

Have a God-like day!

SEPTEMBER 15
ENDEAVOR

Endeavor is to attempt, to venture, and to try to achieve an outcome or goal.

Many years ago, my endeavor was to seek help and find my true self. My journey began with doctors, psychiatrists, hospitals, psychologists, social workers, groups, workshops, retreats, and friends to assist with my endeavor to find peace of mind. I retreated to a cabin in the woods near a river where I found a safe, peaceful environment; there, I was able to clean up the clutter in my mind and know peace. I have learned to trust God, and God's energy, frequency, and vibrations, as I endeavor to live a quiet, humble life.

The journey continues each day into eternity. My self-knowledge and acceptance have opened my heart to live in a God-like manner; contemplating, writing, and singing all spark me into healthier consciousness. Living a spiritual lifestyle has opened many new pathways for me. This week, my endeavor is to grow more, solidify my learning, and share peace among friends, old and new alike. Today, my endeavor was to pray, meditate, and to make a labyrinth in the sand at the Mavillete beach for a retreat of many soul sisters, and one soul brother, who gathered in love and harmony. We also endeavored to do some creative artwork, poetry, journaling, singing, walking Labyrinths, and guided workshops. It was an empowering retreat and fantastic endeavor.

Have a day of endeavor!

OBEDIENCE

Obedience is acting faithfully and being devoted to obey, which means to behave with a good direction to implement change and fulfill a request.

Obedience: to act accordingly comes from surrendering to the creator, who guides, directs, and protects us on our journey. I believe we come to this life to learn, and we continue to grow by sharing. We give back in gratitude, with obedience to practise good orderly living each day. We learn to trust the process, clean up our thoughts and behaviors, and help others along our path. For me, obedience is to honor my wellness and listen to my calling to share my blessing, the joy of living.

I've come across many crossroads; I now choose to walk the walk of a good life and go forth in obedience with trusting faith. Once I had connected with my inner child and healed the trauma, I was able to let go and move forward with comfort, compassion, and salvation. Today, my obedience enriches my soul, and I am a free spirit, living happily, joyously, and without inhibitions.

Welcoming the sunrise each day with obedience, courage, strength, and prayer, a great day becomes my reality. I enjoy my days and am surrounded by love, as I choose to travel the path of kindness with obedience to take care of myself. Life is love, God is love, and I am love.

Have a day of obedience!

SEPTEMBER 17
SURRENDER

Surrender is to give up control of people, places, and ideas, to cease resistance, to hand over, submit, cut loose, discontinue, vacate, and withdraw.

We find ourselves dealing with issues, problems, and crises, and we wake up in a state of trauma and tragedy, living discontentedly. We surrender our obsessions and old ways by accepting life on life's terms. We do not abandon our health, but rather we surrender to let go and let God, using our gifts to apply our hearts in compassion, peace, and love to new solutions. In doing so, we build up our wellness, surrendering to inner transformation and letting miracles happen. Facing reality, creating our own reality in a healthy direction, we surrender and know peace; we build our self-esteem, knowing we are coping and learning the lesson. In giving up our struggles and obsessions, thinking we are in control, we let go and trust the growing process. We trust our instincts and feel the shift.

By creating new coping strategies, surrendering negative thoughts, and becoming willing to move forward in a state of wellness, I have blossomed. I benefit by surrendering ways that do not serve me, and I go forth enjoying the moment in the wellness of higher vibration.

Have a day of surrender!

GRATEFUL

Grateful is feeling or showing an appreciation of kindness. Grateful is being in a state of feeling thankful, glad, obliged, indebted, and filled with gratitude.

Life can present us challenges, and, in sensing defeat, we can feel ungrateful, thankless, loneliness, depression, and impoverished states. Hitting a low bottom opens new possibilities, if we are willing to grow, transform, elevate, and inspire ourselves to get help. Becoming grateful to accept life and being grateful for finding a program of improved living skills, and grace, I share this hope with folks I meet on my journey.

In my life, I appreciate becoming awake, being grateful for love and lively energy. I'm grateful for the diversity, acts of kindness, personal growth, pain, failures, rejections, and, especially, for my unconscious mind for holding space so that I'm less overwhelmed daily. My tears may show happiness or sadness; either way, I'm grateful for my ability to share deep emotions. I'm most grateful for my senses, which allow me to see the sea, hear the waves, smell the salt air, taste delicious seafood, and feel the breeze or frigid air on my skin. I find living with a grateful attitude of gratitude improves my well-being. I am grateful for my mind that allows me to think clearly, process experiences, and create with a grateful heart, which is soothing and brings me great peace.

Have a grateful day!

SAVED

Saved is to be rescued from danger, injury, loss or harm, regenerated, released, healed, and secure. For me, saved is surrendering to God and being delivered from spiritual death.

When I lived with abandoned trust, it was living hell on earth, dysfunctional and dark, and I was one of the walking dead, lost and fallen apart. I was confused, hurt, ashamed, and afraid, burning up in anger and resentments. I had no peace. I was a broken spirit who found help, or I should say help found me, and I was saved, rescued from living in hell on earth. I was saved in learning that there was hope in honesty, if I would accept myself and be open to new knowledge that I am loved. I have learned that, in acceptance, I find hope, which leads me to faith, and my trust is restored. So it is; I am saved from myself!

Wow, I know peace! God's divine grace influences me as I experience the promises and blessings to rebuild and create a healthy reality. Being saved gives me the strength to cope and deal with my trials. I accept being saved and enjoy my new life, person, and spirit as a healed soul; I now live in the light, doing God's will: being kind, compassionate, caring, safe, and protected. I am saved by God's grace, and I share God's love, forgiveness, and comfort. I am saved through prayer and meditation.

Have a day being saved!

SELF-CONFIDENCE

Self-confidence is having feelings of trust in our capabilities, lacking doubt, and showing confidence in our worth and composure. To have self-confidence is to be self-assured, positive, assertive, and to believe in myself.

To build self-confidence, I learned from my mistakes. I learned each day to take care of myself, avoid negative self-talk, become a power thinker, and live in a solution-based manner. The key is being focused on my gratitude, connecting with loving friends, going on road trips, being grounded, and transforming to live my best.

"What can I do to improve my self-confidence?"

Well, I would say: "Share your life experience with others, be open and honest, and do not fear or worry about what others think about you. Your life is between you and your higher power!" My self-confidence is nourished through public speaking, writing, creating, painting, making quilts, playing music, singing, and many more gifts with which I am blessed. I am confident just being me, because I am secure and happy with an open heart and mind. I rocket into the 5th dimension of living, and I feel empowered. My spiritual self-confidence is my sense of sureness that protects me. The result is I am oozing with happiness.

Have a day of self-confidence!

OOMPH

Oomph means having enthusiasm and lively energy, high spirits, vibrancy, and spunkiness.

When my dog died, I was grief stricken. It was in March, and the ground was frozen so I could not bury her; I had to release her to be cremated. I received her ashes and placed them away for a warm day later to decide where she would be buried in the spring. I left it for later when my intuition would know the time and place, and spirit would guide me to let go of her with oomph.

Acceptance draws us closer to our hearts and frees us from all hesitation; acceptance raises our consciousness with oomph. Dancing with oomph, we glide along the grass as free spirits, taking time to raise our hands, to hear our chimes, and rejoice in the spirit of wellness. What an experience of oomph!

Today was a day of oomph for my spirit, receiving blessings when letting Gracey go with the wind. Jean Paul guided me to a wonderful place for an experience of oomph. Oh, what a sweet day for letting go with enthusiasm. My serenity is blessed with a sunny, windy, warm, and peaceful day; such a different experience from the stormy, snowy, cold, and heartbroken day in March when she passed away. Thank you, Spirit, for my oomph and my sheltie dog; you are forever in my heart.

Have a day of oomph!

SEPTEMBER 22
POWER

Power is having the ability to act with energy, strength, and authentic authority.

Yesterday, I rested under the power of the sun; it warmed me and supplied me with a comfortable rest as it restored my energy. At supper time, Jean Paul had the power of suggestion when he asked me if I would make bread; without a thought, out rolled the answer "yes." I only made bread once in my life. Over 20 years ago, I made bread under the direction of my little sister Kathy. I went to the store and bought a big pan. I didn't own bread pans, so we had used empty cans that made lovely round loaves. Mostly living alone, it never occurred to me to make bread again.

This morning, with the wonderful colorful greetings from the powerful sunrise, and last night's power of suggestion, I was guided to make some bread. First, I made a gluten-free loaf from a package, which made me feel very accomplished. The power of the instant yeast made the loaf rise so high I had to remove the upper rack in the oven. Then, I felt a powerful urge to also make some bread from scratch. I got out the supplies, and the power to produce homemade bread continued. Five loaves and one pan of rolls later, I realized the joy of breadmaking. Jean Paul's kitchen-aide machine helped make this experience possible because it did the kneading for me. Wow! I am so powerfully blessed with another passion of creation.

Have a day of power!

SEPTEMBER 23
OUTGOING

Outgoing is expressed through being friendly and socially confident, talkative, lively, affectionate, unreserved, gregarious, easygoing, extrovert, warm, approachable, open, and enlightening.

Living with an outgoing personality was not always my way. As a child, I was extremely shy and unapproachable. At school, I was a slow learner and sent to the resource class. Going there shut me down even more because I felt embarrassed, reinforcing my low self-esteem. My attitude became dark and self-destructive. Today, I have grown to be aware of my mind states.

I nourish my outgoing personality now, having learned to communicate my needs. It is very important for me to be socially confident and to protect my energy because I am no longer a doormat nor shy. I speak my truth and maintain my spirit by being selective in where I spend my time and the company I keep. Being outgoing, approachable, and warm are gifts, precious and cherished. I must protect myself and live speaking my truth, know my limits, and enjoy my life. Learning to communicate through the language of love, honesty, hope, faith, and open-mindedness enable me to experience an empowering, easygoing, and outgoing personality.

Have an outgoing day!

SEPTEMBER 24
PRUDENCE

Prudence is the quality of being cautious and prudent, to have foresight, understanding, perception, common sense, sagacity, sharpness, and good qualities.

Prudence is accepting a virtuous life as opposed to being vicious, reckless, neglectful, ignorant, stupid, inattentive, and squandering. Accepting self, learning one's limits, and having healthy boundaries enables us to change, to make right decisions, and take good actions with precaution and circumspection.

Learning to live with acts of courage is a blessing; we need to have the courage to use prudence in healthy decision-making and know that we must be sharp to maintain serenity at all cost. My self-esteem has given me the ability to act accordingly in my life, and I am able to make the right choice for me without feeling guilty. I am prudent to let go of worrying about others' beliefs, the past, and rocking the boat. I trust my own judgment and enjoy prudence. Recognizing issues that interrupt my serenity are key to maintain my gifts through assertive communication. I need to fully trust my instincts and capacity to solve problems, by asking for help and preserving my own dignity.

Have a day of prudence!

BELIEF

Belief is having trust, faith, confidence, acceptance, certainty, optimism, feeling, hopefulness, understanding, reliance, and freedom from doubt.

My experiences drive my beliefs and behaviors. When I believed I was less than others, I was shy and introverted, afraid to communicate with people and unable to develop healthy social connections. Thus, my beliefs seemed true and justified in my mind, and I was stuck in time feeling low self-esteem. Once I became aware that my self-limiting beliefs that I wasn't good enough and fear of rejection were making me sick and mentally ill, I was able to develop new social skills and belief in myself to raise my self-esteem.

I found a new way to live built upon spiritual lines and principles that helped me to change my beliefs; these changed beliefs helped me find meaning in life and make connections with others. I learned that I could repair my mind, thoughts, and behaviors through knowledge that I was not alone. My commitment to improve my perceptions with an attitude of gratitude eventually enabled me to develop new beliefs, especially confidence, patience, and understanding. I value my beliefs about what's important to me, which include peace, love, forgiveness, cooperation, and hopefulness.

Have a day of belief!

DESIRABLE

Desirable is what we wanted or wish for because of being attractive, useful, or worthy. Some desirable characteristics include being adorable, beautiful, preferred, lovely, golden, enticing, alluring, charming, tempting, most fitting, glamorous, wise, sensible, and prudent.

My character was not very desirable when I didn't believe in myself. I was actually undesirable, harmful, hurtful, unattractive, injurious, and unprofitable. When I found myself in a bottomless place, wearing "I love me" jackets and mad at the world, I knew something had to give. I reached out, found help, and was able to mend my life through building new skills and pleasing qualities that were much more desirable. I looked at the changes I wanted to experience and began growing into a self-confident and desirable woman with higher self-esteem.

The first step was to accept myself and believe in myself. I was hopeful having reconnected with my God and accepted love and forgiveness. I communicated and matured to become hopeful, adaptable, flexible, motivated, dependable, persistent, consistent, humorous, kind and emotionally open, but most of all to be a team player and share my thoughts. The key is to believe that I am desirable.

Have a desirable day!

SEPTEMBER 27
BLESSED

Blessed is to be connected with God, to be enjoying happiness with contentment. To be blessed is to have a sacred nature of bringing honor, welcome, and appreciation into our daily living.

Being blessed in unconditional love, we learn to flourish with grace, the spirit of love, peace, serenity, and abundance. Growing out of dysfunctional existing and moving into spiritual living has been a blessing. It all started with acceptance, a belief and surrendering to faithfulness, truth, and light. The solution was reconciliation with a God of my understanding and being anchored in conscious contact. I experienced freedom in letting go, unity with other human beings, revived wisdom, forgiveness, and the blessing of Grace!

Salvation opened me up to receive blessings. I am forever growing and learning the art and joy of living. I am blessed with the power of belief, action, and service, while I share my love with soundness of mind. I am blessed to live each day in serenity, peace, and hope. Today I am blessed with a sunny day, a bonfire, or simply being content in the moment. Tonight, we will be blessed with a universal change as we watch the super moon lunar eclipse.

Have a blessed day!

Toughness is to be firm, strong, durable, and not easily broken. Toughness in a person is when they are hardened, unyielding, and not easily influenced.

Life's challenges, trauma, car accidents, miscarriages, divorces, and death harden our hearts to a state of toughness. With new knowledge and understanding, we deal with our toughness to be restored to compassion and sanity. Awareness and understanding guard us from further insanity. We accept ourselves in our toughness, and we are blessed in wisdom to know the difference between toughness and strength; we let go so that we may be open to our journey of spiritual growth.

My growth through toughness and into gentleness was a long journey. Today it is my perspective of faith that grants me positive toughness: being firm, fair and friendly in my daily living. I am blessed to have been tested and to have persevered and matured to live a life of courage, strength, and having hope for better days. By accepting my toughness, hopefully I have grown to become the best person I can be, living life in the spirit of love.

Have a day of toughness!

MODEST

Modest is to be an unassuming, humble, and meek person. It also may refer to an amount, rate, or level of something.

Modest is a way to live free from arrogance, pride, vanity, egotism, and boastfulness. Transformation through spiritual growth opens us to learn about being humble and having the ability to be modest. It is a slow progression but the benefits of living modestly help keep us psychologically well. It is a wonderful feeling to be content with living a modest lifestyle, carefree and blessed.

Recognizing our modesty and self-consciousness helps us acquire new perspectives and opportunities. We develop and grow to find love, harmony, and unity, while we are of service to others and make the world a more serene space to live. We rejoice in our personal growth and development and humbly share our experiences. We are modest knowing that we don't really know anything and that we are here to learn, to walk authentically with an attitude of gratitude, being humble and modest.

Have a modest day!

ROOTED

Rooted is to be established deeply and firmly while being constant, continuing, tenacious, ever-present, ingrained, persistent, and settled.

Rooted in a healthy lifestyle involves a clear understanding of the world around us and how we understand and treat other people. Life is enjoyable when we create a healthier outlook and become rooted in goodness, understanding, compassion, and consistent gentleness. We embrace being rooted in God-consciousness and live well one day at a time, sharing our helping hands, hearts, and health.

Living well and rooted in grace, integrity, faith, hope, and love, we are equipped to show kindness, gentleness, and peacefulness. Being rooted opens opportunities to carry forward our spiritual blessings because we have learned to trust the process. Slow is fast, as we weed out the negatives in our lives and nourish ourselves with new, positive ideas, being open to feedback. Blossoming, we live a rooted life of beauty, creativity, joy, music, adventures, and trailblazing. Oh, how sweet it is, the serenity of living in the now, rooted in a positive, grounded, and centered space.

Have a rooted day!

OCTOBER 1
REWARDING

Rewarding is something that is satisfying, fulfilling, peaceful, worthwhile, productive, and gratifying.

Each day is a rewarding day because I live in hopefulness rather that desperation, courage rather than fear, faith instead of despair, and peace of mind and serenity instead of being lost, lonely and confused. I have found a deeper meaning of life through a spiritual journey of self-reflection and daily meditation. I have learned to have self-respect, self-confidence, and to let go of helplessness.

Learning to grow a bit each day and listening to hearts and minds with respect and a clear conscience are positive goals. Sharing a blessed way of living through love, compassion, and understanding in soulfulness is my purpose to achieve and maintain enlightenment. Gathering with others in retreats, prayer, meetings, and special occasions are activities that renew my spirit. Sharing my journey with others with the joy of living in deep gratitude revives my heart and soul. It is rewarding to be content and happy in the now, at peace with myself.

Have a rewarding day!

ELOQUENCE

Eloquence is to be fluent and effective in speaking, writing, and presentation with ease and grace.

As an artist, I feel it is an art form to know how to speak to my audiences when sharing my talents. I have the courage to share my life experiences with fluency and have developed wisdom to tap into others' feelings through identifying. I have become patient, passionate, informing, motivating, and affective in expressing my thoughts.

Teaching grade eight classes with 36 students was challenging, and I did not always perform with eloquence because, at the time, there were difficulties in my life. Being firm, fair, and friendly was the best policy, and I thrived with eloquence most days.

As an artist, I paint my thoughts in my mind and share easily and spontaneously, which serves me well. I have passion for my subject matter and feel it is wise to speak in a simple, clear, precise, and graceful manner. I get my audience's attention and hook them into the feelings, and then I am successful in conveying my message with effective communication. Eloquence is a talent and a gift I must share. The universe fires me up, and I shall go forth writing and speaking my voice. I am strong and eloquent.

Have a day of eloquence!

WARM

Warm is to have, display, or express a pleasant, affectionate, graceful, and pleasing loving kindness. A warm personality is a gift and a blessing.

Communication is pleasant when talking with a person with a warm spirit because it is easy to talk with them. They might possess an attitude of gratitude, taking time to listen lovingly, making us feel welcome with their open-heartedness and huggable, generous, and giving presence. A warm person is confident, authentic, empathetic, and trustworthy.

Changing for the better has been an inside job to grow spiritually and to be warmer in my acceptance of myself. Developing confidence has opened my heart to have the courage to improve my perspective. I feel I am much wiser as a result of aging and enjoy sharing positive perceptions and radiating my inner beauty. This has been possible because I was willing to forgive and move on to know peace. I maintain my warm heart through loving unconditionally and sharing the gifts I have received.

Have a warm day!

PERSONABLE

Personable means having a pleasing, encouraging, positive, nice, kind, and pleasant personality.

A personable human being is welcoming, authentic, and true to their heart, living in harmony with people, plants, and animals in the universe. Someone who is personable has a glow and shines with blessings. They make people feel at ease and share positive energy.

I remember when I met some personable folks who were God- driven and happy, I thought to myself, if they can be happy, maybe I can be too. These personable folks were so caring and listened to my rattled stories, and we had conversations about bringing on change. Sometimes we laughed, and other times we cried; in the end, we had hope. They gently invited me to receive hugs and loved me back to life.

In my shame, as a kid and teenager, I was shy but, through my healing, have grown to be very outgoing. I missed out on a lot of socializing due to my isolating, but I have grown to be very personable. I am content to be loving, patient, and kind. I am grateful to have found such a wonderful path and show my thanks by paying it forward and being personable.

Have a personable day!

OCTOBER 5
LUMINOUS

Luminous is to be intellectually brilliant, enlightened, enlightening, shining, glowing, and radiant.

A luminous person has an open heart, a balanced and quiet mind. They are calm and elegant, living happily and joyfully. Confidence shows in their ability to move through life with ease, living with freedom in the now, awake in the moment with radiance and bright auras.

My human experiences have transformed me to live in solutions and a comfortable flow; dispelling any confusion and chatter, I prefer to live in clarity. I believe we are all unique individuals and experience luminosity from time to time.

I find that keeping the faith and being open to continuously grow each day feeds me with good thoughts, knowing I am developing to be my very best. Most days, I see my luminous light in the mirror and, other days, I tell my soul to dig in. My aim is to simply be; most days, I spend quietly in nature because I love the peace. I walk my labyrinth, let go of all low energies, and welcome the blessings to return renewed.

Have a luminous day!

OCTOBER 6
HELPFUL

Helpful is when one is giving and ready to help, benevolent, cooperative, supportive, kind, friendly, pleasant, considerate, accommodating, thoughtful, hospitable, caring, and neighborly.

I ask myself questions. How can I be helpful? Where can I be helpful? What would God have me do? What is a helpful solution? This helps me to exercise my power of choice to maintain my sanity and well-being, especially when I ask myself, "Is this good for my mental health?" I remain open and go with the flow to allow miracles to happen.

The key to my helpful kindness lies in my gratitude for health, happiness, and continuous growth. I strive for progress: being assertive, firm, and willing to extend my happiness along the way. Being relentless to improve life and restore faith through sharing, inspiring, and encouraging those who travel along with me on my path and journey. It is helpful that I am settled in my mind and able to help others. It is a blessing to be helpful, but equally important to spend time in nature to rejuvenate my spirit. I especially enjoy time in rest and solitude where I can walk my labyrinth, pray, and let my light shine in gratitude. I invite you to join me when opportunity arises.

Have a helpful day!

TAILOR-MADE

Tailor-made is to be made specially, suitably, custom-made, comfortable, and perfect for an individual person, group, or purpose.

Spiritual retreats are tailor-made to include quiet time, guidance, direction, good nutrition, music, fellowship, workshops, and blessings. Taking time to attend a retreat allows us to sigh and relax and be in the moment, knowing our time has been tailor-made. Meeting new friends and rejuvenating our creativity, talents, and gifts, while sharing our experiences and strengths, is a true gift.

I enjoy having friends from Montreal, as well as family visits, because we create our tailor-made vacation with quiet times, beach visits, lake-side camping with bonfires, backyard hammock naps under the trees, adventures to Smugglers Cove, village excursions, and then some beautiful Nova Scotia highlights such as Kejimkujik National Park and Peggy's Cove.

I attended a wonderful retreat, which was especially tailor-made for my growth in my spiritual journey. It was called Labyrinth-by-the-Sea retreat and held here in Clare at our Mavillette Beach and area. New friends, music, meditation, walks, bonfires, and workshops on releasing, receiving, and renewing were tailor-made for me at this time in my life. I enjoyed playing my drum and guitar, and I was sparked into creativity to bring love and serenity to the space.

Have a tailor-made day!

OCTOBER 8
COURTEOUS

Courteous is marked by being polite, respectful, considerate, well behaved, thoughtful, gracious, discreet, civil, kindness, and being of good service to all with love.

It's unfortunate that some experiences in life drove me to anger, hate, jealousy, self-pity, and guilt. I let go of past hurts, saw beyond limitations, and used my awareness to grow; as well, I let go of the "should have, would have, could have, and if only" attitudes. Learning to accept my life and develop a balanced life, I continue to grow a little each day in trust, hope, and healed wellness.

I feel God's grace endow me with spiritual respect to live in the now. I'm learning to be focused with inner calm, knowing that I am loved and able to be courteous. Being courteous is an honor to accept others without judging and demanding them to conform.

Having a blast with pleasant and gracious friends is good for my mental health. Also, enjoying life in a balance of rest and play strengthens my social, emotional, and mental wellness. Being disciplined to be courteous maintains my balance. Sharing time, food, and joy on a regular basis, and using manners, being discreet, and obliging, are great acts of courteous behavior. Practising daily prayer and meditation nourishes my mind, body, and spirit to open my heart to be courteous.

Have a courteous day!

OCTOBER 9
PROGRESS

Progress is the process of growing each day, improving, evolving to achieve or complete something with ongoing movement, amelioration, betterment, gaining ground, stepping forward, and enrichment.

Life has its challenges with its ups and downs, trials, and traumas. Making mistakes are part of life and valuable to learning lessons. Acceptance to change and to be the best person we can be gives us hope and faith, as we build up our self-esteem and self-confidence. Learning to cope, and to live in the now, allows progress and awareness.

Taking stock of my behaviors helps me see where I need to resolve any anger and resentment so that I may continue to progress, flowing forward. The breakthrough was for me to accept myself and my intuition, which opened my heart to let miracles manifest; I was able to build virtuous characteristics such as kindness, compassion, forgiveness, and love.

Experiencing deep love in my heart, seeing the good in others, and sharing this love bring bliss and happiness and are works in progress each day. Creating inner calmness and serenity in my life through prayer, meditation, walks in nature, listening to spa music, and resting, nourish my soul; these activities reward me with a balanced and harmonious life, and I am able to better cope with life. I am humbled and continue to strive for progress, living peacefully, sharing my story for my enrichment, and perhaps inspiring those who cross my path.

Have a day of progress!

Dynamic is to be positive, full of energy, full of get up and go, action-packed, passionate, higher powered, lively, productive, and progressive.

Once upon a time, I realized I was part of the walking dead society, lost and in despair. I was unable to communicate and had withdrawn with a broken spirit. When I acted to bring change to my life, I reconnected with God, providing me with good orderly direction and planting a dynamic lifestyle. My insurance for a life of abundant love is to please God by continuously weeding and hoeing during my ups and downs. My support tribe and team encouraged me to build coping skills, develop self-esteem and self-confidence, learn to select my thoughts, become motivated to learn about a new way of life, and develop an attitude of gratitude.

I have learned to communicate with assertiveness, lead rather than bully, learn from mistakes, and embrace failure and their lessons with honesty, develop a sense of humor, manifest love rather than resentments, create goals with objectives to be the best me, and share this pleasant way of life. Being dynamic is a blessed characteristic with many good outcomes. In music, changes in volume are dynamic, whereas in life there are dynamic changes in spirit. Enjoy your dynamic personalities being funny, energetic, active, and excitable, which are contagious. Being dynamic is a life-long, progressive process to be shared freely with unconditional love.

Have a dynamic day!

OCTOBER 11
PURPOSE

Purpose is the reason, grounds, justification for which something is done or created, or for which something exists. As well, purpose is to have an objective, motive, or intention.

What's my purpose for writing each day? What's my purpose for sharing my words? There are many reasons for my motivation. First, my motivation came from many folks suggesting to me, "Why don't you write a book?" I asked myself, "Where do I start?" My resolve was to make a list of words and write a page about what each has meant to me on my journey. My purpose and objective were to write 365 word summaries as an exercise to challenge my brain injury fog. I started this mission on January 1, 2015 and was successful until July 21st. On this day, I fell, experienced another concussion, and my brain fog put my writing on hold. My project continued over the years and is coming to completion soon in 2019. The next year, hopefully, I will write my life story as a novel.

The main purpose to write each day is a process of journaling to work my brain, review my life, take stock, and to share my experiences. I share my words because it is in giving that we receive. My writing project has shown me my destination, direction, design, and objectives of how and where I'm headed on my journey. An unquestioned life lacks challenges. My purpose is to be the best me and share God's love with vibrant energy.

Have a day of purpose!

RECOVERY

Recovery is the act, process, and return of health in mind, body and spirit. Recovery includes learning, healing, readjustment, rehabilitation, restoration, improvement, reconstruction, and readjustment.

One day I woke up to find myself yellow in the eyes, weighing 97 pounds and needing help to walk out of the hospital after seventeen days. I realized that I was going to need help to recover. Liver failure due to alcohol hepatitis can heal, if one changes to cultivate new ways of living.

My recovery began by letting go of old ideas, changing my cognitive and emotional patterns and behaviors, and developing improved self-esteem. My transcending to create happiness, joy, and bliss came from therapeutic sessions, practising new principles through programs, attending life skills workshops, and becoming accountable for my actions, mind, thoughts, gratitude, honesty, self-discipline, and group participation. I focused on the good in life. In changing my behaviors, I began to handle life with grace.

Then one day, after 14 years of joyous recovery, I survived a near-fatal car accident, which created a new journey of physical and mental injuries. I used my tools of gratitude and dug into recovery with therapy, physiotherapy, massage, etc. I have learned that if trauma doesn't kill you, it will make you stronger, providing you are honest, open-minded, and willing to act with acceptance, hope, faith, and courage!

Have a day of recovery!

OCTOBER 13
SPONSORSHIP

Sponsorship is the act of supporting someone, being a backer, having a one-on-one relationship of trust with honesty, encouragement, and guidance, while sharing the gift of experience, strength, and hope.

A spiritual sponsor may be a Godparent, or a recovery mentor, who is a role model and blessing of direction and support. Characteristics of a sponsor include having hope, faith, patience, honesty, humility, and willingness. A sponsor shares the teachings of courage to open our hearts to a way of living in love, joy, compassion, honesty, and mercy with God. Sponsorship is a journey of helping another to find peace and serenity while navigating our path.

Having a buddy system helps us navigate our path through looking at behaviors that build courage, faith, and hope, transforming us to live a serene life. Studying our habits, we learn to improve and change. We encourage healthy attitudes of gratitude in facing life's challenges share how we live with God-consciousness. A sponsor encourages us to love, to feel the power in faith, and the freedom of our spirit. The gifts are deep healing of body, mind and soul, as we support each other because it is in giving that we receive blessings. Be a sponsor: watch, suggest, support, and assist another human being and live the miracle of growing together.

Have a day of sponsorship!

Individual refers to a single being, special, specific, separate, personalized, respective, lone, free, and different.

Individuals sometimes get off the track of healthy growth and find themselves abandoned, companionless, friendless, unassisted, on their own. They live like a hermit in their own head, which can lead to "me, myself and I." When the pain gets us to the point that we reach out, we accept that we can't live alone in our heads with our limitations. It takes courage to get out of our comfort zone, getting out of feeling stuck in a box with all the "should haves, could haves, would haves, and what ifs." Opening up to free ourselves from feeling stuck, dealing with emotions, feeling our feelings, and letting go, releases our blocked energy. It is in letting go of the past and embracing this moment that allows us to create a new reality of living in the light.

Waking up from darkness to know that it was time for change was my greatest gift. With this new awareness and acceptance, I can now reach out to do the work that resets my mindset to an attitude of gratitude, which is conducive to growth. Looking at where I need improvement and learning to listen to others' journeys opens my heart to empathy, which is the ability to understand others' perspectives. My individual knowledge grows as I build self-esteem, self-confidence, and pursue goals to be my best. I love living in confidence, being resilient and bouncing back with happiness, joy, and freedom. Letting go of limitations and accepting my individual gifts, I live in the flow of vibrating energies of love and peace with perseverance, persistence, and consistency. I walk the new walk one day at a time. I am willing to fight for my peace and stand tall, healthy, and motivated to share blessings.

Have an individual day!

Praises are expressions of approval and admiration for someone or something. Praises include applause, flattery, kudos, compliments, tributes, congratulations, and respect.

When I find myself with negative thoughts, false opinions, and ugly attitudes, I am far away from praises. Finding a higher power, creator, source, and godliness blesses me with freedom and praises. It's important to grow in my journey, in my case, to restore me to sanity, right perspective, and empowerment. Praises in daily morning rituals include thanking God for this day with gratitude, comfort, forgiveness, and an open heart. I feed my soul and spirit when I give praises to God. My day is a gift to be enjoyed in the moment, which empowers me to live in the light.

Praises feel good; I feel great knowing I am respected and valued. Recognition of a job well done, with praises, motivates me to continue. Praises bring encouragement and assure me to continue building confidence.

These acts of kindness propel me to thank God and sing praises of thanks. My love of the creator, source, and God's energy empower me with love and grace. I praise my God, love myself, and have hope, faith, strength, higher vibrations, and positive connections. My universe and world open me to experience praises, as I enjoy my gifts and talents.

Have a day of praises!

MULTIDISCIPLINARY

Multidisciplinary involves combining more than one discipline of learning, such as writing, talking, art, programs, spiritual practices, and therapy.

Using multidisciplinary habits, practices, and exercises, we can grow in understanding and rebuild our life in celebration, study, journaling, fellowship, self-examination, gratitude, prayer, and meditation. We become free from self-destructive habits, distractions, and addictions as we open up to new opportunities to change our behaviors and attitudes. We are free to be our true self, confident and sure. We find meaning in deep living, being awake and developing peace within our hearts.

A typical multidisciplinary day for me starts with prayer and meditation, followed by breakfast and silence. Then it is writing time, journaling, and self-examination, followed by celebration and sharing my word of the day. A great start to a new day, then it's the physical, mental, and social disciplines to go walking, swimming or bowling with friends, sharing the joy of living through participating. Preparing a great meal is another discipline. Afternoon disciplines include artwork, painting, biking, playing music or quilting. My evenings are open to volunteering my time with others, visiting shut-ins and playing music, while reading, praying, and resting ends a good day!

Have a multidisciplinary day!

Funny is having the ability to cause laughter and amusement while being silly, whimsical, ridiculous, playful, comical, droll, jolly, diverting, clownish, clever, and entertaining.

Mostly, we are funny as children, laughing freely, being silly and playful with the joys of life. As adults, sometimes we become serious and lose this gift; we get off the beam and fall into creating unhappy, dramatic, and melancholic realities in our minds. As we create our own illusory reality, we find it's not very funny to feel all alone, sick, sad, and lonely. Realizing we are in bad company in our own head and taking time to create a new reality releases us from self-pity; staying stuck in old ways, without changing, is not so funny. Each day is a good time for a change to get back on the beam to live a happy, amusing life and make the best of each day.

When I learned to let go of the past and future and began living in the moment, I opened up to living in the light and became free to laugh at myself and move on. The new reality to be cheerful and relaxed was enlightening. The positive side effect of laughter creates good feelings and positive mental functioning. It is funny to remember that, when I decided to change, I was only half the weight I am today, so I guess that makes me twice the woman I used to be!

When visiting my sisters, Godchild, and other children, we were celebrating a birthday and talking about ages. My grand-god-baby, who is five, said "Well, how old are you?" I replied 58 years old and soon to be 59. She looked at me, and then her mother and then back at me, and said, "You're almost dead!" Funny how kids think! It's all about perspective and point of view!

Have a funny day!

EMPOWERMENT

Empowerment is the act of qualifying, allowing, commissioning, delegating, accrediting, and investing in someone or something.

When we experience rejection and disapproval, we don't feel empowerment. We are denied peace, and we feel hopeless. To feel empowerment, we learn to let go of the roadblocks of blame, shame, and guilt that drive us to act with anger, resentment, and feel out of control. We shift our consciousness from reacting, resisting, and blaming to growing and rebuilding our life so we are grounded, centered, and self-motivated. We experience empowerment, and we humble ourselves to participate in our community, living and serving as opportunity arises. We feel welcomed and wanted in our social circle. Our self-confidence comes with education, and we become responsible to take care of ourselves and to be generous. In our soundness of mind we grow to self-actualization and feel our empowerment.

Our empowerment increases as we mature in our awareness, perspectives, self-development, thought management, and connection to live in happiness and wellness. The process of becoming authentic, self-aware, strong, and confident opens many doors, and we reclaim a healthy lifestyle. We learn to set goals, fulfill our potential, and humbly share our awakening. Feeling empowerment comes from communicating clearly, demonstrating trust, opening up, reclaiming your voice, learning flexibility and adaptability, embracing change, and taking responsibility to have an improved life, being powerfully aligned with all.

Have a day of empowerment!

AMUSING

Amusing is to cause laughter and entertainment by being funny, humorous, hilarious, lighthearted, interesting, comical, wacky, and whimsical.

When life is boring, desperate, and stale, I lack amusement. Recognizing my reality and becoming open to participate in changing habits is the path to amazing new beginnings. Joining groups to connect with people gets me out of self, and amusing incidents take over. I have connected with my lighter side, having fun laughing and releasing endorphins that heal my pain, even though I have lived with physical pain from serious injuries. Laughing for no particular reason is also fun and amusing because it causes a spiritual shift that results in feeling good. It's amusing to have friends who enjoy sharing the same vibrations, such as my "Boho tribe" who gather at the Log Cabin in our "can't stop laughing" attitude of gratitude.

It's amusing to be part of bluegrass, country, and folk festivals, singing harmonies and connecting with lighthearted souls playing music. Joining retreats is another amusing experience, because we enjoy our sharing the same path and wavelength. The best amusement is sitting on the bench at Cape Saint Mary in the summer and meeting tourists, sharing stories, and enjoying the fresh ocean air while nourishing body, mind, and soul with amazing, amusing folks. I must say, today, I love my family and the amusing dynamics that arise among thirteen adult children.

Have an amusing day!

OCTOBER 20
ACKNOWLEDGING

Acknowledging is accepting, admitting, or recognizing something or someone.

Becoming conscious of, and acknowledging, our self-destructive habits and having acceptance in our life jump-starts a new beginning. What we do about changing is an individual choice. I have learned that escaping this world through self-destruction was a permanent solution to a temporary problem; with counseling, I learned to deal with life in a healthier way. I began to appreciate the possibilities and realized that it's an inside job to achieve happiness and serenity.

Acknowledging the power of God and good orderly direction to start the day is a comfort, knowing there is a source empowering me to be the best I can be. I stand tall, acknowledging that I am now confident, sure, grateful, patient, and brave enough to experience new adventures and cope with life's challenges. I apply intention to have good days, acknowledging the importance of prayer, pacing myself, writing, exercising, eating healthy meals, and loving life.

It gives me great pleasure to acknowledge all the folks who helped me rebuild my confidence to enjoy each day. Professors had faith in me at Nova Scotia Teachers College and applauded me at my graduation, even though I did not achieve honors marks; rather, they acknowledged the fact that I completed my program, despite having had two suspensions. Acknowledging my true self kept me going to become a loving daughter, sister, aunt, niece, friend, and teacher.

Have a day of acknowledging!

DEDICATION

Dedication is having the quality of being dedicated or committed to a task or purpose while, at the same time, having feelings of strong loyalty or support for someone or something.

My dedication to writing my words with zeal, persistence, and perseverance comes from the joy of growing; sharing them fertilizes my growth. Being dedicated to complete my word book with a passion is making my achievement possible.

In my growing, I have learned to live with principles and discipline and live courageously, learning about life connectedness, fact finding, releasing, forgiving and moving toward living in the light.

Acceptance combined with celebration brings me joy and hope, while surrendering brings peace of mind. Faith and solitude allow me to let go and rest in a state of love. Courage and study are dedicated to teachings and lessons. Integrity and confession allow me to share and heal. Willingness and fasting from old behaviors give me the opportunity to change my characteristics and accept positive attributes. Humility and worship open the door to humbleness, and I feel blessed. Brotherly and sisterly love, along with simplicity, help me to be myself, plain and simple. Justice and guidance increase my ability to be forgiving and have forgiveness. Perseverance and meditation are practices that give me freedom and sensible direction. Spirituality and prayer keep me awake. Service and giving keep me dedicated to serve wholeheartedly.

Have a day of dedication!

ANONYMOUS

Anonymous is to be unidentified, unnamed, unspecified, nameless, incognito, unaccredited, unknown, unacknowledged, and undesignated.

Anonymous is having anonymity and is used in groups for recovery to indicate the confidentiality in the fellowship community. It is very important to each individual as they transcend ego and addictive behaviors and move forward with mindfulness. They become aware of living consciously and non-judgmentally and attaining emotional wellness. Having anonymity allows individuals to have a safe environment where they can stop clinging to old behaviors and learn new ways through sharing experiences, strength, and hope.

Over time, I have learned the importance of being connected to self, living awake in the moment, and experiencing serenity. I have stopped living in secrecy and have let go of the need to be anonymous by hiding away from people. I have stopped clinging to what I thought I was and have blossomed, opening up to be the best I can be. Inner emptiness grew into infinite possibilities as I grew in the acts of love, hope, courage, humility, letting go, faith, kindness, generosity, and spiritual connectedness. After all, I know I was born to shine with a twinkle!

Have an anonymous day!

Vibrations are perceived by feelings or emotions and can be sensed or experienced by quivering, trembling, twitching, shaking, shuddering or shivering.

The following are examples of living with low vibrations: addictions, fears, anger, guilt, shame, low self-worth, resentments, jealousy, judging, being unforgiving, and having conditional love. We all have the ability to change, to lose bad habits, to reprogram, and create higher vibrations. Once we are conscious of our thoughts, emotions, and feelings, we are able to change our behaviors, energy, and vibrations. Being mindful, awake, and conscious allows us to create higher vibrations, rather than being stuck in habitual living, which is numbing and the result of living unconsciously with low vibrations.

Becoming conscious of how I live each day invites higher vibrations. Paying attention to my thoughts, being grateful, calm, sharing in acts of kindness, and shining my light vitalizes myself and others. Other people sense my healthy emotional energy, and I connect joyfully with others. Time passes quickly when I live in higher vibrations. I manifest my vibration frequency with daily prayers, clearly communicating good thoughts, letting go and letting God carry me. Stay awake!

Have a day of higher vibrations!

SAFETY

Safety is the condition of being secure, free from harm, invulnerable, unthreatened, safeguarded, supported, unmolested, housed, and saved from injury, risk or danger.

When we lack safety in our life, we might be left with negative behaviors with which to cope. We might feel insecure and alone; if you can identify with another person, you are not alone. Some of us go down the road of self-destruction and feel afraid and confused. We may not be aware we are on such a road because of the insanity that overcomes us from trauma. If we feel we lack safety in our lives, there is help. We need to reflect on unsafe behaviors affecting our lives and know there is hope in changing. We must all act wisely to protect ourselves from danger and develop safe environments in our lives.

I have found a path to safety through the benefits of communicating with doctors, psychiatrists, psychotherapists, friends, family, sponsors, programs, and sweat lodges. I have learned to take stock, evaluate and reflect, create boundaries, act with awareness, review and analyze situations, find my voice, share truths, progress with time, and manage my feelings. Learning decision-making skills and how to implement corrective actions, and having positive feedback, helps me experience the comforts of safety. The key is not to get hungry and angry because I might over-react, losing the ability to respond positively. I must take care of myself so I am able to observe, monitor, improve, and identify signs of danger. Today, I live in safety; I am blessed with a feeling of security, free from harming myself, and recovered to sanity. I have safety in believing in God, enjoying the love of God, and life itself.

Have a day of safety!

SELF-ESTEEM

Self-esteem is having positive thoughts about self and feeling worthy and valuable. A person with a healthy self-esteem has confidence, self-respect, dignity, morality, modesty, humility, and meekness.

Self-esteem is built on positive self-affirmations that a person feeds into their consciousness. Some folks have to rebuild themselves from feeling less than worthy. It is important to weed out the old habits and negative programming that have allowed us to feel that we are not good enough. We start feeling, and living with, improved self-esteem.

We build self-esteem by getting into the habit of thinking positive thoughts. We can do anything we want to, as long as we are willing to do the work, which might involve changing. We realize that we are enough as is and continue to be accepting and pleased with who we are. We treat ourselves like worthy folks, give ourselves praise, and even reward ourselves from time to time. We accept that we are not perfect and feel okay if we make mistakes because we are human. We have fun because we know our lifetime is short, and we must make the best of it to be our best.

I accept my self-esteem as being healthy today because I have learned to accept my feelings, which gives me personal power. Feelings may be good or bad, but I feel them and cope with them in healthier ways. Feeling strong in self-esteem allows me to identify feelings such as being interested or excited, enjoying myself and being joyful, being surprised or startled, distressed or anguished, fearful or terrified, angry or enraged, ashamed or humiliated, and contemptuous or disgusted. These feelings will pop up in our lives but it's the level of self-esteem and responsibility that will guide us in our coping.

Have a day of self-esteem!

TRUSTFUL

Trustful is having or showing trust, ability, reliability, simplicity, and being optimistic, unsuspecting, unwary, and undoubting.

Respect and appreciation are a must for healthy boundaries to maintain a unified and trusting friendship or relationship. Trustful inner characteristics of love and kindness feed wellness to bring about peace and become positive habits. Growing trustful is not easy and takes time to rebuild after trauma and let downs. Having readiness to trust others is a blessing. However, sometimes people make mistakes in trusting when others manipulate us to get what they want.

I have learned that people come into my life for different reasons, and I trust they are teaching me lessons. What happens is karma, and my relationships bring me lessons. It's great to be open to grow, work through, and learn from the lessons. When something ends, it ends because the universe has new directions for me in which to grow. I trust that I must move forward. I respect my inner gut when it tells me to rest, take time out, and pace myself.

Have a trustful day!

RESPECT

Respect is a feeling of admiration, appreciation, esteem, honor, cherishing, value, consideration, thoughtfulness, politeness, civility, recognition, awe, and attentiveness.

I did not always respect myself because I suffered from low self-esteem, jealousy, envy, and was trapped in a mindset of self-centered ideation. As the result of therapy and program modification in my behaviors and thinking, I built self-confidence and learned to respect myself.

Learning to respect myself grew from letting go of sarcasm, bullying, and lashing out. It was interesting to gain respect by being kind, polite, and courteous. I began to feel a sense of safety rather than being suspicious. I started to trust, and my well- being improved. I have learned the healing power of using good manners, being considerate, and dealing peacefully with others, rather than with anger, insults, and disagreements.

Respect is a positive feeling and respectful actions convey a sense of recognition and admiration for another. I hope that, if you respect me, you will treat me well, greet me with love, and understand that I am human with the right to live my life in serenity.

To maintain my self-respect, I must follow the "Golden Rule" of respecting all people exactly as the universe presents them to me. When I am doing what is good for me, my tribe understands and cherishes my energy, encouraging me in my well-being and growth to be the best me. The universe and life are good: respect with love!

Have a day of respect!

SYMPATHETIC

Sympathetic means attracting acceptance from others, being likeable, pleasant, agreeable, friendly, companionable, simpatico, and easy to get along with.

Showing kindness and compassion was a skill that I lacked in my life when I lived in anger and dysfunction. I lived in a toxic state: damaged, broken and unlovable, being defensive and stuck in a negative loop of judging and being unnourished. I found hope and courage to become disciplined. Learning the virtues of principled living strengthened me through having faith and connecting with God, my higher power. Slowly, the transformation to live in the light became a way of life, and I excelled with passion to live courageously.

Learning to be still, praying, meditating, and nourishing myself brought me peace and joy. Freedom from victimization and progressing into survival caused my psyche to blossom, and now I thrive in contentment. Natural enlightenment grows with greater awareness.

Generally, I am confident in being lovely; my heart is warm and glowing with white light and positive emotions. My goal is to be sympathetic, growing every day in loving gratitude and respect for myself and others.

Have a sympathetic day!

SECURE

Secure means to feel safe, protected, free, confident, assured, and free from fear and anxiety of any harm or danger.

Once upon a time, I would wake up feeling unworthy; I lacked self-confidence, maturity, and acceptance, which had been driving me down a road where I was frozen in fear, anger, and resentful ways of dysfunctional living. Secrets fed my mental and emotional illnesses, and I was living deeply out of balance with negative emotions of shame and guilt. I did not feel secure.

Graciously growing with this insight and awakening, I sought help and began my journey of getting well. I changed my way of life and started healing when I accepted that my addictive behaviors were going to kill me. The biggest thing that freed me was learning to forgive myself and others, so that I could let go of the old vibes and get busy with truthful living.

Doing the healing work to change with the help of doctors, psychologists, life skills programs, self-help programs, and new friends all helped me to put back together my frayed spirit. I grew in self-confidence and sprouted to feel secure, which has become my new normal. Feeling accepted, being heard, and feeling hopeful each day is a wonderful state of mind.

Have a secure day!

WELL-READ

Well-read means a person is knowledgeable, learned, educated, literate, cultured, intellectual, trained, scholarly, self-taught, and well-informed as a result of intense reading and studying.

As a child, I was not a big reader. I was placed in a resource program throughout my primary and junior years in school. These were traumatic years in my life and continued into high school. I was determined to learn about myself, once I found a recovery group and therapy, which became a turning point in my journey.

I began to read many available self-help books, and this reading opened my mind. Eventually, my broken heart began to heal with the nourishment from identifying with others' stories and using new techniques for personal growth. I learned that I could become what I read; I shaped myself to become enriched, developed, enlightened, refined, and opened my heart to the light. Being a patient learner allowed me to develop a respectable mindset, while journaling helped me enrich my personal growth and enhance my joy of living well.

Reading provides mental stimulation, which helps me focus and concentrate and improves my memory. A good book in a cozy chair is a travelling journey that enhances my creativity by presenting healthier perspectives. Being well-read is a spiritual discipline that keeps my mind awake, vibrant, and balanced.

Have well-read day!

VIGOROUS

Vigorous means having mental or physical strength or energy. To be vigorous is to live actively, dynamically, energetically, eagerly, enthusiastically, strongly, heartily, and with wellness and great effort according to our ability.

My psychological state was fragile at one point in my life. I thought negatively, could not handle pressure, and did not believe in myself. My attitude lacked focus and I went every which way from pillar to post.

It is with gratitude that I found my way to mental wellness, developed self-confidence and belief in myself, overcame obstacles, and found my resilience. I learned to change my attitude, accept myself, and adapt a new mindset. My focus on growing taught me to deal with life, both the good and the bad. I developed habits to make things happen by letting go of the past, learning the lessons, and I stopped criticizing.

Having developed a vigorous attitude of gratitude and being happy in relationships without whining, I now share with others while maintaining a balance. I play vigorously at self-improvement and personal growth and enjoy retreats, sharing my contentment. I also retreat into quiet time and meditation to stay grounded.

Have a vigorous day!

FUN

Fun is the experience of having enjoyment and amusement. Fun is enjoying people, places and things that are interesting, hilarious, humorous, ludicrous, droll, and entertaining.

I must say that despite all the troubles and traumas in my life, I still had a lot of fun. However, when I crossed the line into dysfunctional living, there was not much fun. Taking stock of my miserable life conditions forced me to go for help. This was the beginning of looking deep within me to see why people no longer were laughing with me but, rather, at me. It was not fun knowing I was making a fool of myself. I grew up, found my self-confidence, self-esteem, and became affectionate, adventurous, courageous, and adaptable. It's much more fun having people laughing with me.

Once I recognized my self-harming behaviors and actions, I was able to take responsibility for my part and work out solutions. I grew to enjoy life one day at a time. Today, my life is full of compassion, zest, and fun. I love having fun because it boosts good feelings. Even in my darkest days, I still create fun. For example, I once spent about three months in the psyche ward. because I was bad and bored. I had the patients follow me in a line singing my song: "We're in the cracker factory now, we're in the cracker factory now; give me pills in the morning to make me happy, happy, happy; give me pills at night to make me sleep, yee-haw!" Although it was fun and funny at the time, I am glad I found my light and love for life!

Have a day of fun!

CLARITY

Clarity is the quality of being coherent, clear, plain, precise, lucid, and comprehensible.

The human psyche can get stuck, blocked, and lost in negativity, which fogs and traps unhealthy feelings. I found myself blocked, worn out, lost, exhausted, and feeling down and out. To change these feelings, I had to learn the law of attraction. When I became willing and acted by changing my character dysfunction, I began to exercise positive behaviors, thinking with awareness, and staying awake, which brought me clarity.

Having clarity came from letting go of my past thinking, my past coping styles, and my need to be right. Meditation brings me to a clearer path. Believing in me, I exercised the habits of positive change necessary for vibrant energy: pacing myself, getting enough sleep, and sharing my kindness.

To maintain clarity, I must stay awake, exercise positive changes regularly, and let go of people, places, and things that dim my light. I try to keep focused on positive living rather than letting myself get stuck in negativity. I like to maintain my clarity physically, mentally, and spiritually because I find it healing. We are what we think, so think love: sparkle, shine, and glow!

Have a day of clarity!

PATTERNS

Patterns are a recurrent way an individual acts. Patterns are habits, practices, and ways that we think and behave.

My patterns for living were destructive; I drove people away from me with my passive-aggressive nature. I fell into the trap of trying to gain control over people, which always ended in a win-lose situation. Having lost my self-respect, I didn't know how to respect others.

When I became disgusted with my own behavior, I accept and own it, then begin my journey to correct my dysfunction. Feeling alone motivates me to accept responsibility for changing my life, my perceptions, my judging, and comparing. I have to let go of my bitter and nasty patterns to free my soul. Growing aware and focused, I begin to transform.

I have learned to be assertive and no longer take part in argumentative communication. I have improved my behavioral patterns to conduct myself in a spirited manner of love, peace, and kindness. I have learned the law of attraction, and no longer sit back passively taking unacceptable behaviors and apologies; they are energy vampires. I stay grounded and am open to living a healthier, quiet, balanced, and peaceful life.

Have a day of progress in patterns!

ASSERTIVENESS

Assertiveness is being self-assured, confident, positive, bold, strong-willed, determined, insistent, commanding, firm, and forceful in personality.

I used to act passive-aggressively and would neither speak my voice nor assert myself, which was harmful behavior. This blocked my mental and emotional wellness, and my thinking was stuck in a self-imposed negative attitude. I wasted so much time and energy, not only for me but for those around me. Recognizing my toxic way of functioning and breaking the cycle was difficult.

Participating in a mental health skills workshop, therapy, reading books, and working on a program to improve my self-confidence and self-awareness opened the door to healthier beliefs, identity, values, and boundaries. Assertiveness came with time and effort. I was able to go back to university and train to be a teacher. I shared knowledge and the importance of learning to communicate in a healthy way. I learned to state my point clearly and directly.

It's an on-going work in progress to improve my realistic self, to understand others, to listen actively, and aim for openly honest growth. It's detrimental to sacrifice myself at the cost of others and console others while complying with their demands. Therefore, I have had to act assertively to let people know I deserve respect. Sometimes my patience is tested, and the response is no to negativity; this is my positive assertiveness for self-care.

Have a day of assertiveness!

INSPIRE

Inspire is to influence, guide, bring out, and draw forth people to awakening, creativity, motivation, and stimulation.

I did not have the energy or attitude to inspire myself when I was at my worst in dysfunctional living with low self-esteem. The whole world was wrong, and me? – I was poor little me, uninspired and feeling hopeless. A medical crisis brought me to find help; I was yellow, 97 pounds, and one of the "walking dead."

I needed inspiration to find peace and contentment in my life. Many dear souls inspired me to change by sharing their stories with me. Listening and learning inspired me to be a better me by developing new healthier habits and patterns. I was inspired to take risks and try different ways of thinking.

Setting goals to grow spiritually, I don't plan the outcome because my new habit is to focus on enjoying my journey. I ask God in the morning to inspire me with what I can do each day; as a result, I am able to go forth and inspire people who cross my path. I enjoy the gift to be inspirational and am truly inspired to share my journey because I know that the world needs more inspiration, love, kindness, and fun. Go forth, inspire, hunker down, and get a better life; then go spread that everywhere and to everyone!

Inspire someone today!

SINCERE

Sincere is to be free from pretense or deceit. Also, it is to be profound, deep, real, frank, direct, heart-felt, true, honest, and devout.

When I was living insecurely and feeling fragile, angry, envious, impatient, vulnerable, and belittling others, I was expressing my low self-esteem. Recognizing that these feelings and behaviors were character defects and understanding that I had a choice to change, I hunkered down to change. I learned to replace despair with joy, to love rather than to hate, and that forgiveness would set me free. I began to grow and identify the blessings of restored faith, grace, solitude, prayer, meditation, and contemplation. I even had a cabin in the woods near a river where, for many years, I went to be out in nature.

My gratitude for a changed attitude was sincere; love of God helped me to grow in patience, sincerity, honesty, reliability, and integrity. My sincere transformation gave me a voice to speak my mind, trust my gut, learn from my lessons, own my flaws and faults, and follow the path to enrich my soul.

It's my priority to stay sincerely grounded, balanced, and centered and live with contentment. My sincere intent is to have relationships that respect my growth and encourage me to continue to flow peacefully like a river; I am forever changing and spreading my love.

Have a sincere day!

Productive is being able to achieve a significant result by being imaginative, original, creative, artistic, gifted, talented, inspired, skillful, mastering, and moving forward.

Learning to persevere through reprogramming, therapy, and opening up my mind was a very long and slow process. I had to learn to be awake to what my thoughts were because these thoughts were driving my mind. Learning to catch myself and change my thoughts brought improved relations. Patience is a virtue for opening up to truth and consequences, which sets me free and allows me to grow. Learning to like and respect myself enough to take care of my well-being was the most challenging. Through a program of reading self-help books, spiritual and religious readings like the Bible, as well as therapy, prayer, and meditation, I developed spiritually and trained myself to be the best me I could.

Today I prioritize my list and focus on one task at a time, because it allows me to be in the moment, giving myself fully to each situation. I pace myself and manage my energy, taking breaks and time out to remain centered.

I have found many gifts as a result of staying sharp and being open to risk trying new things. Staying awake, sharp, and in tune with the vibrations, I open myself to a loving heart. With peace and love, I sit down to write in my journal, then I might paint a picture, bake some bread, go out into nature, sew a quilt, share my time, play some music, sing, or read.

Have a productive day!

Being loyal is giving or showing firm and constant support to someone. Loyalty is being constant, true, devoted, dependable, reliable, trusted, obedient, and fair.

Loyalty does not include comparing, judging, jealousy, assumptions, demanding, disrespecting, and criticizing.

Being jealous in a friendship is crossing the line and being disrespectful. Loyalty does not include entitlement, doubt, and judging. Demanding that my friends be yours and making assumptions is unhealthy. Taking responsibility to take care of myself includes processing what is happening in my friendships. Sometimes I have to walk away, take time out, and evaluate my part. I need to be realistic and go to any length to support and be firm to maintain my well-being.

Clarity in all my relations is the key for communication in respect, and love builds healthy boundaries. Understanding each other's backgrounds, we can be there for someone, no matter the education, age, or race, because we are all one. Loyalty is being genuine and loving, forgiving, and encouraging, being a good listener, offering solutions, practicing empathy, and supporting each other in Godly ways of kindness, patience, and compassion.

Have a loyal day!

RESOURCEFULNESS

Resourcefulness is having the ability to find quick, adventurous, original, active, sharp, talented, inventive, and creative ways to overcome difficulties.

Years ago, I was numb and my life empty; I was down and out, living in a box of my own making, on the sidelines, suffering depression, and aching to be accepted and to feel wholeness. I learned that I had to make some choices to change, so I dug in, adapted, opened my mind, developed confidence, identified alternatives, and learned resourceful ways to cope and deal with my issues.

I grew a new mindset and ability to act effectively by training myself to have an attitude of gratitude with the ambition to learn, grow, energize, and ground myself. Having faith opens my soul to be resourceful, hopeful, goal-oriented, aspiring, an eager beaver, energetic, zealous, and to be a ball of fire creating and enjoying my life. Painting and playing music raise my vibration and nourish me to ward off depression. Respecting self is a necessity, and I must be persistent in caring for myself. Spending time in Mother Nature is a journey with my Higher Power and walking my Labyrinth connects me with my ancient ancestors, which keeps me grounded to overcome my difficulties.

Have a resourceful day!

AMICABLE

Amicable is having a friendly, polite, easygoing, sisterly/brotherly, harmonious, cooperative, civilized, peaceful, conflict-free and good-natured spirit between two people without serious disagreements.

Letting go of quarrelsome, sad, cold, mean, and argumentative behaviors is critical to become peaceful and pleasant. Disrespect does not solve issues; rather, it creates frustration, which breeds stress and drives people away. Learning to find healthy boundaries is a lot of work. I have learned that I can only tolerate being misunderstood for so long; if I can't find agreement for common ground then I must walk away with dignity.

Growing and nourishing my soul to be outgoing, smiling, interested, and personal creates loving conversations that are mutually respectful, warm, and comforting. Greeting people is extremely important to set the tone to feel love. Being sensitive is extremely difficult at times because of the energy I feel and take in, so I must take care of myself, knowing I am highly sensitive. My brain gets overwhelmed with excessive talking, so I must take time to re-charge so I can be amicable and express peace and joy. It is my character to work at progressing and to manifest kindness, gentleness, and love in all my meetings and greetings.

Have an amicable day!

VIBRATION

Vibration affects and reflects a person's emotional state, such as love, peace, serenity, hate, fear, and greed. As well it can be the atmosphere of a place or space.

Recognizing the characteristics of lower vibrations, we can learn to raise the vibration to love, forgiveness, and compassion. I tune into the energy, feel the energy, and know I am vibrating in good energy. I am able to show love and be forgiving, which enables me to have compassion. When I walk into a lower energy space, I feel the vibration and cover my chest to protect myself from the negative vibrations. Becoming self-aware of my energy, I am extremely sensitive and need to guard myself from being unbalanced; it might lower my own vibration and energy. Being conscious of my thoughts and finding appreciation in all my relations is the key to my well-being; indeed, I am no doormat.

To nurture my harmonious vibrations, I must read inspiring books, smile to spread my love, share my healing, spend my time in nature, be excited to live each day in gratitude, get proper rest, eat healthy, drink lots of water, be kind, and act with kindness.

It's so much more fun living in higher energy and harmonious vibrations, resonating in love, peace, and improved health. Time flies when I'm having fun, so I am creative, productive, grateful, and contentedly live in the flow. I matter and am made of matter, so I connect with the divine love of God and know peace.

Have a day of higher vibration!

SUCCESSFUL

To be successful is to achieve the results for which we worked, wanted, or hoped. To be successful is to be fortunate, acknowledged, blooming, thriving, flourishing, rolling, outstanding, fruitful, and happy.

Feeling disempowered takes up precious energy, time, health, and happiness, which is costly, and leads to unsuccessful and unhealthy living. Success comes when we let go of our self-defeating behaviors and thoughts and train our mind to understand that most problems are little problems and obstacles. Sometimes we run into roadblocks, but we learn to cope and figure out other options.

It has been my experience to learn to observe and identify my thoughts, acknowledge and sift through them, and to accept the ones that make me happy and empower me. I choose my thoughts as I run my thinking ship; I drive my own bus, and I use understanding to be successful. Living with an attitude of gratitude keeps me spiritually fit and maintains my wellness. To continue living successfully, I tell myself positive affirmations: I can, I will, I want to; I'm patient, reasonable, open, honest, confident, sure, loving, and compassionate. I feed my brain with music, good books, and reading. I fertilize my brain through writing, listening, learning, accepting, staying focused on priorities to meet my goals, working out, keep moving, and meditate daily, which results in successful, contented living.

Have a successful day!

Playful is the spirit of giving and being high-spirited, fun, loving, vivacious, energetic, whimsical, good-natured, lively, and having joyous pleasure and amusement.

It's difficult to be playful in a dark, depressed, dispirited, inactive, lethargic, lazy, and unhappy mood or space. I know the feeling of being totally blocked, stuck, and stagnant in my living, which created my mental illness.

The problem is not having mental illness; it is in not recognizing it and getting stuck in it. I could not change until I awoke from the darkness; I could not connect with my playful spirit until I was ready to act. When I bottomed out, I knew I was blocked by insanity. I found hope in believing that I could grow and transform, and I made healthier choices that became good habits.

Creating a healthy life, through learning the art of living joyously, took a lot of hard work, meditation, medications, and adapting. Learning to manifest playful blessings came from learning self-love, self-care, and mental healing. Awakening flicked a switch to become alive and sparkle with the ability to enjoy passionate living.

My playful inner transformation came from being aware of my inner child and having a spiritual awakening. I found true contentment, happiness, and a lighthearted spirit to begin playing productively through journaling, art collages, music, guided relaxation therapy, behavior modification therapy, a principled and disciplined program, finding meaningful connections, quilting, painting, and celebrating life in gratitude!

Have a playful day!

Reputable means having a good reputation, being thought of well and being highly respected, reliable, principled, virtuous, upright, conscientious, esteemed, and dependable.

Living an emotionally and mentally dysfunctional lifestyle came from being detached and straying away from God-consciousness. My perceptions, distortions, and darkness fed my negativity. My unstable feelings created wreckage of precious time and energy, which stole a good chunk of my years; it did not reward me as being reputable. I recognized my self-will destruction of beating myself up and living off the beam; I sent the devil packing. I was no longer selling my soul to the devil. My reputation slowly changed.

My spiritual development began after major liver malfunction. I had to accept my serious physical, mental, emotional, financial, and social problems. I became willing to change, grow, transform, and accept God-consciousness in my life. Being connected to God's plans for me to be right-minded, intuitive, and living in the light is so much more rewarding. It's a lot of work to change and move forward, live with principles and disciplines, to raise my level of God-consciousness, and to be willing to share my story. By doing the work, I am able to keep growing and perhaps help someone on the way. It is by giving that we receive; my service is to be reputable and enjoy what's left of my journey.

Have a reputable day!

HUMOR

Having humor is having the quality of being funny, amusing, and comical.

Laughter is such good medicine; it lights me up, releases endorphins and reduces pain, feels good, changes my perspective, and lightens my mind. Humor ignites my frame of mind, and my spirits are aroused. Being funny is a social thing and comes naturally to me.

I have learned some basic habits that create humor, such as: being silly and playful, being illogical to use nonsense rather than sense, contradicting myself, and stimulating others by acting contrary to their expectations.

Once I was travelling with three women when we got caught in a snowstorm and pulled off the highway to get a hotel. We were tired and stressed after seeing transfer trucks, cars, and trucks flipped in the ditches. We were exhausted and edgy when we were in our room. I was wearing a red shirt; I took it off and held it in front of me like a bull fighter and started shaking it and danced around the room. The energy changed as we all began laughing. One woman even went into the bathroom and locked herself in, so she could stop laughing and wait for us to settle down. Finally, we all had a good rest.

Have a day with humor!

MAJESTIC

Majestic means having or being awesome, great, superb, striking, dignified, proud, impressive, beautiful or dignified.

I no longer live slumped down in an attitude of defeat, believing nothing is possible. It gives me great pleasure to live in a changed mentality, which gives me strength and courage to believe in possibilities. I stand tall in confidence with an attitude open to majestic possibilities. Living with majestic experiences comes from living a compassionate lifestyle, fostering connections, sharing time, inspiring creativity, and enjoying blissful experiences.

A friend called me, wondering if I had time to drive her to visit her friend. I said, "Sure." It was compassionate to help her to foster connections that day. As we were sharing time, we talked about fishing, and I mentioned I loved fishing. It's such a majestic experience to go to the woods, sit quietly along the lake, and fish.

So we went to the store where I bought my license, and we were lucky to find some boots, hats and warm jackets in my van's tickle trunk. We created moments to enjoy a blissful experience. Oh, the sweet smells, as we hit the dirt road, rolled down our windows, and crept over the potholes, parked on the edge of the road, and hiked to the lake. The scene at the lake was majestic, as well as our catch!

Have a majestic day!

WELL

Well is to be free, healthy, strong, vigorous, sound, thriving, blooming, bursting, in good condition, and hearty. To be well-meaning is to have good intentions, having the desire to do something good.

Letting go of old habits and learning to be well is a lifelong process. Finding my true self and accepting my beauty have helped me to be well. My gratitude is sharing random acts of kindness to give back to society. My service and calling are to pay it forward by being inspiring, causing laughter, volunteering, offering my time, donating time and food, reaching out to the lonely, and giving compliments and encouragement.

Becoming well and a well-meaning human is a blessing after crawling out of hell on earth. Learning to be compassionate and spontaneous rewards me with the most awesome feelings. Living in the light and doing things that I would like others to do for me brings me out of self, and I am rewarded tenfold. Good intentions nourish my soul, mind, and body, and I know peace! Over time, I have developed a well-meaning spirit and continue to progress. It is my spontaneous nature for me to live well!

Have a well day!

THINKER

A thinker is a person who thinks deeply, cleverly, intellectually, and philosophically. A free thinker is a person who forms thoughts based on reason, independent of authority and tradition, and is revolutionary, questioning, far-out, and progressive. A thinker might also direct, organize, manage, and plan.

My thinking was a major problem in my life at one time, and my life was extremely unmanageable. I thought I was out of my mind but, with help, was able to return to my senses with a team of healers. Once I was able to change my thinking, I became free to personalize my experience, find my strength in connecting with my higher power God, and I had hope of a better life.

Connecting to a greater purpose, and retraining and reframing my thoughts, have ignited my mind to be a healthier thinker. I think creatively with curiosity and am wiser, loving self and others. Thinking open-mindedly, challenging my misperceptions, understanding and being humble opens my heart and mind to think more positively so I can listen to, and care about, others. I am what I think, so I choose to think clearly, simply, honestly and with humility. To maintain healthy thinking, stimulate joy and calmness, I bathe in nature and plug in outdoors as much as possible, which exhilarates my human experience!

Have a day being a thinker!

NOVEMBER 19
STUPENDOUS

Stupendous is to be extremely impressive, amazing, astounding, remarkable, wonderful, mind-blowing, awesome, and phenomenal.

Living in the past or future stagnates my journey's progress. I have learned that it is very important to quiet my mind, so that it can open up the circuits of creativity, imagination, and be free flowing. It is in the art of silence, meditation, and a quiet mind that I was able to learn to be positive in my thoughts, which changed my life miraculously.

Taming the brain in meditation enabled me to face the truth of how I was living. I grew through quieting my mind, worked through my challenges, and learned to appreciate the gift of living. It is stupendous that I could adjust, eliminate, move on, and learn to be still and know peace.

I have a habit of making up songs on the spot, in the moment; my words flow into a song. My friend Herby would say, "Alison, that song shows stupendous talent!" I believe it is God's grace and direction from my ancient ancestors that guide me. It's stupendous what a person can do with a quiet mind.

Have a stupendous day!

Mind is a person's mental capacity, which includes consciousness, imagination, language, thinking, judging, memory, understanding, reasoning, sense and psyche.

My unconscious mind drives my body functions to operate on automatic pilot; my sleeping, breathing, and heart work on their own. My cognitive faculties were also on auto pilot, sparking dysfunction with emotions, responses of fight or flight and irrational thinking. I was living in a state of sadness and unhappiness, feeling disturbed and dissatisfied with gloom, misery, and pain. My ego became habituated to being stuck; this state was certainly not conducive to having peace of mind.

I needed to recognize and understand that my dark thoughts were taking me down the road of self-destruction before I could change to live more consciously and be awake and aware. Learning to let go and change strengthened my self-confidence so that I could make healthier decisions and have peace of mind as a result. Learning this lesson improved my feelings of self-worth; now, I experience fewer emotional reactions. Taking care of my thoughts feeds my mind, enabling me to demonstrate greater abilities and the freedom to speak up with my true voice. Meditation quiets my mind to a healthier consciousness, sparks me up and keeps me awake and living in higher spirits with fulfillment, contentment, well-being, joy, tranquility, and serenity.

My mind loves to express the energy that comes from being mindful; the side effects include equanimity, even temperedness, and being polished and levelheaded. It's important to continuously weed and cultivate my mind with loving expressions of cheerfulness and delight. Actually, I feel like I'm living in seventh heaven; how sweet it is to have peace of mind, vibrating in serenity.

Have a taking care of mind day!

Divine, as I understand it, means to be God-like, to live experiencing truth, goodness, supernatural power, and what is sacred and holy. Divine means developing a relationship to our higher power, creator, God, and spirit to transcend our human capacities, to be blessed with beauty and divine intervention.

Learning to live with respect for the divine force in my life has brought healing, strength, and hope. Prayers, positive thoughts, and the willingness to accept the divine action of living in a God-like way brings me closer to miracles. Spiritual awakening made me aware of miracles in my life. I grew out of dysfunction and disconnection with divine connections to a new vision. I let go and let God, and my heart opened to the divine reality of infinite awareness.

Walking the labyrinth is a great way to feel my feelings, my awareness, and make divine connections. I am blessed each day as I choose to walk with the ancient spirits and live in a divine reality of being simple, aware, and opening my heart to the presence of one God, one people!

Have a divine day!

NOVEMBER 22
SELF-TAUGHT

Self-taught is to learn a skill on one's own, primitive, natural, independent, standing on one's own feet, self-made, and without instruction.

Self-taught habits come from actively thinking, creating, and being motivated to achieve an outcome. When I was in residence at Teachers College, I found a piano in the basement hall next to the laundry room. I thought I should buy a book and learn to play this piano while my wash was on. So I went to Mingo's Music store to buy a piano book. However, a man named Albert was playing a guitar, and I commented that it sounded good. He said, "Try this guitar." I said, "Oh, I don't know how to play guitar. I came to buy a piano book." He said, "It's easier to carry a guitar to festivals." Instead of the piano book, I came back to my room with a guitar, tuner, capo, strap, case, and a book of country songs.

That afternoon I went to the Down East Bluegrass jam and followed along, teaching myself the chords and strumming. I studied how they strummed with a boom-chuck motion. I went back to my residence and drove the other students crazy as I practiced changing chords and strumming. Over the years, I recognized the process of learning each day and accepted my progress in being self-taught. I surrendered to my instinct and let go of the uncertainties; I felt peaceful simply to play the best I could. My hope and belief in myself and my self-taught ability grew with encouragement from other musicians. My faith vibrates with my spirit and I am free to shine my light. I love to play. Today, I share my self-taught talent with gratitude and am grateful for this wonderful, joy-making, self-taught hobby.

Have a self-taught day!

Comical is to be funny, hilarious, humorous, droll, waggish, priceless, a hoot, and foolish in a strange and silly way causing laughter.

Once upon a time, I took my friend with me to visit my aunt and uncle in Mattie Settlement in Antigonish County. We would do the laundry, clean up the house, make some meals, and help out so that they could stay in their home comfortably.

One evening the sun was shining, and it was beautiful with all the spring growth. My friend and I went for a walk up the back woods road, crossed over the flowing river and cut across the field to my Grammy's old homestead that was vacant. It was the last house at the end of the road.

It was a most memorable evening, so peaceful and such a serene walk. As we walked through the woods she asked why the grass was all patted down in places. I replied, "Oh, that's where the deer sleep at night." As we came down the hill, my other uncle was at the old homestead getting ready to mow the grass. He said, "You should not be walking up there with all the hungry bears." My friend almost passed out as she looked at me and said, "Allie, you said they were the deer beds." I said, "Yes, I realized once we were back there that my uncle had told me there were a lot of bears this spring, but because we were already far in the woods I figured it would be best not to scare you, my dear friend." We can now laugh over this experience, which is comical in retrospect. We almost became bear burgers that night!

Have a comical day!

PHYSICAL

Physical relates to the body or flesh and is solid, phenomenal, visual, touchable, tangible, sensual, sensible, sexual, material, real, gross, and natural.

Life is physically demanding, and I worked hard at being physically fit: walking, hiking, cross-country skiing, alpine skiing, water skiing, biking, swimming, cleaning, building, and dancing. Then, in the blink of an eye, I was seriously injured, physically exhausted, dazed, foggy, lackadaisical, dreamy, listless, and lethargic, as the result of a car accident.

To recover my physical strength, and once again to have a get-up-and-go attitude, and be alert, snappy, merry, and lively, I had to have physical therapy. First, I had a physiotherapist and a masseuse work on helping me improve through manual therapy. Then, I went for exercise therapy based in the gym and at the pool. All these physical therapies helped my movement and my ability to manage the pain. They focused on isolating specific joint and tissue pain and encouraged me to keep moving.

My abilities were challenging but having had a strong, physically fit body, and being tenacious, I progressed to a state of well-being, feeling vigorous and lively. I found my get-up-and-go spirit and am content in my physical space living one day at a time with all my kinks and pains. I live in the countryside, overlooking the ocean, and have built a labyrinth in my back yard. It motivates me to get out for a walk daily. My physical health nourishes my mental and spiritual health too. My senses are awake; I am grateful and love all of me, even my "Buddha Belly" because my human structure is temporary, just for today. Acceptance is the key to my freedom, peace, and serenity!

Have a physically healthy day!

MODERATION

Moderation is living in middle ground, balanced, composed, poised, tolerating, steady, mild, and reasonable and avoiding excessive and extremist behaviors.

Letting go of extreme and excessive habits is the key to spiritual growth; moderation creates balance and harmony. Obsessiveness, indulgence, irrationality, and unrestrained behaviors bring on neuroticism. Growing, changing, and staying grounded in the moment and becoming agreeable, patient, calm, and cool develops a positive attitude. I live in the flow with higher vibrations. Eating and drinking in moderation opens my energy paths so that I can be mindful, attentive, and sharp in all my relations.

Moderation enhances my ability for self-control and to communicate with consistency and fairness. Taking it easy is a process of pacing myself that promotes wellness. Understanding my cognitive style and personality traits helps me make healthier decisions. Learning to be self-disciplined, optimistic, helpful, forgiving, emotionally secure, and conscientious leads me to moderation, stability, contentment, and growth so that I can be of service to others. We are all one! Let's all flow and grow together one moment at a time!

Have a day of moderation!

LOVELINESS

Loveliness is the quality of being beautiful, attractive, charming, respectful, delightful, fair, and highly pleasing. It also a word used to describe a group of ladybugs and seeing such a group is supposed to create good luck.

Letting go of disagreeableness, nastiness, offensiveness, and unbecomingness opens our hearts to let loveliness blossom. I had to find peace within myself by implementing good orderly direction in my life to overcome some difficult behaviors and thinking patterns. I chose to clean house in the way I lived; I cleaned out the clutter and chatter in my brain and found space for creating a spirit of loveliness that feeds my beauty, creativity, and spontaneity. I have learned to love myself but remain humble, knowing that I really don't know much in relation to everything there is to know. Nonetheless, I am open to continuously learn and, therefore, am contented, growing each day and radiant in loveliness.

Finding a group of women, gathering to communicate about our journeys, and weeding, feeding, growing, and inspiring each other, is fantastic. Sharing our stories nourishes our strength, which is a true blessing. We gathered for a "Ladybug Picnic" one fine Spring day, and we shared loveliness. We walked down to the creek enjoying the smells of the forest; we relaxed doing yoga; we walked up the road to find words to unscramble; we shared a BBQ lunch; we sang and rejoiced as we bathed in pure loveliness. A calling to share the deep beauty of our hearts and minds, once again, has been delightful. Thanks to the team at the Log Cabin Entertainment, Rawdon Hills, Nova Scotia for such a fabulous Ladybug Picnic.

Have a day of loveliness!

Witty is being quick, clever, sparkling, ingenious, brilliant, entertaining, ludicrous, teasing, epigrammatic, diverting, joking, crazy, funny, facetious, and penetrating in inventive verbal humor, timed just right in the moment.

The heaviness of living can be lightened by this divine gift of being witty. When I release the pain of the human condition of living seriously, prudishly, constipated in my thoughts of past hurts, and being self-grasping, self-important, and egotistical, I lighten up to enjoy laughing. It feels good to be witty, sharing humor to rise above the pain, and encouraging people to enjoy the blessings of better connections with others. It is certainly a gift to be awakened, keen, and resourceful with a natural ability to quickly weave in jokes and sharply respond to create humor and end on a high note. Creating vibrations of positive energy are beneficial to increase higher mood endorphins, release stress, and enjoy living.

Living in joy sure beats being alone and feeling lonely. When I'm alone in my stinking thinking head, I'm in very bad company. I realize I need to invite my Creator into my head, move my thoughts to my heart, feel the gratitude, and get on with enjoying my sparkling energy. I'll risk almost anything, as long as it keeps me growing!

Have a witty day!

MIND CLEANING

Mind cleaning involves clearing one's head from the chatter and clutter of negativity, anxiety, memories, fear, denial, hate, pessimism, doom and gloom.

My mind has cognitive faculties of languages, perception, judging, thinking, consciousness, memory, and imagination. Cleaning up my mind involves tidying up my thoughts, letting go, scrubbing out past thoughts, getting more sleep, and healthy eating. Staying awake and focused spiritually have been a direct result of rebuilding my brain through the process of mind cleaning through reprogramming my mind for self-confidence, motivation, and a lust for living well. Choosing positivity, peacefulness, courage, acceptance, and love have nourished my mind, body, and soul with side effects of joy, serenity, optimism, and radiant vibrations.

Learning to function with a clean mind gives me the ability to be clearheaded, coherent, sane, stable, balanced, rational, and right-minded. It's a process of continuously learning, clarifying, improving, sharpening, elevating, and polishing my thoughts and feelings. Being aware of my body and intuitions and learning from the lessons along the journey are keys to having a clean mind space. I feed my mind with positive affirmations, choose healthier thoughts, decide consciously with the best intentions, meditate, walk, and have room for love and peace within. Cleaning our mind is really an inside job. Operating from acceptance, appreciation, gratitude, and brightness allows me to breathe easily and be open to share the languages of love.

Have a mind-cleaning day!

RESILIENCE

Resilience is having strength, flexibility, toughness, adaptability, buoyancy, and ability to endure to recover from difficulties.

The first step is to recognize that one has an issue, problem, or trauma that needs attention. Next is to accept it by acknowledging it and feeding it with positive self-talk to think about solutions. Then, deal with it as best as possible, perhaps with the help of a support team of encouraging people. Finally, go forth to develop a healthier perspective for a happier and more contented life.

Having resilience opens us to new ideas. I guess I have developed a strong resilience as I am oozing with new ideas, coping skills, and a sense of calmness, gentleness, loveliness, and compassion. I developed these skills by getting out of my head, because my thinking caused "dis-ease" in my interactions. I have moved into my heart, which allows me to hold space, light fires, and align myself with a quiet mind.

Connecting with my mind, body, and soul returned me to centered living and knowing my true self. The greatest gift is to be emotionally, mentally, and spiritually stable. There is nothing in the universe and my world that I can't overcome. Experiences of trauma have been consistent, but with spiritual maturity and letting go of selfishness, greed, and envy, I have room for continued transformations. Knowing all experiences are lessons and not obstacles, I live compassionately with resilience!

Have a day of resilience!

Unstoppable is to be unbeatable, bulletproof, unconquerable, inevitable, unavoidable, inescapable, and continuous. Being unstoppable is being secure, safe, guarded, and protected from being stopped or prevented from developing.

Learning to rise above all trauma, letting go of the characteristics of being insecure, powerless, defenseless, vulnerable, exposed, helpless, doubting, and distracted opens the door to moving from limited life skills to limitless possibilities. Being resilient and unstoppable allows me to move towards growth and deal with life challenges and problems. I am able to develop new perspectives that encourage me to reach healthier goals. I have learned that I am a unique, creative, loveable, and humble being. I can do anything I want to because I am my own superhero in a healed state of wellness.

The road to being unstoppable came from changing my thinking and developing active learning to trust and accept my intuition. Challenging myself to practise new thinking patterns and let go of the idea of perfectionism allows me to live outside the box. I now strive for progress, which enables me to build self-confidence and self-respect doing the best I can each day. There is no destination, because yesterday is gone, and tomorrow is not here. I live in the gift of today – the present, the now; in this moment, I am continuously open and growing. I continue to do deep work on myself with no fear of failure because I have come to realize that it's all about learning the lessons. No more blaming and beating myself up, but rather acceptance, attitude adjustment, action, and participation for contentment!

Have an unstoppable day!

OPENNESS

Openness is living with lack of restrictions and secrecy; it is the ability to live being honest, direct, open-hearted, unreserved, unguarded, straightforward, frank, blunt, transparent, and free.

My openness journey began once I became willing to be open to new ideas and changing some of my constrictive and uncooperative ways of living. Learning to have an attitude of gratitude and a flexibility to study my perceptions, patterns, and perspectives opened my life to infinite possibilities. Growing confident to have a voice and feel comfortable in communications, being clear and frank, learning to listen and ask myself if something makes sense, helps me to adapt my behaviors to be the best version of me I can be. These changes rewarded me with openness.

Learning to understand myself helped me develop new habits, some of which are: accepting new ideas and methods, managing cooperatively, having courage to act and openness to question and be awake, making better decisions, being in tune with my feelings and emotional health, and being creative, artistic, and respectful. My biggest teacher comes from travelling, going on adventures and meeting new people, enjoying other cultures, and joyfully tasting different foods. My openness rewards me with a healthy imagination, reliability, talkativeness, affection, and emotional stability.

Have a day of openness!

ADORABLE

Adorable is being able to inspire great affection, being delightful, charming, captivating, appealing, ambrosial, precious, lovely, beautiful, and enchanting.

It has been a long and arduous trip to outgrow extremely reactive, impulsive, intense, and dangerous behaviors. I needed release from a distorted self-image, feelings of intense emptiness, loneliness and neediness, and dissociative states stemming from a borderline personality disorder. However, I am here to share with you that it is possible to change and achieve emotional stability. Acceptance to recognize the problem, optimism to learn new functioning skills, determination to master self, and willingness to become open and conscientious have afforded me deep transformation.

My new skills have changed my ways, and my habits have evolved to include an attitude of gratitude to live in the light, upbeat, cheerfully, and optimistically. Being generous, curious, wide-eyed, sparkling, and spreading kindness and compassion are much more conducive to my emotional well-being. Practising acts of kindness, repetitively and rhythmically, and, understanding that life is a process of learning keeps me unconditionally open. Being lovable, sweet, childlike, friendly, and fun are adorable qualities. Cultivating my personality has been a slow but rewarding journey to mindfulness, tolerance and emotional stability.

Have an adorable day!

DECEMBER 3
SACRIFICE

Sacrifice is to forgo, offer, spare, surrender, drop, and give up something that is valuable to oneself for the happiness and opportunity to help another.

When I hit my lowest living in an unhealthy lifestyle, I realized I needed to alter my fixed mindset, perfectionism, toxic behaviors, dependency, and egotism. I had to let go of my need to be liked, my need for control, and habit of saying yes. I had to learn to say no! I had to come out of denial, let go of shame, blame, and guilt, and free myself from restlessness and regrets. My comfort zone no longer served me, and I had to break down my walls, make a plan, become disciplined to improve my skills, and learn to live in a right mindset. Sacrificing is having willingness to put the time into grooming myself. Living in the moment and deciding to live successfully with contentment to open my heart and serve others. I was able to give back in gratitude for what others gave me; the more I give, the more I receive.

To sacrifice my time to change and to do the work to move forward was a hard program of studying, learning, and sacrificing to learn to love myself and live successfully. Increasing self-esteem enables me to give and sacrifice my time, sleep, quiet times, and desires, as long as they are beneficial and reasonable to us all. I have learned the art of sacrificing in a good way by performing acts of kindness, which has become my second nature. My living is authentic, and I have a clear conscience in creating connections to continue growing in freedom. To sacrifice is to make sacred and to share love.

Have a day of sacrifice!

IMPARTIALITY

Impartiality is having fair-mindedness, neutrality, detachment, and justice for equal treatment.

Living with bias, prejudice, criticism, and judgment is the opposite of impartiality and takes away from seeing the whole picture. I have learned that it is better to be honest with myself to learn the facts and to have constructive doubt when necessary. It is far healthier to take no part, stay in a neutral attitude, and to have mercy. Learning to have an epistemological perspective of truthfulness, tolerance, and freedom of opinion allows me to live harmoniously, faithfully, freely, and interconnected to others so I'm able to treat all people equally.

Decency comes from thinking independently, learning to take action to maintain stability and self-control, learning that we are all one, developing a deep understanding of life skills to have mercy, developing people skills, and feeling our feelings. All of these skills have improved my life so that I now embrace living in harmony. The true blessing and miracle of healing is to be affectionate, compassionate, and loving. All this prepared me for the day I came face to face with the man who shot and killed my brother. He was dying in a hospital bed, and I told him I was not the one to judge him. We talked about what happened. This moment, my friends, was my blessing to experience the virtue of living with impartiality.

Have a day of impartiality!

DECEMBER 5
PASSIONATE

Passionate is to show and express strong feelings and enthusiasm in a loving, blazing, intense, vibrant, dynamic, awake, energizing, eager, devoted, hungry, vigorous and zealous way.

Once upon a time I lived very nonchalantly, cool, lethargic, unexcited, indifferent, and emotionless going from pillar to post, drifting along like a zombie with no passion to live. Eventually, I woke up and started to live in a new light by being honest and facing my thinking problem. I knew it was time to find my true self, life purpose, and path. I went back to school and became a grade eight teacher with a passionate heart. It took courage to start learning and become devoted to follow through, living every day with anticipation of wonderful experiences, incidents, and adventures.

The keys to becoming passionate were my truth, courage, self-motivation, determination, and tenacity. Changing my thinking habits brought about a passionate life, blazing with family and friends, loving what I do in life, painting, writing, singing, playing music, and socializing, which keeps me hungry for more passion. Living connected to the source, God gives me happy joyful vibrations, I am what I think, and today I am loved and aligned with passionate love. My heart and soul are passionate each day for new blessings.

Have a passionate day!

INTENTION

Intention is something you intend, hope, desire, aim, plan or target to do.

A sense of hopelessness had blocked my ability to live happily and contentedly. Finding a healing process and a support team encouraged and empowered me and opened the door to new beginnings. Setting positive intentions paved the way to sanity. Learning to do the work by being creative, brave, and self-disciplined with tenacity fired up a new healthier version of my life, which enabled me to develop intention to find my talents and gifts. My method included implementing a daily routine, building positive self-talk, developing an attitude of gratitude, practising better self-care, recognizing my calling in life, answering the call to be a teacher, and living as a missionary of peace. Sharing my life and my skills with unconditional love is my resolve.

My intention is to live fully and responsibly to manifest forgiveness, happiness, contentment, love, and unconditional love, abundance, being a leader, seeing the good in people, and encouraging them to be their best. My inner conversations are now prayer, peace, and patience, from which I develop a mindset free of chaos and crazy chatter. My skills include meditation, staying awake, letting go, detachment with love, trusting my source, taking action, and doing God's will! My intentions are my aspirations, dreams, determination, and motivations for continuing to share happiness, peace, and serenity.

Have a day of positive intentions!

RESPECTED

Respected means being appreciated, praiseworthy, admired, esteemed, important, valued, well thought of, and honored.

At times in my life, I found that I was disrespected as a worthy human being. I hit my bottom in despair and had no respect for myself. I learned that being respected starts with respecting myself, which is an inside job of changing my thinking and behaviors. On this journey, I learned that respected people are not always liked because they stand tall to protect their boundaries! Being taught to respect elders can sometimes be a barrier to speaking up, but it's important not to be snowplowed by their aggressive behaviors because, then, we are disrespected and ill-treated.

To be respected, I must understand what respect means; it is to have consideration, thoughtfulness, attentiveness, and politeness, as well as being courteous. To build a personal sense of worth through discovering my personal qualities and talents helps me to be respected. By becoming an active listener, practising tolerance, and appreciating our life's journey, whatever it is, we build respect. The value of living with respect and honesty is wonderful and has become a way of life that is ever so blissful. Being mindful helps me to show consideration for others, and I am, hopefully, respected.

Have a day being respected!

DECEMBER 8
UNDERSTANDING

Understanding is having the ability to be aware of others' feelings, to be tolerant, good-natured, approachable, supportive, merciful, considerate, compassionate, sensitive, kindly, patient, and forgiving.

Living in a selfish, inconsiderate, unfeeling, intolerant, and disagreeable way only leads to frustration, judging, and self-destruction. Awakening to live a peaceful and serene lifestyle came from learning to listen to others and identify my defects. Navigating through my issues and traumas with the help of a support team opened new opportunities and awareness. With my new knowledge, I was able to gain insight to change my bad habits and construct a new way of living. Sharing my truth with others taught me how to distinguish my good and bad behaviors; with this insight, I was able to transform and let go of trying to be perfect. Welcoming God into my life helped me mature and build confidence and self-esteem.

Speaking my truth and sharing my journey with loving grace and humility ensures my continuous growth to live in goodness. Learning to listen with empathy, reflection, and validation, and developing healthy negotiating skills is a blessing. Being a human being, I do make mistakes, but I am able to grow out of them because I have a toolbox of coping skills to manage my life today. My understanding is cultivated by prayer and meditation.

Have a day of understanding!

ACCOMMODATING

Accommodating is the ability to be cooperative, adaptable, considerate, generous, willing, hospitable, helpful, polite, kindly, neighborly, and willing to fit in with someone's needs or wishes.

Living in disharmonious ways shifts and traps us in negativity. I have learned that I must protect myself from anxiety, fear, loneliness, depression, and anger so that I do not fall into vengeful, bitchy, selfish, demeaning, and hurtful behaviors. A few years ago I had surgery, experienced anxiety, and I was not in sound mind; I retaliated in anger. The results were negative. I now understand that I need to be accommodating to myself to stay sincere, truthful, and centered; my feelings are important, and I need not become a doormat. I must not participate in dysfunctional chaos but draw the line with healthy boundaries.

I can't accommodate others if I am not grounded in wellness; therefore, I choose to sit back, watch the storms, pray for healing, and hold space. Living in wellness is a practice in humility; people find it easy to get along with me. Learning to give and taking time to be accommodating create openness and peaceful experiences. It's a pleasure to be mentally grounded in a healthy mindset and be inspirational with a virtuous lifestyle, while accommodating myself and others. It is in taking care of me that I am able to be accommodating to others, and we might live peacefully.

Have an accommodating day!

PURIFICATION

Purification is the process of refinement, rebirth, grace, atonement, release, and forgiveness making something spiritually clean.

Spring cleaning is good for housekeeping and a healthy home. Mind purifying is good for alignment to see a healthier world from a higher perspective of confidence, hope, love, and vision. Letting go of negative energy, negative attitudes, and old ideas opens the door to purifying and creating soundness of mind. Learning to connect with my conscious self and my heart helped me to develop the art of compassion and positive energy. Awakening to life and living with divine intention allows me to focus on my spiritual transformation of rebirth with grace.

Oh what a journey! What is this life about and what's the value of living? Finding my purpose and enjoying what I do with my life has been a long process of lessons and personal growth. This is what my life is about today: I have transformed through finding answers; I live in lightness and experience stillness and peace; I am at one with myself and connected to all beings with a loving spirit. I maintain this way of life by purifying my mind daily to reflect and contemplate peace. The value of my life with purification comes from sharing and caring and being of service to mirror the joy of being still and knowing peace.

Have a day of purification!

ENLIGHTENING

Enlightening is the practice of providing knowledge in an informative, educational, illuminating, and instructional way to give understanding and insight.

Living in ignorance and oppression feed a constipated, blocked, narrow, unbecoming manner, and low self-esteem. Learning is enlightening and leads to knowledge. It was enlightening when I began waking up to feelings, having a sense of connection, seeking a support team, becoming aware of my patterns, letting go of attachments, and developing an attitude of gratitude. It was enlightening to learn to laugh at myself, focus on my own business, choose to let go, and get on with living in the light.

It's wonderful to understand and know that I am a part of the whole, because we are all connected in this universe. Constantly growing in the truth that we create our own reality, I learned to make better choices, listen to my gut, trust God, stay awake, and observe how I think, feel and act. Daily meditation increases my intuition, and I live in peace with a playful spirit that sparks higher vibrations and frequencies. This is the way for me: enlightening ways of sharing my love, kindness, and serenity.

Have an enlightening day!

COMMUNITY

Community means to live in a neighborhood, society, clan, affiliation, fellowship, union, and group of people in the same place, while feeling group spirit, team morale, and shared openness for the common good.

Being mentally ill, with delusional thinking that I was all alone, fed my aggression and unhealthy behaviors. These destructive behaviors kept my mind in a prison of desperation, withdrawal, retaliation, and unhealthy coping skills, and limited my progress in maturing.

Learning that I am part of the whole and becoming connected with common interests, attitudes, and goals improved my union with others and taught me to live in right action for the good of all. Volunteering, doing favors, gestures of good will, and spontaneous acts of kindness improve my sense of belonging in my various communities.

I thrive when I am open to my feelings and emotions. I have self-confidence in speaking my voice. I feel accepted in sharing mutual goals to be my best authentic self, building community spirit in my tribe, my community, and with all my human relations; I am empowered with self-confidence, knowing I am part of the whole. Feeling accepted feeds my desire to be involved and maintains my willingness to participate. Living in a healthy community encourages me to live, love, and laugh with magnetic energy in life's infinite possibilities. I am blessed to express happiness in unity with my community.

Have a community day!

DECEMBER 13
SCRUPULOUSNESS

Scrupulousness is to have a strict, attentive, focus on doing things morally correct with carefulness, closeness, conscientiousness, meticulousness, and heedfulness with high standards of excellence and ethics.

This sounds like obsessive-compulsive and bipolar personality behavior. I used to be flying around, trying to have things my way while running over others, which was not attractive. Therapy helped me to see these disorders and opened my mind to new perspectives. The secret is to become centered and feel the vibrations, finding a balance to work towards letting go of the character defect of perfection. I am now living healthier and know that I don't have to be perfect and meticulous about my plans and details. I am now free to live grounded and well-balanced.

To maintain good physical health I must drink mountain water to wash out toxicity and also exercise; my emotional stability is scrupulously maintained by my dealing with stress and anxieties through relaxation and having healthy boundaries. My aspiration for good mental health reminds me to take it easy and spend lots of time in nature and be humble with an attitude of gratitude. I appreciate the beauty in life and look for the beauty in others with scrupulousness. Slowing down to be scrupulously aware and conscious of the flow and vibrations heightens my frequency. I serve others through acts of kindness and generosity. All of us, my tribe and community, benefit from the scrupulousness of living in a healthy manner with comfort, peace, and serenity. I know I am love; this is my way!

Have a day of scrupulousness!

AUTHENTICITY

Authenticity is having the quality of living accurately, with certainty, factuality, dependability, and being sure, real, truthful, faithful, original, and genuine.

Immaturity, lack of confidence, doubtfulness, being unrealistic, falsifying, and unreal living in fear created a desperate life, and I was living on hold. Letting go of these dysfunctional characteristics and ways, like "stinking thinking," allowed me to accept myself; I started to grow up and mature to the point of changing my beliefs and welcoming self-worth. Living in openness relieved stress, anxiety, and especially intolerance. I feel at home in my body, mind, and soul. My greatest change, and growth, was when I stopped being concerned about what others thought; I let go of fearing what others thought about me. Becoming authentic, I can be my true self, and my spirit flows in authentic freedom, peace, and serenity.

My concern is to live in authentic wellness, being mindful, stable, wise, impartial and nonjudgmental. Taking care of myself includes being aware, awake, honest, trustworthy, introspective, kind, and respectful with good intentions in the moment. Accepting myself as a mature, talented, and wise woman gives me the ability to accept others unconditionally. I accept that I am perfectly imperfect and open to new lessons. I am free to release, receive, and renew my vibrations each moment, free to share my feelings and emotions, and blessed with authenticity!

Have a day of authenticity!

DECEMBER 15
LOYALTY

Loyalty is having the qualities to be loyal, true, devoted, dedicated, committed, and supportive to a person or cause.

Building healthy friendships and relationships are based on mutual love and respect. How do we love and respect when trust is broken and betrayed in deception, manipulation, greed, jealousy, and selfishness? At a young age and vulnerable, I lost my loyalty while being sexually disrespected and, as a result, withdrew into a realm of dysfunctional characteristics. Today, I am more functional and use my skills to deal with issues.

I healed with my support team's encouragement, and I grew to be a loyal person who demanded honesty, courage, kindness, faithfulness, sacrifice, service, and spirituality. To learn to build healthy boundaries, I had to learn to trust myself and others.

As a result, I am able to stand up, use my voice, be respectful and trustworthy, and share my honest opinion with integrity and sincerity. I am growing in compassion to take care of myself, as well as taking care of my family and friends, so that we all may grow together. My loyalty to myself is to continue improving myself and sharing my gifts with love, the virtue that keeps me connected and empowered with my source and authentic self.

Have a day of loyalty!

OPEN-MINDED

Open-minded is the quality of a person to be accepting, unbiased, tolerant, non-judging, unprejudiced, flexible, and humble, knowing that they don't know everything and are willing to grow in insight, love, wisdom, and compassion.

When we are opinionated, prejudiced, narrow-minded, and judgmental, we have our authentic curiosity squashed and beaten down, and we withdraw into black-and-white thinking. Sometimes, we might even dissociate, losing connection with healthy thinking. Opening up to explore and cultivate an open mind requires courage, honesty, and a nerve to be authentic. We are open-minded when we have a willingness to consider things differently with new perspectives to improve our critical thinking skills.

My world now flourishes with infinite possibilities because I have learned to free my mind from limited thoughts and have the courage to live outside the box. Knowledge strengthened my confidence and I am open to consider others' beliefs. Wisdom makes me willing to listen without judgment. Open-mindedness gives me an abundance of energy.

Have an open-minded day!

MANIFESTATION

Manifestation is an event, action or object that clearly demonstrates an existence, reality, or presence of something.

When I am sick, I might have the manifestation of symptoms that indicate a medical condition. I have learned to be awake, turn my attention to reprogram my brain and think differently. Learning to visualize my body healing through higher vibrations brings healing and recovery.

Manifestation is a great illustration, expression, demonstration, and appearance. I train my thoughts and manifest my dreams to become my reality. Once I figure out what I want, I open my thoughts to God, Source, Creator; I am blessed with the spirit to act. I am persistent and consistent in my blessed intentions, and I manifest peace in my communication. I focus on manifesting peace, abundance, and continued blessings. It is an ancient principle of life to manifest your reality. So attract, create, and manifest; you are the master of your destiny!

Have a day of manifestations!

VIRTUOUS

Virtuous is having or showing honest, good, upright, moral, principled, admirable, scrupulous, trustworthy, respectable, right-minded, and honorable standards.

Learning to live virtuously involves developing the habit of doing good things not only for ourselves, but also sharing and giving back by doing random acts of kindness for others. Letting go of anger, envy, false pride, and resentments creates more space for virtuous acts. It's not always easy to be straightforward in all situations but it's necessary to be truthful to be virtuous.

It is one thing to be intelligent, self-taught, and educated, but it's another thing to be virtuous in habits of everyday living. The biggest character empowerment comes from implementing and living in honest, courageous, kind, hopeful, faithful, respectful, forgiving, and blameless principles. It feels good to live with good moral virtues and to merit the gifts of good behavior; being virtuous is conducive to my well-being, happiness, and contentment.

Make it a virtuous day!

DEITY

Deity is a god or goddess who is an almighty, divine being, creator, and maker. God is the highest power in the state of being divine. God is all powerful, omnipotent.

I have learned to live in God's image; being God-like in my journey rewards me with living contentedly. God teaches me to have the mind of a deity to be loving, understanding, caring, compassionate, patient, and humble. When I act in the spirit of love, I am pleasing to God and blessed with enlightenment. I raise my energy through prayer and meditation and receive divine messages! How sweet it is to be awake to the manifestations of creation, happiness, and bliss in the name of God.

It is helpful to be open to change; the deity teaches me how to deal with anger, jealousy, injury, loss, and discontentment. I am fortunate to have ups and downs, both from which I learn. I deal with obstacles by asking God for guidance and thinking about what the deity would have me do. I am strengthened by living my true God-self and moving forward with hope. To live God-like, I am honest in revealing myself, inviting my heart both to give and to receive. I am blessed knowing my higher power is with me and sometimes carries me.

Have a day with deity!

Breath is the air, life, life force, vital force, spirit, and inspiration taken into and expelled from our lungs while breathing is the process of inhalation and exhalation.

I did not and do not always breathe easily, but I have learned to let go of life barriers such as worry, fear, doubt, depression, age, race, religion, nationality, sexual orientation, and anything that causes anxiety for me or others. Learning to accept life, people, and places on life's terms allows me to breathe fresh air into my life and others' lives. I've learned to accept feeling relieved, release guilt, and to move on to live in the light. I breathe life's energy of love and compassion, which bless me with harmonious living with all in unconditional love.

It was a long process to quiet the chatter rolling in my brain and the worry about being socially accepted. I had to take time and space for healing and learn to identify dysfunctional patterns and work at changing them to reprogram my brain. One day I woke up, started living consciously and started to more fully and naturally breathe. I learned self-discipline, and how to study, meditate, and grow to be of service to others. Breathing in white light, love, patience, kindness, faithfulness, self-control, gentleness, and forgiveness; I exhaled worries and anxieties to renew my vital force so that I might breathe fresh air.

Have a day of breath!

DECEMBER 21
CONSIDERATION

Consideration comes from being careful, reflective, attentive, contemplative, factor- based, detailed, concerned, caring, understanding, and having friendly thoughts.

My life is much more harmonious now that I have learned to have consideration; I put out my intentions, let go, open my heart, detach from outcomes, and accept God's will. Having consideration for my blessings, I live in gratitude.

Consideration for living a healthy lifestyle and finding contentment in life came from having had a spiritual awakening. In consideration of my many blessings I give thanks. These blessings include meditating to be mindful, thoughtful and resourceful; listening to the morning breeze and birds; singing praises for a happy, joyous and free spirit to shine; and breathing fresh air. Consideration of being balanced compels me to journal, eat well, walk my labyrinth, stroll on beaches and through forests, feeling interconnected with all sentient beings.

Have a day of consideration!

SIMPLICITY

Simplicity is having clarity, directness, straightforwardness, understandability, easiness, manageability, uncomplication, and freedom from pretense.

At a young age, life became complicated, leaving me lacking self-worth and confidence. I trudged a lonely, dark path for many years. Deep within me I was screaming for help, but I did not find my voice until I was hospitalized several times due to my self-destructive behaviors. Having my stomach pumped in emergency was complicated and desperate. I longed for simplicity. Fortunately, I had a divine intervention and became willing to change.

I matured and learned to say no to negativity and to take care of myself. I improved my relationships by studying my blueprint and designed a new way of living in simplicity. I choose to learn every day, to focus on loving thoughts, and simply to be there for others. I had to understand that my empathy takes on other people's pains and sadness because I so consciously identify. I have learned how to protect myself. I find that simplicity promotes my being able to manage my life. My journey of intentionally manifesting simplicity results in the flow of higher vibration frequencies of love, compassion, and grace.

Have a day of simplicity!

GRACIOUS

Gracious is characterized by being polite, well-mannered, considerate, thoughtful, charitable, accommodating, elegant, tenderhearted, forgiving, kind, pleasant, and graceful.

As many of you know, I was not always a gracious woman. I developed some hard characteristics and dressed in a masculine fashion and used unattractive language to act tough to protect myself. However, like layers of an onion, I peeled a few of my layers, cried as I would peeling an onion, and began developing confidence, strength, and gentleness. I learned to dress attractively and sometimes elegantly and graciously.

Mending my energy vibes, I slowly began reaching out and, with my support team's encouragement, learned through life skills programs to find a new way of living graciously. I became much more gracious in my expression after accepting, learning, practising, and growing. I was able to tone down my harsh ways and use a loving voice, practise tolerance, and become supportive to others. Letting go of the fear of not being good enough and growing to a healthy feeling of self-worth gave me confidence to walk in the light graciously, sit with grace, and be comfortable in my own skin. Oh, how gracious, merciful, and forgiving is this divine intervention!

Have a gracious day!

DECEMBER 24
SACRED

Sacred is being connected with God, divine, blessed, dedicated, spiritual, devotional, and considered of worthy of spiritual respect.

Living a sacred life comes with awakening and the sacredness of being connected to all life with unconditional love. It is sacred to share our happiness, joy, and love of God, and let go of our trials and traumas. We learn and begin changing one day at a time; we live in gratitude, respecting ourselves and all beings. This gratitude is sacred to living fully and deeply with compassion, grace, kindness and spirituality.

Create a sacred space for each blessing; perhaps a small space could include artifacts that help a person feel quiet or an environment that helps us to focus on the sacredness of life. Create a life of inspiration and get out into nature to connect with the universe and God's blessing, where we can listen, feel grounded, and experience the light of God.

Creating a sacred space to live in peace and joy is very important for building a positive vision for our life, as is retreating from the noisy chatter of life. A sacred space allows us to connect with our inner child and spirit, which is pure love. I believe we are all born as a sacred blessing, and the journey is to reconnect to this feeling of inner bliss. We are connected with energy and vibrations and are, therefore, intrinsically sacred.

Have a sacred day!

DECEMBER 25
HUMBLE

Humble is to be simple, polite, gentle, ordinary, unassuming, and courteously respectful.

Letting go of negativity, ego, and arrogant, aggressive ways frees me to change my view on life. The nagging low opinion and self-sabotaging destructive habits had to be weeded out so that I could cultivate a positive character and learn admirable qualities.

How does a person learn to be humble?

I have learned that being humble comes with being teachable, and adopting respect, patience, self-control, and integrity to recognize I am not running the show. I have learned that to live humbly I needed to maintain a quiet confidence in my assets without needing others' approval or acknowledgement. As well, I have learned to get out of myself and be there for others without expecting praise. I am open to focus on what I can bring to others through volunteering, which keeps me humble. I understand that we are all one and have learned to treat everyone as I would like to be treated, because we are all equally discovering our own journey's path in humility.

Have a humble day!

DECEMBER 26
HARMONIOUS

Harmonious means being able to be friendly, agreeable, easy, peaceful, good-natured, well-balanced, cultivated, creative, rhythmical, mellifluous, and free from disagreements.

Learning to integrate with others harmoniously grew out of learning to let go of having my own way. One of my saving graces was my love for being in nature, which soothed my heart and grounded my spirit to live harmoniously with the other inhabitants of this world. I now feel connected and rejuvenated; I am deeply blessed with harmonious interconnection with all people, places, and things in my life.

How did I achieve harmonious living?

It was by being a learner. I had to learn to accept differences in people and adapt to the world cultures around me. I needed to be humble and open to understanding where my place is in the world and that I have my individual purpose as do others. Learning to adapt harmoniously comes with maturing and being open to others' perspectives. Learning to be compassionate, loving, respectful, honest, and humble enhances my harmonious spirit. So it is, in opening my heart that my mind follows, and I stay awake and harmonious!

Have a harmonious day!

DECEMBER 27
UNCONDITIONAL

Unconditional is unquestioning, wholehearted, positive, complete, and unlimited to any condition.

Harmony graces me with the ability to love unconditionally. To be loved unconditionally is to be accepted in our authenticity. I have learned to love myself without conditions, to accept my past, and let go of shame, blame, and guilt. Previously, I trusted no one; love and relationships were conditional, and few people got close to me. My spirit had short-circuited and left me in darkness and despair. I desperately longed for unconditional love.

I recovered from despair with the unconditional love of divine consciousness. In experiencing unconditional love, I knew better how to love others without conditions. My changes in attitude and daily awareness contributed to expanding my understanding of how unconditional love could manifest. Offering peace and generosity were expressions of unconditional love. I learned to accept and love others as they were, without any conditions.

Have an unconditional day!

DECEMBER 28
SERVING

Serving is encouraging, sharing time, being still in quietness to bring peace offerings to help others. Serving is to hear my calling to refine my character to be a serving, sharing person.

I experienced hard times in dysfunctional living and through suffering, eventually, I woke to my senses. The rewards of healing, transforming, and manifesting new perspectives and a healthy mindset came in the form of knowing and feeling a deep peace, which radiates patience in unconditional love. These changes strengthened my desire and ability for serving others.

I met a woman who was a role model for serving. She took me under her wing and showed me unconditional love and acceptance. She helped restore my confidence and was a catalyst for my becoming a loving, kind, compassionate, and gentle woman. She was a mirror of what I deeply desired to be like and, from her example, I followed the path of serving others.

I changed my attitude to one of gratitude and became a person happy to serve others. I was able to witness miracles, experience joy, and feed my soul. I thank my God every day for being able to serve others. By serving, I hope to radiate peace, love, and harmony.

Have a serving day!

TRUTH

Truth is pure, precise, frank, open, honest, authentic, sincere, genuine, and factual with an aim of belief.

Fear, shame, deception, and falsehood were consequences of being unable to accept life as it was served to me and to cope with the trauma. I lost respect for myself, my life, and even attempted to take my life. The cold hard truth hurt as much as the tube shoved up my nose in order to pump my stomach.

The facts could not be changed, but my attitude and behaviors could be modified with the blessing of therapy and encouragement from support groups. In my recovery, I looked at my standard of living and created new goals to be true to myself. I learned to respect my values and live by principles that connected me to truth, justice, and peaceful living. The truth is, I have learned that I am perfectly imperfect, and it is best if I acknowledge that I am a work in daily progress, being healed to shine my light.

I acknowledge my feelings; as the truth sets me free, I continuously make amends so that I can engage in healthier and more meaningful relationships. Most times, I am able to be forgiving; other times it may still be a work in progress. Acceptance opens my heart and truth sets me free; I am willing to grow into the best me I can be.

Have a day of truth!

PRINCIPLES

Principles are fundamental truths that serve as a rule, basis, ethic, golden rule, foundation, prescription, and source for satisfying and healthy living.

Principles were few and far between in my darkest days of dysfunctional living. I was drowning in depression and despair, feeling hopeless and resentful. Acceptance was the medicine that allowed me to wake up and focus on moving forward in an improved and healthier way. The secret to progress is to be honest, accepting life on life's terms, and being guided by the inner spirit to live with higher principles.

I must have faith, be reasonable, and let go so that I can get on with my life and have the courage to live with truth, be authentic, and shine. I must continue to be open-minded and admit wrongs to live with integrity. Adhering to principles of goodness strengthen my positive character attributes. Principles remind me to show gratitude and appreciation. I must be forgiving, tolerant, and seek justice through reviewing my actions and asking for forgiveness. Then I must stay awake and persevere in being spiritually fit through prayer and meditation to maintain a proper attitude. Preserving a state of wellness, I must share all these principles and spread them everywhere with love, compassion and grace.

Have a day of living with principles!

DECEMBER 31
UNITY

Unity is the state of being in union, unification, integration, and amalgamation with cooperation, togetherness, synthesis, like-mindedness, and peace while living in harmony with all in a complete and satisfying wholeness.

Living with mental and emotional illness is difficult because it creates disorders of shame, blame, and isolation. I did not feel in unity with others until I was willing to do the healing work to do something about my condition.

To heal myself, I accepted me as I was in the moment and prayed for wellness, honoring myself while learning to be grateful for new opportunities. Through opportunities of sharing with others, I began to feel a new unity and connection, realizing I was not alone with my problems. I learned to let go of rigid walls that kept me isolated. I developed a new confidence and became optimistic to see the good and look for the good. A new way of seeing opened me to experience unity with others.

Having connection with myself, and being grounded and centered, I am now able to have unity with God and my fellow human beings. Unity allows me to be true to my core identity, comfortable in my oneness and singleness, and, yet, have integrity to live as part of the whole. The action of learning to live in unity and be wholesome has been a sweet blessing.

Have a day of unity!

Happy New Year!

INDEX

Easygoing – *May 6*

Education – *Feb. 28*

Efficiency – *Jan. 28*

Elated – *Feb. 25*

Eloquence – *Oct. 2*

Emotional – *Apr. 2*

Empathetic – *Apr. 15*

Empowered – *Aug. 15*

Empowerment – *Oct. 18*

Endeavor – *Sept. 15*

Endurance – *Aug. 31*

Energy – *June 9*

Enhancing – *Mar. 29*

Enjoyable – *July 31*

Enlightenment – *Dec. 11*

Enrich – *July 11*

Enrichment – *July 12*

Enthusiasm – *Aug. 12*

Epigrammatic – *May 29*

Equanimity – *Mar. 1*

Expansion – *Sept. 10*

Fabulous – *Mar. 24*

Faith – *May 11*

Fearless – *Apr. 5*

Flexibility – *Mar. 28*

Focus – *Jan. 26*

Forbearance – *Aug. 23*

Forgiveness – *Jan. 8*

Fortitude – *July 3*

Fortunate – *July 2*

Freedom – *Jan. 15*

Fun – *Nov. 1*

Funny – *Oct. 17*

Generosity – *Jan. 17*

Gentle – *Aug. 4*

Gentleness – *June 29*

Gifted – *Aug. 10*

Giving – *Jan. 13*

Gleaming – *Apr. 29*

Godlike – *Sept. 14*

Good-Natured – *Mar. 1*

Good-Hearted – *Mar. 21*

Grace – *June 18*

Graced – *Aug. 16*

Gracious – *Dec. 23*

Grateful – *Sept. 18*

Gratitude – *Jan 14*

Grieving – *Jan 12*

Guardian-Angel – *June 14*

Happiness – *July 5*

Happy-go-lucky – *Sept. 7*

Harmonious – *Dec. 26*

Harmony – *Apr. 1*

Healing – *Feb. 1*

Helpful – *Oct. 6*

Hilarious – *Feb. 8*

Honesty – Apr. 7

Hope – *Feb. 2*

Hospitable – *Aug. 25*

Humble – *Dec. 25*

Humor – *Nov. 15*

Idealism – *July 28*

Identify – *Apr. 18*

Imitate – *July 12*

Impartiality – *Dec. 5*

Improvement – *Jan 27*

Individual – *Oct. 14*

Informed – *June 3*

Insight – *Feb. 21*

Inspiration – *Feb. 17*

Inspirational – *Aug. 17*

Inspire – *Nov. 5*

Instrumental – *June 26*

Integration – *May 3*

Integrity – *Mar. 8*

Intention – *Dec. 6*

International – *Mar. 4*

Intuitive – *June 28*

Joy – *Jan. 10*

Justice – *May 13*

Kindness – *May 21*

Laugh – *Aug. 24*

Level-headed – *Aug. 19*

Liberated – *June 20*

Light – *May 23*

Likeable – *Aug. 3*

Like-minded – *Apr. 24*

Listening – *Mar. 22*

Love – *Jan. 3*

Loveliness – *Nov. 26*

Loyal – *Nov. 8*

Loyalty – *Dec. 15*

Luminous – *Oct. 5*

Magnanimity – *Feb. 13*

Magnificent – *May 1*

Majestic – *Nov. 16*

Manageable – *Aug. 21*

Manifestation – *Dec. 17*

Maturity – *May 26*

Meditative – *May 28*

Meekness – *Apr. 23*

Mellifluous – *Feb. 6*

Member – *May 22*

Memorable – *July 13*

Mending – *July 22*

Mental – *Sept. 3*

Messenger – *Aug. 6*

Metaphysical – *June 6*

Mind – *Nov. 20*

Mind-Cleaning – *Nov. 28*

Mindfulness – *Jan 16*

Moderation – *Nov. 25*

Modest – *Sept. 29*

Modesty – *Mar. 31*

Multi-disciplined – *Oct. 16*

Musical – *Mar. 25*

Neat – *Mar. 27*

Neighborly – *Apr. 17*

Neutral – *July 29*

Nice – *Apr. 10*

Noted – *July 20*

Nurturing – *May 31*

Obedience – *Sept. 16*

Omnipotent – *Apr. 14*

On the beam – *Mar. 14*

Oomph – *Sept. 21*

Open-minded – *Dec. 16*

Openness – *Dec. 1*

Optimistic – *Apr. 30*

Orderliness – *June 10*

Outgoing – *Sept. 23*

Passionate – *Dec. 5*

Passionately – *Sept. 6*

Patience – *Jan. 24*

Patterns – *Nov. 3*

Peace – *Jan. 4*

Peace of mind – *May 9*

Persistent – *Jan. 25*

Personable – *Oct. 4*

Perseverance – *Apr. 28*

Physical – *Nov. 24*

Pioneering – *Mar. 9*

Placid – *Mar. 6*

Play – *July 9*

Playful – *Nov. 13*

Poise – *Feb. 23*

Polite – *Apr. 19*

Potential – *Aug. 28*

Power – *Sept. 22*

Powerful – *July 16*

Praises – *Oct. 15*

Prayer – *Jan. 18*

Principles – *Dec. 30*

Privileged – *June 30*

Production – *Sept. 11*

Productive – *Nov. 7*

Program – *Aug. 30*
Progress – *Oct. 9*
Promises – *May 7*
Prompt – *July 19*
Prudence – *Sept. 24*
Purification – *Dec. 10*
Purpose – *Oct. 11*
Purposeful – *June 5*
Quiet – *June 23*
Radiant – *July 1*
Rational – *May 12*
Realistic – *June 17*
Reasonable – *Apr. 13*
Reassuring – *Sept. 8*
Rebuilding – *Feb. 5*
Reconstruction – *Apr. 27*
Recovery – *Oct. 12*
Redivivus – *June 12*
Rehabilitation – *Aug. 1*
Rejoice – *Jan. 1*
Rejuvenated – *July 23*
Relaxed – *Feb. 22*
Release – *Jan. 19*
Renewed – *Feb. 24*
Reputable – *Nov. 14*
Resilience – *Nov. 29*
Resilient – *June 4*
Resolved – *July 20*
Resourcefulness – *Nov. 9*
Respect – *Oct. 27*
Respected – *Dec. 7*
Responsibility – *May 4*
Restful – *Mar. 17*
Rewarding – *May 17*
Rewarding – *Oct. 1*
Rooted – *Sept. 30*
Rugged – *May 24*
Ruminant – *Feb. 10*
Sacred – *Dec. 24*

Sacrifice – *Dec. 3*
Safety – *Oct. 24*
Sagacious – *Feb. 15*
Sanity – *May 30*
Sapient – *Mar. 18*
Saved – *Sept. 19*
Scrupulousness – *Dec. 13*
Secure – *Oct. 29*
Self-Acceptance – *Aug. 26*
Self-Confidence – *Sept. 20*
Self-Control – *Aug. 11*
Self-Esteem – *Oct. 25*
Self-Possession – *Feb. 9*
Self-Sacrifice – *Aug. 14*
Self-Sufficient – *Feb. 20*
Self-Taught – *Nov. 22*
Sensitive – *Sept. 12*
Serenity – *Jan. 2*
Service – *Aug. 27*
Serving – *Dec. 28*
Shaping – *Feb. 4*
Sharing – *Apr. 11*
Silence – *May 14*
Simplicity – *Dec. 22*
Sincere – *Nov. 6*
Sisterhood/brotherhood – *Feb. 3*
Solicitous – *June 27*
Solutions – *Sept. 2*
Soulful – *July 15*
Special – *Mar. 11*
Spirit – *Mar. 19*
Spiritual – *Mar. 20*
Spiritual Abundance – *Jan. 9*
Splendid – *Mar. 26*
Sponsorship – *Oct. 13*
Spontaneity – *July 17*
Stable – *Sept. 5*
Stillness – *Mar. 12*
Strength – *Feb. 12*

Stupendous – *Nov. 19*

Successful – *Nov. 12*

Supportive – *May 15*

Sure – *Sept. 9*

Surrender – *Sept. 17*

Sympathetic – *Oct. 28*

Tailor-made – *Oct. 7*

Talents – *Mar. 30*

Tasteful – *Aug. 13*

Teachable – *June 25*

Tenacity – *Apr. 4*

Tenderness – *Feb. 19*

Thankful – *June 24*

Therapeutic – *Mar. 5*

Thinker – *Nov. 18*

Thorough – *May 2*

Thoughtfulness – *July 24*

Thrilled – *Mar. 2*

Toughness – *Sept. 28*

Trailblazing – *June 2*

Transformation – *Feb. 14*

Travelled – *Mar. 13*

Treasured – *Mar. 10*

Tremendous – *July 25*

Trust – *Feb. 7*

Trustful – *Oct. 26*

Truth – *Dec. 29*

Truthful – *May 27*

Unassuming – *May 25*

Uncomplicated – *Apr. 22*

Unconditional – *Dec. 27*

Understanding – *Dec. 8*

Unique – *July 14*

Unity – *Dec. 31*

Universe – *Feb. 16*

Unselfish – *Aug. 22*

Unstoppable – *Nov. 30*

Usefulness – *Apr. 25*

Valiant – *Mar. 23*

Valuable – *Sept. 4*

Vibration – *Nov. 11*

Vibrations – *Oct. 23*

Vigilant – *Apr. 20*

Vigorous – *Oct. 31*

Virtuous – *Dec. 18*

Wanted – *July 21*

Warm – *Oct. 3*

Warm-Hearted – *July 4*

Welcoming – *June 19*

Well – *Nov. 17*

Well-Grounded – *June 7*

Well-Intentioned – *Apr. 16*

Well-Liked – *July 27*

Well-Read – *Oct. 30*

Wide-Awake – *Feb. 18*

Willingness – *Jan. 7*

Wisdom – *Apr. 12*

Witty – *Nov. 27*

Wonderful – *Mar. 15*

Worshipful – *Apr. 3*

Worthy – *Aug. 8*

Zeal – *Aug. 7*